INDIANA

GETTING STARTED GARDEN GUIDE

Grow the Best Flowers, Shrubs, Trees, Vines & Groundcovers

First published in 2014 by Cool Springs Press, an imprint of Quarto Publishing Group USA Inc., 400 First Avenue North, Suite 400, Minneapolis, MN 55401

Library of Congress Cataloging-in-Publication Data

Coronado, Shawna.
  Indiana getting started garden guide : grow the best flowers, shrubs, trees, vines & groundcovers / Shawna Coronado.
    pages cm
  Includes bibliographical references and index.
  ISBN 978-1-59186-608-4 (sc)
  1. Gardening--Indiana. 2. Plants--Indiana. I. Title.

  SB453.2.I6C67 2014
  635.909772--dc23

                              2014012726

Acquisitions Editor: Billie Brownell
Design Manager: Cindy Samargia Laun
Layout: Kim Winscher

Printed in China
10 9 8 7 6 5 4 3 2 1

INDIANA

GETTING STARTED GARDEN GUIDE

Grow the Best Flowers, Shrubs, Trees, Vines & Groundcovers

Shawna Coronado

COOL SPRINGS PRESS
Home and Garden Experts™

MINNEAPOLIS, MINNESOTA

DEDICATION AND ACKNOWLEDGMENTS

This book is dedicated to several strong, wonderful women in my life who have truly made a difference in how I view the world. They have given me laughter, love, advice, and the strong belief that a single determined woman can save the world.

Thank you Barbara M., Delores C., Eileen L., Jamie V., Janet R., Linda R., Lisa S., Narda C., and Samara S. I am glad you are my family, but more important, I am glad you are my friends.

There are many people who have helped inspire and help with the completion of this book, and I am eternally grateful for their support. My editor Billie Brownell, Tracy Stanley, and all the staff at Quarto Publishing Group and Cool Springs Press have been outstanding. Thanks for believing in me.

Jim Kleinwachter from The Conservation Foundation continues to be my mentor in everything conservation-oriented; his help and counsel have made this guide a better book. Practical publishing advice from James Rollins and David Sylvian-Czajkowski truly helped me form a book plan. Kate Szekely has been my ever-faithful marketing assistant and helped me in a million ways—I am so thankful for every minute she has spent helping me in the office. My dear friends from the Dirty Glove Society have been with me every second of every day cheering me on; your support has touched me and brings tears to my eyes. Thank you for all you do.

Thank you to all the readers of my newspaper column, blog, and social media. Your support, love, and unending dedication to me are a balm for my soul. I am very grateful for you.

Various horticultural experts at The Morton Arboretum, Chicago Botanic Garden, and Purdue University offered fantastic tips and guidance. A special thank you goes out to these organizations for having excellent online databases and wonderful experts with detailed scientific knowledge. I also spent hundreds of hours taking photos at their gardens as well as at the Ball Horticultural test gardens. The grounds for all these locations are stunning and the photos reflect that. Thanks to Dan Heims for his advice on echinacea.

Huge thanks go to my husband, Luis—your laughter, love, and support are important to me. Luis is also my computer man, and I am forever grateful for his frequent and heroic computer rescues during the book-writing process. My children and all of my family have endured without complaining the very long hours when I have been buried in research and writing for weeks on end. Thank you, my sweet family; you are fantastic.

CONTENTS

WELCOME TO GARDENING
IN INDIANA

When I was a little girl growing up in Indiana, my greatest joy was the time I spent outside in nature: climbing trees, hopping fences, catching crawdads, and gardening. Without a doubt, my fondest memories were the moments spent with my grandmothers in their beautiful gardens. Living in rural farm country in Indiana, we landscaped with trees and flowers and love. My escape from the pressures of the world was always the gardens, trees, and the land

Above: Growing native and pollinator-attracting plants in the city can be quite beautiful and easy to accomplish. This family has an amazing home in an urban area and has incorporated native, ornamental edible, and pollinator-friendly plants into a play area for their children. **Opposite page:** Swallowtail butterflies represent both beauty and usefulness as they pollinate flowers in Midwest gardens. Attracting pollinators such as native hummingbirds, bees, and butterflies to your garden encourages stronger flower and fruit formation, and therefore a more productive garden.

that makes up Indiana. When I grew to be an adult, I became a passionate gardener and I am convinced that is because of the time I spent as a child learning the value of a lovingly tended bed of plants. Gardening teaches a beautiful and unique understanding of the world. I discovered that knowledge with dirty knees, ripped jeans, and my hands grasping a coffee tin filled with fresh peonies on my grandmother's front steps.

Why Is Gardening Important?

Gardening is important to building community. Indeed, a garden is more than a garden; it is an incubator for positive community growth. Building a more connected community by growing a garden is possible because beautiful landscaped areas within your community encourage both businesses and potential home buyers to come into that area to establish their presence. Landscaping improves economic viability within a community by improving your home's value and improving the look of the neighborhood. An important study conducted by the University of Illinois at Urbana-Champaign in an urban area of Chicago afflicted by violence and aggression shows that crime reduction can happen in the homes of people who are exposed to landscaped areas. Gardening encourages pollinators to come to the flowers, trees, and landscapes, thereby helping the environment. Nurturing plants on your property that create food and homes for the native species of wildlife in your community is particularly important. Additionally, the act of working in the outdoors is good for one's health and encourages positive exercise patterns for people of all ages who garden regularly. In other words, gardening is good for you, your urban community, and the environment.

Contending with a full range of seasonal weather changes, from freezing winters to incredibly hot and humid summers, is a part of the Midwest gardening condition. While Indiana is known as a rich farmland, conditions for gardening vary upon site and a gardener can find both hard-packed clay and a wet boggy soil side-by-side. Therefore, planning becomes the key to success for the most successful garden: know the seasons and plan landscape plantings accordingly, choose the right plant for the right zone and sun location, and most importantly, amend and improve soil for the best growing success.

Indiana Getting Started Garden Guide helps you with your plan. This book covers a variety of trees and plants, divided into 11 informative chapters, that will perform well in the Hoosier landscape. Determining which plants will work in your specific landscape means having an understanding of an individual plant's basic requirements and the conditions in which it can survive.

Welcome To My Garden

While I have traveled all over the world educating and speaking about gardening, my entire life I have called the Midwest home. There's nothing more joyful than sitting in my quiet suburban garden with a cool drink in hand watching the lightning bugs on a summer's evening. Traveling triggers inspiration, and I often bring the ideas and techniques I learn from international gardens back to my little piece of the Earth and try them. Gardens are the same in many aspects all over the world, but how they are different is the unique soil, plants, and native wildlife diversity that make up the region that the garden is a part of. Most urban homes have very little biodiversity in their gardens. This is unfortunate because the more planting diversity, the more a garden can support wildlife and encourage environmental stewardship. When considering a garden, the Earth needs this biodiverse support and so does your community.

This is my sustainable front lawn vegetable garden, which incorporates ornamental edibles, pollinator-friendly flowering plants, a variety of herbs, traditional perennials, a rain barrel, and a rainwater cistern into its design. It provides between 120 to 150 pounds of ornamental herbs and produce annually, which I donate to local food pantries.

Within my own personal Midwestern garden, my goals in gardening and landscaping have been to understand the needs of my soil, make room for and encourage native wildlife such as birds and pollinators, and grow diverse plants that are low in maintenance and high in visual appeal and that work well within the constraints of an urban neighborhood.

In my front lawn ornamental edible vegetable garden and all my perennial beds, for instance, I practice no-till soil maintenance. That means that after the first planting of the garden bed, I do not till the soil over again. By turning soil over annually in your garden, you are destroying the microbial system that helps make your soil a rich and nutritious resource for your plants' root systems. By understanding that soil is a living, breathing part of the garden, we are better able to have growing success.

My home's landscape is a mix of native and non-native bushes, trees, and perennials. Annuals, ornamental edible vegetables, and tropicals have a place in my Midwestern garden, in containers and directly in the soil. My front yard contains very little grass. There's a large flowering crabapple tree surrounded by a front lawn vegetable garden and perennial beds on one side, while a 500-gallon rainwater cistern and sedum-filled herbal cocktail garden fill out the rest of the beds. There are dozens of bird species that come to play seasonally in the fountain that sits on top of my rainwater cistern. Robins, redheaded woodpeckers, cardinals, cowbirds, yellow finches, doves, sparrows, wrens, and hummingbirds come to visit. Their babies peep at us from nests in the apple tree and within birdhouses set around the property.

Echinacea and black-eyed Susans are fantastic drought-tolerant plants that attract pollinators and provide a solution in dry garden areas.

Behind and to the side of the house is an extensive shade garden surrounded by flagstone paths and wine bottle borders where I grow shade-loving perennials, annuals, and ornamental edible vegetables in raised beds, paths, and vertical gardens. If you open the back fence and step to the sidewalk you will find a lush 200-foot-long prairie garden filled with native and drought-tolerant perennial species and sunflowers. This garden is planted along a difficult and hot "hell strip" sidewalk with little or no water access, yet it grows lush and thick every season for the public's enjoyment.

My daughter has faithfully noted and documented several hundred different varieties of wildlife that come to visit the garden. Ultimately, my personal joy in a garden comes from the beautiful presence of life. Part of the goal with a garden is to give the visitor a taste of the natural, sharing a delightful cocktail for the soul, which he or she can take home in the form of memories and laughter. Your garden is your personal statement of your relationship with nature and your community. Building a landscape that supports community, both environmentally and socially, is a part of what makes your garden special for your neighborhood.

How To Get Started Gardening
Sun Needs

Gardening can be an amazingly rewarding experience, but to be successful at growing, a gardener needs to understand the basic needs of a plant. Within this book you will find plant profiles that tell you the particular needs of each plant listed, and this will give you a helping hand in getting started with the landscaping and gardening process. My recommendation for homeowners is that they live in a home for at least a year before they start making dramatic landscaping changes. This gives you time to understand the sun requirements and growing conditions that exist on your specific property and enables you to make smart choices about garden design. For example, full-sun plants need at least six hours of direct sunlight per day. Part-sun plants often prefer filtered light during the day, but still need four hours of sunlight per day. Shade plants can live with little or no sunlight, but still prefer indirect light to no light whatsoever. By watching the sun conditions on your property for one year, you can determine the evolution of the sunlight your garden might have and then determine the best specific plants for the conditions you have.

Utilizing sustainable solutions is a wise choice for the modern urban landscape. In my back garden I have incorporated wine bottles as path edgers and have reused bricks for a patio, as seating, and a raised garden area. Ornamental edibles are placed in vertical wall spaces and raised garden areas.

Considering sunlight also means you will make more sustainable planting choices in your designs. For instance, planting all the sun-loving plants in one garden bed means you will have more growing success because all the plants within that bed that have the same light and watering requirements will be grouped. Similarly, basing your design plan on a centralized shade tree on your property, then planting specific shade-loving plants beneath that tree will also be more likely to guarantee success.

Designing with light exposure in mind can also save you money and resources. Shade trees play an important part in that concept because trees that shade a building during the summer can lower air-conditioning bills by blocking the sun from roofs, exterior walls, and windows. Air conditioners cooling a well-shaded home don't need to work as hard as those in a house that is more fully exposed to the sun. Trees that lose their leaves during the cold season can help you save money because their bare branches allow more sunlight to hit a house and warm it up, reducing the amount of time a furnace has to run.

Plant Hardiness Zones

Indiana is a land filled with weather extremes and challenging soil for growing conditions, yet gardening is quite enjoyable here because of regular annual rainfall,

Container design can easily be incorporated into the landscape. Non-traditional ideas include a stacked design such as this blue container tower. Mix annuals and ornamental edibles together for an attractive and unique look.

consistent sunshine, and the prolific variety of plants Hoosiers are able to cultivate. Indiana hardiness zones range between Zones 5a, 5b, 6a, and 6b. A zone indicates the lowest average annual temperature at which a plant might be able to live through existing weather conditions. (Refer to the Hardiness Zone Map on page 25.) Microclimates can exist within your garden area that might support zones higher than those recommended based on that area's wind, humidity, and soil conditions. Creating microclimates for better plant growth takes good planning and a thorough knowledge of a plant's needs. Understanding the conditions your plants can grow in can often mean the difference between failure and success for a tree, perennial, or annual plant.

Watering

Rainfall is incredibly variable annually, and the amount of water you need in your garden varies as well. Summers in Indiana can be swelteringly hot, and drought is a regular concern in late July and August. Some plants, like roses or begonias, will need constant attention during these months. However, other types of plants, like sedum or prickly pear cactus, thrive in the heat and lower rainfall. Planting beds according to watering requirements is as important as grouping plants according to their sunlight requirements. Placing plants with other plants that have very similar water needs will help you enjoy more long-term growing success. As a rule of thumb, it is better to water your plants deeply once or twice per week—at least 1 inch of water—rather than water shallowly every day of the week.

Have you ever noticed that you can water a plant for weeks with city or tap water with no real increase in plant size, then it rains for less than an hour and your plants grow an inch? This is because of the chemicals like fluoride and chlorine found in most city water are not a plant's preferred nutrient choice. Consider using a rain barrel, which collects and stores rainwater from rooftops, preventing less strain on our overtaxed storm water systems. This stored water can be used later for watering your landscape. Storm water runoff is the leading type of residential non-point source pollution and is a big concern for those monitoring our Earth's oceans and water systems. Typically, water from your roof flows through roof gutter downspouts and becomes storm water runoff, ultimately moving onto paved surfaces, collecting oil and other chemicals, on its way to a storm drain. And all that storm water eventually ends up in our lakes and rivers.

Rain barrels allow you to collect and use fresh rainwater instead of city water, thereby keeping water out of storm water systems. Rain barrels are excellent garden helpers as they save money and provide your garden plants with a drink they really enjoy. Another reason to use a rain barrel is that during the summer months, residential water use increases approximately 40 percent because of outdoor landscape requirements. Using a natural resource like rain barrel water is a common sense choice for saving money.

Plants seem to perform much better with rainwater rather than city or tap water. This is because rainwater lacks the chlorine and other chemicals that are typically found in tap water. This rain barrel is stacked on top of concrete bricks to encourage a stronger gravity-generated water pressure.

Although rain barrels save only a small percentage of water, every little bit counts. Instead of sending water to the ocean, we should be trying to replace the water in our water aquifers, thereby keeping our water in a more natural state of replenishment while simultaneously reducing overuse of the storm water systems in our communities.

HOW TO INSTALL A RAIN BARREL

1. Find an area under a downspout on your home that is flat and level.

2. Place cement blocks or a stand of some sort on the level ground where your rain barrel will sit. Keep in mind that most rain barrels weigh more than 400 pounds when full. By setting the rain barrel on a raised surface, you can fit a watering can below the spigot, and you will also have more "gravity pressure" should you want to use hoses for watering various parts of your garden.

3. Place your empty barrel on the blocks or stand and measure where you need to cut your downspout to allow for an elbow or a diverter to drain water into the top of the rain barrel. Draw a line on the downspout.

4. Move the barrel aside and cut the downspout with a hacksaw where you drew your line.

5. Slide an elbow or diverter that will allow the water to drain into your barrel over the downspout.

6. Remove the old downspout and save it for later use. Rain barrels cannot be used during winter, so you will change the system back in the fall.

7. Attach a short hose to the top overflow spigot and direct the water away from your foundation. A hose can be attached to the bottom spigot as well for watering purposes.

8. Slide your barrel under the newly reconfigured downspout, and you are done.

9. Once installed, rain barrels are fairly maintenance free; in the fall, drain your rain barrel completely so the water does not freeze and crack the container. Many prefer to turn their rain barrels upside down to make sure the barrel stays drained. Be sure to reattach the downspout when you remove the rain barrel. When you plant your garden in the spring, flip the rain barrel over and start the process all over again.

Soils and Soil Testing

Good soil is the secret to success and the most important ingredient in the garden. If a plant's roots are healthy and strong, then it's more likely that the plant will survive drought and other harsh conditions. Improving soil is something you should be doing annually to build and grow a strong soil system that will support healthy roots, and therefore, healthy plants. Soil improvement starts with organic matter such as compost, leaf mold, rotted manure, dried grass clippings, and chopped leaves.

Testing soil to discover your soil's pH and fertility needs will help you decide on additional or special soil amendments. Local County Extension Service offices and garden centers will sometimes test the soil for you or will send your sample away for testing.

If you are gathering the sample soil, pull a core sample about 8 to 12 inches in depth in several locations around your landscape. Gather samples of the soil seasonally if you are able, taking samples from various locations throughout your yard and garden. The test results will help you determine what specific soil amendments you might need. However, by and large, no matter your pH reading, natural organic matter should be your primary soil amendment whether you have sandy, clayey, loamy, or silty soil, to help expand and recover your soil's microbial growth.

The Soil Ribbon Test

Once you have had your soil tested and understand its nutrient content, it is critical to understand its consistency so that you can determine what soil amendments you might need. If you have sandier soil, you might need to add more compost or rotted manure, which will help improve its structure and so support stronger root systems. If you have extremely heavy and poorly drained soil, you might need to loosen the soil to improve its aeration ability.

This ribbon test will help you determine the type of soil you have.

1. Gather a handful of soil. Add enough water to make the soil shapeable.
2. Form the soil into a tight ball.
3. Gently press the soil between your fingers and allow it to roll slowly out of your hand. A stream of soil that resembles a ribbon will begin to form and will eventually form a break. If the soil crumbles and refuses to form a ribbon, you have sandy soil.
4. If a ribbon forms that is more than 1 inch long before it makes a break, you have silty soil.
5. If a ribbon forms a 1- to 2-inch ribbon before it creates a break, you have clay soil.
6. If a ribbon forms more than a 2-inch ribbon before it breaks, you have extremely heavy and poorly drained soil.

Composting: "Black Gold"

One of the best ways to encourage microbial growth is to add compost to your soil. Compost provides a complicated microbial structure that helps roots grow stronger. Considering that food scraps and yard clippings make up one-quarter of the United States' solid waste piling up in landfills, every gardener should have a compost pile. When organic matter is discarded in landfills, it decomposes without air and produces methane, a greenhouse gas 20 times more potent than carbon dioxide. Composting is the way to cleanly convert kitchen and garden waste into productive soil matter

Compost is made from a mixture of natural brown and green ingredients combined with moisture. It is good for the environment to recycle leaf trimmings and pulled weeds. Throw them into the compost pile to be transformed into compost for the landscape.

without producing byproducts. Making compost is easy and it saves money.

When adding material to the composter or compost pile, you must maintain an even ratio of nitrogen-rich materials, or "greens," carbon-rich materials, or "browns," and moisture. Below is a list of browns and greens you might use in your compost pile. Never use meat or bones. Never use dog, human, or cat manure/feces as they can contain pathogens or diseases that could be harmful.

Examples of Brown Materials for Compost

- Aged grass clippings
- Brown paper bags and shredded cardboard
- Newspaper (black-and-white soy print is best)
- Shredded cotton and paper-based tissues and towels
- Straw
- Dead leaves from healthy plants (do not use leaves from diseased plants)

Examples of Green Materials for Compost

- Coffee grounds
- Barnyard animal manures such as llama, cow, horse, goat, chicken, sheep, and rabbit
- New grass clippings
- Pulled weeds and plant prunings (do not add prunings from diseased plants)
- Tea bags with metal staple and string removed
- Kitchen scraps; avoid items that will root, such as potato skins and onions, unless ground completely

Speedy composting happens with a good balance of carbon and nitrogen and by turning the pile regularly. On average, it takes between three and four weeks to make your own compost. If your pile is hot to the touch, that's good because it indicates a heavier activity level in the decomposition process. To increase activity, add green materials and place your composter in the full sun. Additionally, keeping the pile moist, but not soggy, is best. Organic waste needs water to decompose. The rule of thumb is to keep your compost pile as wet as a wrung-out sponge.

Soil pH

Plants are highly adaptive organisms that are sensitive to soil pH conditions. Soil pH describes the levels of soil acidity, alkalinity, or neutrality. Determining soil pH via soil testing can be very helpful in understanding which plants are more likely to survive in your landscape. Soil is considered neutral at a pH level of 7.0. While many plants prefer a slightly acidic pH reading of 6.0 to 7.0, the reality is that the majority of soils throughout the northern part of the state are quite frequently alkaline. PH readings of 8.0 or higher are uncommon.

Using plants that will tolerate, and even prefer, a higher alkalinity will generally improve performance. I gave up years ago on having blue hydrangeas in my Midwestern garden because of my highly alkaline soil: growing blue flowers requires an acidic soil. While it is possible to add a sulfur amendment to increase acidity, it takes regular effort and amending to make the blue appear. I prefer to keep my pink hydrangeas and lessen my work.

Planting Techniques and Tips

Planting a live plant in the ground is one of the greatest joys for the gardener. There is something wonderful about placing your hands in soil and connecting with the earth. Planting techniques vary; however, the best techniques are the simplest. Below are some easy tips for planting an annual, groundcover, native plant, ornamental grass, perennial, shrub, or vine.

1. Before wildly digging holes all over the garden, start by laying out the plants (in their containers) in the landscape to see if the design plan works according to your wishes.
2. Water the plant in its existing container before planting so that the roots absorb the moisture. Dig a hole where you wish to plant that is twice the size of the plant's root system. Gently pull the plant out of its container and tease the roots to loosen them so they will spread and adapt to their new environment. If the roots are potbound with a very dense root system, use a knife to slice through two or three sides of the rootball. Do not worry about damaging the rootball; the freshly cut roots will regrow.
3. Most plants require that you plant them at the same depth they were in their containers. Gently place the plant in its hole and backfill the soil, forming a well around the base of the plant to help it collect and absorb water.

(continued)

4. With annuals, pinch flowers and buds once the plant is placed in the ground so that it can focus its efforts on growing strong roots. If you are planting a groundcover, native plant, ornamental grass, perennial, shrub, or vine, leave the flowers and buds in their natural state. Mulch the area surrounding the newly installed plants and water well.

Bulbs, Rhizomes, and Tubers

Bulbs require a slightly different planting technique. Prepare the soil bed, making sure the soil has the recommended amendments based on your soil tests. For most bulbs and corms, dig a hole three times deeper than the circumference of the bulb. In other words, if the bulb is 2 inches around, plant the bulb 6 inches deep. If it is 3 inches around, plant the bulb 9 inches deep, and so on. Be sure the bulb is placed with the pointy end up. Add organic bulb fertilizer in the planting hole if you like, and top off the planting with a nice layer of compost or mulch.

Rhizomes like to be soaked in warm water for an hour or so before planting. Prepare the soil while your roots are soaking. Add organic slow-release fertilizer to the planting hole. Plant the rhizomes pointing upward about 2 inches below the soil surface. Follow package directions for distance between plants. Top with a layer of compost and mulch well.

Tubers vary in their planting depths and soil needs. Consult package directions for more specific instructions on planting depending on the tuber you have.

Natural Fertilizers and Soil Amendments

After you have amended your soil with organic matter, you might also consider fertilizing your plants and adding additional soil amendments to enhance plant growth depending upon their

This compost pile has rotted manure incorporated into it, which gives the compost an additional boost of nitrogen. Turning "hot" compost regularly encourages a speedier transformation into a more soil-like additive that has been nicknamed "black gold" for a garden.

needs. Adding organic matter to your soil encourages less use of other fertilizers; they simply are not necessary in some circumstances. Observe your landscape and if you feel it is warranted, use organic fertilizers and soil amendments, which are always the preferred choice for your landscape because they are better for the environment and your garden. Organic fertilizers are most likely to come from minerals, plants, or animals and have varying N–P–K (nitrogen, phosphorus, and potassium) values. Organisms within the soil break down the organic fertilizers so the plants can access them. While there are many fertilizers and soil amendments, below are a few of my favorites that I like to use in my Midwestern garden.

Plant-Based Fertilizers

Plant-based fertilizers have nutrients that are typically made available as soon as you place the amendment in the soil. Most can be found at a home-improvement or garden center; however, some can be found at your local feed store.

- Alfalfa meal – Pelletized alfalfa is made from alfalfa plants and has 2 percent nitrogen and 2 percent potassium as well as some trace minerals. Roses love this fertilizer; mix 4 to 5 cups of alfalfa meal into the soil at the base of each plant. Apply every eight to twelve weeks.
- Humus – Humic acid or humates are organic compounds scientifically proven to increase soil microbial activity and soil structure. Humus products do not have an N–P–K fertilizer value, but I place them in this category because they are stimulants that support the plants, much like a vitamin. Look for products that add humates to soil. One I use contains humic acid with beneficial bacteria

(continued)

and iron. I place a handful in every planting hole. Another has humate sugars for plant food and calcium carbonate for soil. I apply 1 pound per 100 square feet.

- Corn gluten meal – Corn is the primary ingredient in corn gluten and is considered a nitrogen fertilizer with a value of 10 percent. It's also an all-natural, pre-emergent weed preventative. I use this later in the spring because it can inhibit the growth of a seed's tiny feeder roots. Apply on gardens and grass on top of the soil at a rate of 50 pounds per 2,500 square feet.

Animal-Based Fertilizers

Animal-based fertilizers are made from the manure, blood, and bones of animals such as birds, fish, and farm animals. Most of these fertilizers contain nitrogen, which encourages leaf growth.

- Manures – Fresh manure can "burn" your plants and devastate your garden. The secret to manure is composting. Garden centers have bagged manure, which has been processed and heated so weed seeds are killed. Local farms raising animals also have rotted manure you can access for free (usually lots!). Simply mix several inches of composted manure in with your soil as a topdressing for existing plants, or as part of your soil mix for new gardens. A preferred manure treatment is to make compost tea and use the tea as a foliar treatment as well as a liquid soil amendment. You can also buy commercially made manure tea treatments.
- Blood meal – This product contains many natural micronutrients as well as about 14 percent nitrogen, which enhances leaf growth. It is made from slaughtered animals, which might disturb you, but I have found it effective in helping perennial plants that have large leaves. While many claim this amendment repels deer, I have found it attracts skunks and dogs.
- Bone meal – Containing about 2 percent nitrogen and lots of micronutrients, bone meal is derived from animal or fish bones. It has 11 percent phosphorus and 22 percent calcium.

Mineral-Based Fertilizers

Mineral fertilizers are an excellent long-term solution to increase soil fertility over time and enhance plant growth. Depending upon your soil test scores, you might find you need differing levels of the various minerals. Mineral deficiencies in soil can certainly be improved by a variety of soil amendments.

- Epsom salts – Epsom salts contains 10 percent magnesium and 13 percent sulfur. Prepare garden soil by mixing up to 1 cup of Epsom salts per 100 square feet of soil. Potted plants can benefit from dissolving 2 tablespoons of salts per gallon of water, then spraying the mix on foliage. For traditional garden application, fill a tank sprayer with a solution that contains 1 tablespoon of Epsom salts per gallon of water. Spray three to four times per season on all gardens.

- Chelated iron – Adding chelated iron to your soil prevents plant chlorosis or yellowing. There are many different products in the marketplace with varying application rates. You can find chelated iron in products that also contain humic acid combined with beneficial bacteria. I place a handful in every planting hole and 3 ounces per cubic foot as a top dressing.
- Soft rock phosphate – Better for acidic soils, colloidal phosphate contains 16 percent phosphorus and 19 percent calcium. This can be added to your compost bin or you can spread 2 to 4 pounds of soft rock phosphate for every 100 square feet of garden. Phosphates should only be added if a soil test indicates a need. Excess phosphate is a major water polluter.

The Percolation Test

Before adding soil amendments, you should also understand how fast water drains from the area you are planning to garden. Poor drainage blocks air from reaching plant roots and creates a less-than-healthy planting zone for root systems.

1. Dig a hole about 24 inches deep × 24 inches across.
2. Fill the hole with water to saturate the soil thoroughly.
3. Let the water drain completely.
4. Fill the hole with water again, letting the water drain completely. The soil should be well saturated at this time.
5. Fill the hole with water a third time. Then mark the time and calculate how long it takes for the water to drain out of the hole.

If the water is slow to drain, taking four to ten hours to seep into the soil, you have poorly drained soil. If you discover that your soil has a slow percolation rate, then you will need to install better drainage (such as a French drain), heavily amend soil to support better drainage, or build a raised planting bed above the poorly draining area.

Weeds

A weed could be any plant that is not wanted in the garden. I was speaking once at an independent garden center when a woman stood up and shouted, "Hey lady, what the heck do you do about the danged weeds?" After the laughter died down I told her what my father used to say: "Weeds happen: Go pull 'em!" In reality, there are many ways to control weeds without the use of chemicals. Hoeing or pulling the weeds is, of course, the old standard and

Mulch is an important component of gardening. Mulching with a natural ingredient helps hold moisture in the soil and prevents weeds. It is eventually eaten by soil microbes and transformed into an important additive for the soil.

represents emotional therapy for me personally. Who needs a psychiatrist when you have weeds to pull?

Regular mulching is probably the number one way to control weeds. Mulch prevents weeds by smothering out the weed seeds. By using natural mulch, you are also contributing to a stronger soil structure in the landscape. As the mulch breaks down, it is integrated into the soil structure, thereby creating a system that helps better support the plants you install. Natural mulches that have a lot of organic matter are best, such as leaf mold, shredded bark, pine needles, straw, wood chips, and grass clippings. Compost can also be considered an effective mulch if a heavy layer is applied as a topdressing over the soil.

If you are preparing a bed for its first planting or are willing to let a planting bed go fallow for a few months in the summer, you can try a technique called solarization. Get rid of what weeds and grass you can, then thoroughly wet down the soil and cover it with clear heavy plastic. Weigh down the sides of the plastic by burying the edges. Leave the sheet in place six to eight weeks, and the sun will bake and kill the grass, weeds, and weed seeds. The soil will then be ready for soil amendments and planting.

Another idea for killing grass or weeds in the area of a new bed is to use a black-out technique. In the fall, after the ground freezes, cover the section to be killed out with old carpet or a thick layer of newspaper so that no light can get through the covering. Weigh the covering down with something heavy and ignore it until spring. In April or early May, uncover the area. The weeds or grass will be dead, and the soil will be ready for amendments and planting.

Once you plant the garden, you can suppress weed seeds by using corn gluten meal. Simply broadcast it over the planted beds until it looks like a fine layer of pollen resting on the surface of the soil. In general, use 20 to 40 pounds of corn gluten per 1,500 square feet for best weed inhibition. Double that rate if you want to use it as a fertilizer also. Be aware that corn gluten meal works on *all* seeds, so if you are trying to sprout desirable seeds in the garden, it will also inhibit their growth. Corn gluten must be gently wetted down after application, then dried in order for it to suppress weeds. So check the weather before you try corn gluten as it can be effective for four to six weeks if there has been a longer dry spell.

Pests

Nature has an amazing way of keeping balance in our landscape, particularly in relationship to pests. There are good bugs and bad bugs, and each has an effect on our gardens. If we are patient enough, the bad bugs are eaten by the good bugs and other wildlife, and a healthy balance of life can develop in your garden. For example, I had a potato beetle invasion several years ago, and I was almost ready to treat the bugs with a spray of some kind. One day I looked out my front garden window and saw birds nibbling all the potato beetles off of my plants. Those same birds stayed around the garden for weeks keeping things in check and delighting me with their presence.

Over the years, I have realized that waiting out a pest problem quite often solves it. When the problem can't be solved by waiting, then I hand-pick beetles, power-hose aphids, and spray insecticidal soap where a particularly unruly group of pests has attacked. If I had sprayed a chemical pesticide on that problem area, it would have killed the good bugs that eat the aphids as well as the bad bugs. Then I throw my landscape into an unbalanced situation that causes more trouble in the long run.

In the natural garden, chemicals are something we choose only as the last resort. We are already overexposed to toxic chemicals. Our world is filled with increasing amounts of toxic pesticides; they are used to manage pest problems almost everywhere. In fact, pesticides are linked to a wide range of human health conditions ranging from nausea, headaches, reproductive concerns, endocrine disruption, and cancer. When exposed to pesticides, humans can get many types of cancer such as those that affect the brain, bone, breast, liver, blood, ovaries, and prostate. Children who live in homes where parents regularly use pesticides are more likely to develop brain cancer versus those who live without the exposure. With that in mind, keeping our home, land, and families as pesticide free as possible is critical.

Think about the natural world before applying a toxic chemical solution. There might be a better way to control pests that is healthier for your family and the environment.

Gardening *Is* Important

There are many styles of gardening and landscaping with many ways to be successful, but the most important and enjoyable part of gardening is the connection a garden brings between people and the environment. Gardening is crucial in environmental stewardship and community growth. I want to encourage diversity of growth and variety in our landscapes and discourage the monoculture of one-plant-only gardening. We can encourage wildlife by nurturing natural food and shelter in our garden design plans. My theory is that a garden is much more than "just a garden"—it is also a place that can change your neighborhood and encourage positive community action. As a gardener, I am a steward of nature, and so are you.

Gardening is a pastime that does more than express beauty. Please garden to make a difference for your community and for the environment.

Native and drought-tolerant plant gardens are good for the environment. They encourage native wildlife, water conservation, and pollinator production. This garden is planted behind my back fence along a busy urban sidewalk that used to be an environmental dead zone.

How to Use This Book

Each entry in this guide provides information about a plant's characteristics, habits, and basic requirements for active growth as well as my personal experience with and knowledge of the plant. This includes a plant's mature height and spread, bloom period, color, sun and soil preferences, water requirements, fertilizing needs, and general care. Because Latin names can sometimes be a challenge, there is a phonetic botanical pronunciation given for each plant selection as well as another common name (if any). Any added benefits that are unique, such as native, seasonal or fall color, drought resistance, deer and rabbit resistance, attracts beneficials, attracts hummingbirds, and edibility are represented by symbols. To help achieve positive results, I will also give my suggestions for landscape design and companion plants.

Sun Preferences

As a quick reference, I have included four symbols representing the range of sunlight suitable for each plant. Full sun means sunlight of eight hours per day to almost all of the day. Part sun is four to six hours of direct sun, preferably in the morning with protection from direct afternoon sun. Part shade is two to four hours of direct sun per day, primarily in the morning, or all day bright indirect light. Shade is shade for most of the day.

Full Sun   Part Sun   Part Shade   Shade

Additional Benefits

Plants can add a lot of special benefits to your garden. Selecting plants that enhance your landscape with special extras have a unique appeal and are indicated with the following symbols.

 Native   Fall color

 Resists drought   Attracts beneficial insects like bees, butterflies and predaceous insects that eat the bad bugs

 Attracts hummingbirds   Edibles

 Deer and rabbit resistant

Try These

These include specific species, varieties, or cultivars that I believe are particularly noteworthy based on size, flower color, or other characteristics adaptable regionally or seasonally. You might want to give these plants a try and see what exciting results might happen.

USDA Hardiness Zone Map

Cold-hardiness zone designations were developed by the United States Department of Agriculture (USDA) to indicate the minimum average temperature for an area. A zone assigned to an individual plant indicates the lowest temperature at which the plant can be expected to survive over the winter.

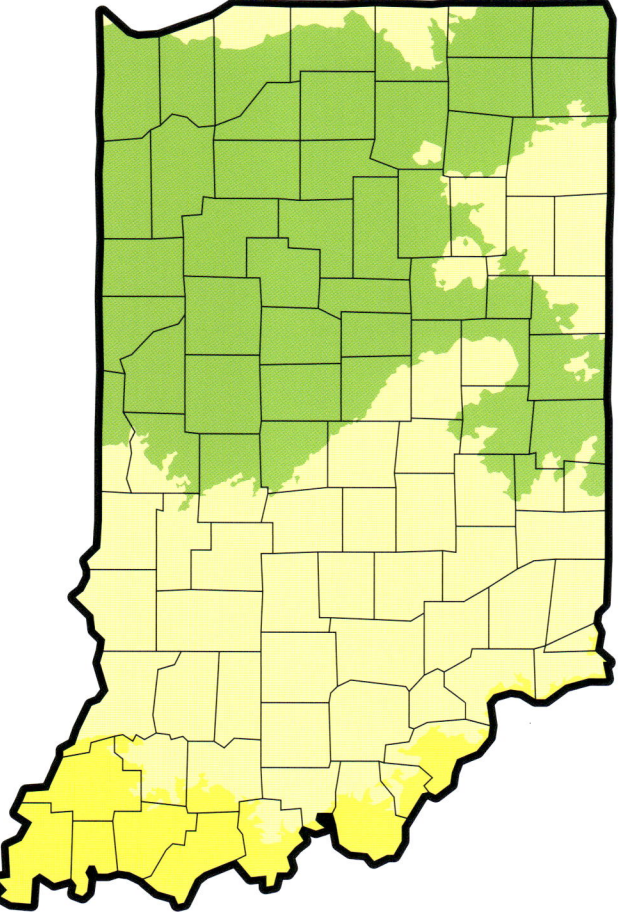

ZONE	Average Minimum Temperature
5 B	-10 to -15
6 A	-5 to -10
6 B	0 to -5

USDA Plant Hardiness Zone Map, 2012. Agricultural Research Service, U.S. Department of Agriculture. Accessed from http://planthardiness.ars.usda.gov.

ANNUALS

FOR INDIANA

Annuals are full of excitement, color, and instant gardener gratification. Most annuals share the benefit of having lasting impact all season long with interesting shades, textures, and shapes. Shopping for traditional annuals used to mean searching through a boring assortment of geraniums, impatiens, and marigolds. Happily, that has evolved with the modern garden center providing hundreds of glorious varieties of petunias, pansy, calibrachoa, ornamental edible vegetables, and tropicals, with many of the plants attracting pollinators and beneficial wildlife.

Mixing annuals with groundcovers, perennials, vegetables, and shrubs in both garden beds and containers can mean an endless celebration of color for your landscapes. For the Midwestern gardener, an annual is a plant that completes its life cycle in a single season. Typically an annual germinates from seed, grows, flowers, and dies all in one season.

Versatile and Interesting

Annuals allow a unique versatility in the garden; you can choose pollinator-attracting annuals to mix in your containers and beds, planting something new every season for the bees and butterflies. There are cool-weather annuals like violas, Icelandic poppies, and osteospermum that bloom brilliantly in the spring and fall but wilt in the heat of the summer. Hot-weather annuals like celosia, cleome, and cosmos seem to explode in celebration of the peak summer heat.

My garden has a significant display of annuals I consider dual-duty plants. Herbs such as oregano and globe basil help encourage bees, which love their scented flowers. Besides functioning simply as a beautifying tool in the garden, ornamental herb and vegetable edibles such as Swiss chard, kale, and purple basil can help feed your community. Every season I donate over 100 pounds of fresh vegetable and herb annuals to my local food pantry. Many lovely annuals such as nasturtium, pansy, and marigold are edible and make an astounding contribution to a salad. Culinary uses for annuals are extensive, and this certainly makes a strong argument for having them in your garden.

How to Plant Annuals

Seed starting an annual is quite easy and a great way to save money. You start seeds inside four to six weeks before planting or sow them directly in soil. If starting your seeds inside, it helps to have a sunny window or grow lights above the seedlings. Use an organic commercial seed-starting soil mix that focuses on organic plant growth. It

Annuals such as the spreading petunias from the 'Wave' petunia series combine brilliantly with Dichondra 'Silver Falls' as an excellent full-sun landscape planting.

is particularly important that your ornamental edible beds are chemical free. There are dozens of seed-starting kits on the market that work fine. Moisten the soil mix, fill the potting cells, and place a single seed in each cell of the seed tray according to seed packet directions. Keep moist until germination, then water regularly. Use organic liquid fertilizer to improve growth. Plant the seedlings in the garden bed once danger of frost has passed.

If you want instant color without having to grow the seeds yourself, simply go to your local garden center and purchase bedding plants. They come ready to plant in containers or flats and are often already in flower. Set out young plants following the recommended sunlight needs and spacing, to prevent crowding later. Prepare the planting hole with any soil amendments or organic fertilizers you want to add. Plants can be potbound when you bring them home, so remove them from their cells or containers and gently tease apart their roots. Place them in the soil and cover their roots. Water thoroughly.

Annuals are delightfully versatile plants and with so many available, the sky is the limit when it comes to planting combinations. My favorite thing to do is mix ornamental edible vegetables and herbs in with my annual flowers for a dual-purpose planting that can help feed my family. Adding annuals to your landscape plan brings color and excitement to your garden.

Alyssum

Lobularia maritima

Botanical Pronunciation
lob-yoo-LAIR-ree-uh muh-RIT-tim-muh

Other Name
Sweet alyssum

Bloom Period and Seasonal Color
Spring, summer, and fall blooms; white, yellow, pink, rose, violet, and lilac

Mature Height × Spread
4 to 8 inches × 6 to 12 inches

Seemingly dainty alyssum is actually a tough little plant known for its explosive flower power. Reseeding is common with alyssum, so plants that flower early could easily spread by the end of the season. Flowers perform best in cool-weather conditions and have a wonderfully sweet scent that attracts beneficial pollinators. Because alyssum has a mounding nature, it functions as a superb edger and the perfect filler in annual and perennial beds. Alyssum plants make excellent rock garden specimens as well, surviving brief periods of drought. They look fabulous spilling out of window boxes and container gardens. Alyssum is edible and tastes slightly like kale. Its flowers look very attractive sprinkled in salads, desserts, and even frozen in ice cubes for cocktails.

When, Where, and How to Plant

Alyssum is killed by a heavy frost, so plant seed in spring and summer after your last frost. It favors cool weather, and it prefers sun or part sun locations with good drainage, although it will adapt to part shade and continue to flower. Its seeds need light to germinate, so sow seeds on *top* of the soil, then water gently until rooted to prevent seeds from washing away. Or start indoors four weeks before planting outside. Be sure to amend soil according to soil testing results before planting seeds or baby plants.

Growing Tips

Water plants regularly for the first week. After the initial week, water as you would the other annuals in your garden. Fertilize once per month with a liquid organic fertilizer to see stronger plant performance. If plants get leggy, simply shear back their growth with clippers; they will grow fresh flowers.

Regional Advice and Care

Known as a low-maintenance annual, deadheading alyssum is not typically needed. Alyssum will grow well in clay and sand, but do better with organic matter added to the soil. Plants grown in shadier conditions might be prone to powdery mildew, which can be treated with an organic fungicide.

Companion Planting and Design

Alyssum is easy to grow, and the plants make a wonderful living mulch as they keep soil cool and attract beneficial insects which will stay for the companion plants. Planting the flowers in between roses, perennials, and even vegetable rows helps keep pests off the companion plantings. Good companion plants include roses, geraniums, zinnias, and edible ornamental vegetables such as kale, cabbage, and Swiss chard.

Try These

'Snow Crystals' is a fragrant, large flowering plant with a vigorous, trailing nature. 'New Carpet of Snow' is delightful in fairy garden plantings because it only grows 3 inches tall. 'Easter Bonnet Lemonade' is a newer variety that has white flowering clumps with pale yellow highlights. These plants stay compact and tidy much longer than other alyssums. 'Easter Bonnet Deep Pink' is the brightest pink available and is relatively frost tolerant through the first of fall.

Angelonia

Angelonia angustifolia

Botanical Pronunciation
an-jel-OH-nee-ah an-gus-tih-FOE-lee-ah

Other Name
Summer snapdragon

Bloom Period and Seasonal Color
Spring to fall; blue, lavender, pink, rose, white, stripes, and bicolor

Mature Height × Spread
1 to 4 feet × 6 to 12 inches

Angelonias are a remarkably drought-tolerant and low-maintenance annual. They are often called summer snapdragons because they resemble a snapdragon in their upright habit; however, they hold up better in heat and drought than snapdragons. They flower most of the spring, summer, and on into the fall with no deadheading required. There are many cultivars within the angelonia family—some are shorter and have tiny blooms and some are taller with large blossoms. All have varying degrees of fragrance that smell somewhat like grape or apple. Because of their strong stems and long-lasting blooms, they make an excellent choice for cut flower arrangements. Hummingbird moths and other pollinators love angelonia.

When, Where, and How to Plant

Angelonias can be found during the spring at garden centers across the state and can also be grown from seed. Plant after Mother's Day to ensure there will not be a frost as the plants really prefer warmer weather. Angelonias grow their best in a full sun location with a bed amended with a heavy level of organic matter. They will perform in part sun, but require six to eight hours of direct sun per day in order to produce hearty plants with lots of flower spikes. There are many different varieties of angelonia, so be sure to check the label of a plant for growth habits to make sure you have the correct height for your growing situation. Outstanding as container plants, angelonias do well as a featured plant or as part of a mixed container design as well.

Growing Tips

Water very well until established. Once established, this plant is in it for the long haul and will require very minimal care. Fertilize with an organic fertilizer every four weeks. Staking is not required.

Regional Advice and Care

Deadheading is not needed for this vigorous flower; however, trimming overgrowth or leaning stems will not harm the plant. Aphids are best treated by squirting a strong blast of water from a garden hose or spraying the bugs with soapy water. Plants grown in shadier conditions might be prone to powdery mildew, which can be treated with an organic fungicide.

Companion Planting and Design

Angelonia's upright habit makes it the perfect taller companion plant for cascading plants such as petunia, calibrachoa, or sweet potato vine. They are gorgeous in front of ornamental edibles, roses, fountain grass, and plume grass.

Try These

'AngelMist™ Purple Stripe' is a white-and-purple striped variety that grows very low to the ground, making this plant an interesting groundcover. 'Serena Blue' grows up to 20 inches high and is a marvelous combination with contrasting plants such as a yellow calibrachoa or gerbera daisy. 'Angelface® White' is a great cut flower and blends well in container plantings.

Baby Blue Eyes

Nemophila menziesii

Botanical Pronunciation
ne-MA-fih-lah men-ZEE-see-eye

Bloom Period and Seasonal Color
Early spring; blue flowers

Mature Height × Spread
6 inches × 12 inches

Baby blue eyes is a wave of true blue color in early spring. In California, it is a wildflower, so it's rather drought tolerant as most natives can be. Here, this flower is often used as a spring annual. Charming little blue flowers with white eyes adorn fernlike foliage and capture the hearts of all. Easy to grow from seed, they are a perfect rock garden addition, do well in hanging baskets and containers, and serve as a brilliant filler in the spring bulb garden. Victorians loved their tiny flowers and sowed seed in early spring and again in early fall for a delightful rebloom. I fell in love with baby blue eyes while viewing it at a botanic garden where their little flower heads bobbed and danced in the wind.

When, Where, and How to Plant
Sow directly in soil in spring to early summer after temperatures consistently reach at least 68 degrees. It prefers cool weather and can be sown in fall. Disturbing the roots of baby blue eyes will upset its growth cycle, so transplanting full-sized plants is not always successful. While the sweet flowers prefer direct sun, once the heat arrives, plants wilt, so it is better to plant in part sun or a location in shade during the heat of the late day. Baby blue eyes can grow in light sandy soils but prefers well-drained soil enriched with manure or compost.

Growing Tips
Water gently when first planted so the seeds don't wash away. Fertilizing is rarely needed, although adding an organic fertilizer when starting the plants can help spring growth.

Regional Advice and Care
Deadheading extends flower power and prevents excessive self-sowing. Snails like the baby seedlings; set out organic snail traps if concerned. Aphids are best treated with a strong blast of water from a garden hose or spraying the bugs with soapy water. Plants grown in shadier conditions might be prone to powdery mildew, which can be treated with an organic fungicide.

Companion Planting and Design
Baby blue eyes is a delightful spring underplanting to bulbs such as yellow daffodils. When planted in a mixed bed with red tulips and white daffodils, baby blue eyes can make an "All American" red, white, and blue design statement, which is perfect for landscape design in public areas. Featured with hyacinth, the gently nodding heads of baby blue eyes seems to spill over the edges of a container. Large masses of baby blue eyes can look like a river because of its undulating movements and spectacular color.

Try These
'Atomaria' is a white variety with black spots, which sometimes has a faint blue tint or blue veins in the corolla. 'Penny Black' is a gorgeous white-rimmed flower with deep purple centers that are such a deep velvety shade as to appear black in certain lights.

Bacopa

Sutera cordata

Botanical Pronunciation
soo-TAIR-ah kor-DAY-tah

Bloom Period and Seasonal Color
Spring to fall; white, lavender, pink, and bicolor flowers

Mature Height × Spread
6 to 8 inches × up to 36 inches

Bacopa is one of my favorite flowering plants, spilling over a window box and serving as an excellent groundcover. Vigorous and drought tolerant, bacopa has grown in popularity as a tough plant that can take a beating and still return after summer's heat has abused it. Hybridizers have developed new flower color combinations beyond the traditional white that include lavender, pink, and bicolors. Bacopa has branchy, cascading stems that can trail up to 36 inches and, if taken care of properly, can have tiny, five-petaled flowers along every inch of stem from spring all the way until frost. There is no need to deadhead or trim the plant unless you are interested in increasing its fullness or branching habit because bacopa is self-cleaning.

When, Where, and How to Plant

Plant in spring after the last frost either from seed or transplants, providing a rich, well-drained soil with compost or manure mixed in for better root development. Bacopa will grow well on its own but enjoys an organic fertilizer once every four weeks or so, particularly if planted in a container. While this plant will do well in sun or shade, it will flower more if you plant it in sun to part sun. Space 8 to 12 inches apart.

Growing Tips

While bacopa is known to be a drought-tolerant plant that will not wilt in the heat, it craves consistent watering. If you do not water the plant regularly, it suffers drought stress and drops flowers and buds from the plant. After the flowers drop, it will take two to three weeks for the plant to regain its full bloom capacity. Therefore, monitor the soil to make sure it never becomes too dried out.

Regional Advice and Care

While consistent watering is important, overwatering will create root disease problems. Deadheading is not needed; however, trimming overgrowth or leaning stems will not harm the plant. Treat aphids with a strong blast of water from a garden hose or spray the bugs with soapy water.

Companion Planting and Design

Bacopa can suffer from flower drop in excessive drought conditions; it's beneficial to plant with companion plants that might provide advance indication of drought. Coleus, petunias, and calibrachoa all wilt when dry, so use these companions as an indicator to let you know when bacopa is drying out. Water immediately if you see wilting companions. Bacopa is great as a low feature with taller plants and grasses in containers.

Try These

'Boutique™ Tie Dye White' (in photo) is a marvelous newer variety that has pale white flowers set off by a hot pink ring and bright yellow center. It's gorgeous paired with other pink or yellow flowers. 'Snowstorm® Giant Snowflake®' is a clear white. 'Big Falls Dark Pink' has large flowers for the species and an intensely bold pink color.

Banana

Musa basjoo

Botanical Pronunciation
MEW-suh BAS-joo

Bloom Period and Seasonal Color
Summer; orange flowers, foilage interest

Mature Height × Spread
6 to 14 feet × 8 to 10 feet

Bananas can definitely be grown as an annual or an herbaceous perennial in the Midwest. If there is a cold winter that goes below -15 degrees, the plant will not survive as an herbaceous perennial and will need to be replanted. Therefore, I treat this plant as an annual; I do my best to mulch well in the hopes that it will return the following year. Seeing the large tropical leaves of the banana is an unexpected surprise in a northern garden bed that can add an eye-lifting level of interest to your landscape. I have found it to be a conversation piece next to my front patio. While the bananas produced are inedible and seedy, the banana leaves are edible and I often use them in culinary dishes.

When, Where, and How to Plant
After the last frost, plant a banana plant from a nursery or online catalog in a sunny spot, out of the wind and in well-drained soil that is organically rich with compost and manure. Windy locations can damage the large leaves, which can grow up to 6 feet long in perfect conditions. If you plant a banana deeper—up to 12 inches—the plant will be more likely to survive through winter.

Growing Tips
Mulch well to help retain moisture; in fact, bananas love water and grow well with a consistently moist soil. Fertilize regularly with organic fertilizer throughout the season. Overwintering a banana is easy if you dig it up after the first frost, wrap the roots in plastic, and store it in a cool, dark, frost-free location like a basement. To keep the plant in the ground, let it die back, then cut off the dead part of stem, mound a layer of mulch around the plant base, and cover the mound with black plastic or burlap. Uncover in spring and see if it has survived. Yes? Fantastic, you saved money. No? Go out and get yourself another banana; it is time to start over.

Regional Advice and Care
Japanese beetles seem to love bananas, but it's mostly pest-free. For an organic solution, handpick the pests and drop them into soapy water. Cut wind- or pest-damaged leaves with scissors to keep the leaf edges looking crisp.

Companion Planting and Design
Great companion plants include hakonechloa and other more tropical plants such as caladium, colocasia, and canna. Planting petunias and other annuals around the base of the plant helps feature the height of the banana. I have seen an upstart cherry tomato use a banana as a support quite successfully, which speaks to the possibilities of adding the banana to an ornamental edible garden as a center feature.

Try These
Other hardy bananas include *Musa xishuangbannaensis* 'Mekong Giant', which can grow 20 feet tall, and *M. velutina* 'Pink Banana', which is a dwarf that grows 6 to 9 feet tall.

Beet

Beta vulgaris

Botanical Pronunciation
BAY-tah VOOL-gah-rus

Other Name
Beetroot

Bloom Period and Seasonal Color
Summer; green or burgundy leaves

Mature Height × Spread
4 to 12 inches × 2 to 8 inches

Years ago I was searching for a burgundy-leaved annual when I came across a six-pack of 'Bull's Blood' beet at a local nursery. I snatched it up and planted it in my containers that year as a tall center balance to white-flowered bacopa in my window boxes. From that point on I was addicted to this ornamental edible, which can be harvested for its flavorful leaf, and then harvested at the end of the season for its root. Versatile, heat and cold tolerant, colorful, nutritious, and an excellent design filler, beets are a perfect ornamental edible and can easily be incorporated into a garden design. Vitamins and minerals found in beets include iron, calcium, vitamins B6, B12, C, and magnesium.

When, Where, and How to Plant
Beets can be planted anytime after the first frost and are exceptionally cold hardy, so they even can be planted and harvested into early fall. While transplants work fine, it is also very easy to grow from seed. Loosely cover the seeds with ½-inch of soil. Plants should be placed in well-drained soil that is richly amended with rotted manure or compost.

Growing Tips
By and large, beets prefer cool weather and will seem to pause in their growth midsummer but will stay fresh looking as long as they are watered consistently. Beets like consistent and even moisture. Mulching enables better moisture retention and protects against weeds. If beets try to bolt, simply cut off the flowering stem at the base of the plant.

Fertilize with an organic timed-release fertilizer at time of planting.

Regional Advice and Care
Plants are typically problem-free but can be attacked by aphids and other pests. Treat the pests organically by spraying them with soapy water or picking them off. Beet roots can get tough and woody if left too long in the soil at midsummer. If you grow the plant for the root, be sure to pull them out at midsummer and replant. However, if you are growing as an ornamental for the leaf, leave the plant in the ground all summer.

Companion Planting and Design
Beets, specifically 'Bull's Blood' with its powerful burgundy leaf and stem, look pretty and provide spectacular contrast when planted with gerbera daisy. Zinnia, petunia, and bacopa look wonderful with beets in window boxes and containers. White-stemmed Swiss chard looks fantastic behind a row of burgundy-stemmed beets. Beets are excellent mixed in with herbs, lobelia, and blue-hued kale in containers.

Try These
'Bull's Blood' is the most colorful beet on the market with flavorful, fade-proof, deep burgundy leaves and stems that flourish from spring until fall. 'Cylindra' has red stems that resemble Swiss chard. 'Touchstone Gold' has golden stems and a brightly colored green leaf. 'Merlin' is a smaller variety with a purple stem and bright green leaf.

Begonia

Begonia × hybrida

Botanical Pronunciation
bih-GOAN-yuh HY-brid-ah

Other Name
Dragon Wing begonia

Bloom Period and Seasonal Color
Spring to fall; red and pink flowers

Mature Height × Spread
12 to 15 inches × 12 to 15 inches

There are many varieties of begonia, from perennial to tuberous, but my absolute favorite heat-tolerant variety of *Begonia × hybrida* is 'Dragon Wing'. This beautiful hybrid from the Begoniaceae family is an introduction that blooms nonstop from May until October. Because it is a sterile hybrid, it does not self-seed and puts all its energy into flowering. Dragon Wing has exceptional tolerance for heat and humidity, performs well in deep shade areas, and has few disease problems. Dragon Wing leaves are elongated, pointy, and waxy with hints of bronze around the edges. When you see the begonia at the first of the season at the garden center they look ugly without flowers, but once planted, they quickly become the queen of the shade annuals.

When, Where, and How to Plant

Plant this flower in the spring after the last frost in a rich, well-drained soil with compost or manure mixed in for better root development. This is a compact plant that forms dense mounds, so be sure to give it plenty of room to grow. While the plant will do well in part sun, it really prefers part shade or shade. Make sure the plant gets afternoon shade if it is in sunnier conditions.

Growing Tips

Dragon Wing likes an organic fertilizer once every four weeks. Dragon Wing prefers moisture but will tolerate short periods of drought. Dragon Wing can be overwintered indoors by cutting the plant back, placing in a low light area, and reducing water to hibernate. Should you want to enjoy the blooms indoors, bring the plant in and place in a container with exposure to a brightly lit area. Begonias enjoy moisture, so misting the plant as well as watering regularly will be critical for the plant's survival.

Regional Advice and Care

Deadheading is not needed for this flower; however, trimming overgrowth or leaning stems will not harm the plant. There are no serious insect or disease problems. Overwatering in shady conditions can sometimes encourage powdery mildew or blight. These fungus issues can be treated with an organic fungicide.

Companion Planting and Design

Since Dragon Wing does so well in shade, I prefer to partner it with colorful shade companions like sweet potato vine and coleus. Ornamental edibles such as lacinto kale and Swiss chard make wonderful container companions as well. Dragon Wing looks amazing planted *en masse* beneath shade trees.

Try These

Dragon Wing™ Red Begonia was the first cultivar and has amazing red flowers that look fantastic massed together in ground plantings. Dragon Wing™ Pink Begonia blends well with purple- and pink-flowering plants. Other cultivars of *Begonia × hybrida* include 'Sparks Will Fly', which has an amazing orange flower, and 'Gryphon', grown mostly for its unusual and colorful leaf.

Calibrachoa

Calibrachoa hybrids

Botanical Pronunciation
kal-ih-brah-KOE-ah

Other Name
Million bells

Bloom Period and Seasonal Color
Spring to fall; yellow, bronze, red, white, lavender, pink, striped, and bicolor flowers

Mature Height × Spread
6 to 14 inches × 6 to 24 inches

When growing calibrachoa, or million bells, expect nonstop explosions of flower from May until October. There are dozens of colors of calibrachoa, which resemble miniature petunias with darling little bell-shaped, self-cleaning blooms. Calibrachoa are frequently compared to petunias because of their similar habit; however, petunias collapse with heavy spring and summer rains, while the calibrachoa will pop back up with vigor after a heavy rain. It loves heat, but if suffering brief bouts of drought stress, calibrachoa stays bushy and compact, therefore making it a great full sun plant both in containers and garden beds. As a trailing plant that is smothered in blossoms most of the season, calibrachoa looks marvelous as an addition to window boxes and containers.

When, Where, and How to Plant

Plant this flower in sun, at least ten hours per day, after the last frost either from seed or transplants, providing a rich, well-drained soil. Calibrachoa sometime suffers from root rot, so it needs good drainage. Calibrachoa prefers a little afternoon shade and likes to feed. Mix chelated iron in the soil when planting to help keep the plant green.

Growing Tips

Add a water-soluble organic fertilizer every few weeks. Water regularly, letting the top of soil to become dry to the touch before watering. If you wait too long to water, the plant will wilt. Container plants typically require more watering. Cloudy days with wetter weather will delay plant flowering.

Regional Advice and Care

Deadheading is not needed for this flower, but pinching stems back will encourage branching. Flowers often close at night and on cloudy days but will open again with the sun. Fight off aphids with a strong blast of water from a garden hose or spray the bugs with soapy water. Pythium, powdery mildew, and other fungus issues can occur with heavy rain or shadier conditions. Treat with an organic fungicide.

Companion Planting and Design

Ideal companion plants for hanging baskets, window boxes, and containers include euphorbia, angelonia, geranium, grasses, sweet potato vine, and other colors and varieties of calibrachoa. Mass ground plantings of calibrachoa look great in front of perennial heuchera, grasses, and shrubs. I like to design a container with a single flowering color theme—all yellow or all orange, for instance. This design idea is quite easy to do with marigolds, cockscomb, and calibrachoa.

Try These

There are literally dozens of varieties of calibrachoa. My favorites tend to be the ones that feature colors that cannot be easily found in other bell-like flower types such as the petunia. For example, 'Minifamous Double Deep Yellow' is a shorter variety with double yellow flowers that resemble roses. Superbells® Tangerine Punch has the most astonishing shades of orange with a burnt orange eye. Superbells® Lemon Slice has an unusual white "pie slice" stripe that runs through the flower.

Cockscomb

Celosia argentea

Botanical Pronunciation
sell-OH-see-ah ar-JEN-tee-ah

Bloom Period and Seasonal Color
Spring to fall; red, yellow, orange, and magenta

Mature Height × Spread
6 to 40 inches × 6 to 12 inches

With bold velvety blooms, cockscomb is the drama queen of the annual world. Some label the plants as gaudy, but I find the happy colors bring personality to a cutting garden. As most royal family lines prove complicated, so is the horticultural taxonomy for celosia. Names for the individual celosias become easier to understand when you compare the shapes of each variety: *Celosia argentea* 'Plumosa' have fluffy plume flowers (see photo); *C. argentea* var. Cristata have crests that look a bit like the anatomical shape of a brain; *C. argentea* var. Spicata have stiff, spiky flowers; and *C. argentea* var. Argentea is one of the most widely consumed greens around the world, particularly in Africa. Young leaves, stems, and flowers are edible with a mild flavor in salads and stews.

When, Where, and How to Plant

Plant seeds in full sun after the last frost in richly prepared, well-drained soil. The plant does not like heavy clay soil and excessive moisture, so amend your soil as required. Celosia plants take about three months after seed germination to flower, so start the seeds indoors six weeks before the last frost in order to have earlier blooms. Seeds are susceptible to damping off disease. Using a seed-heating mat to provide warmth will help the seed growth.

Growing Tips

Celosia are drought tolerant and produce striking flowers without requiring much fertilization. Use an organic water-soluble fertilizer such as watered-down fish emulsion as a nutrient boost once a month. Water moderately.

Regional Advice and Care

Some celosias may need staking if the variety is particularly tall. These varieties are susceptible to windstorm breakage. Spider mites can be a problem during hot dry weather. Use a soapy water mix to spray on the spider mites. Treat the entire plant, including the tops and bottoms of leaves, every six days until eliminated. Celosia is susceptible to root rot if it is planted in soil with poor drainage.

Companion Planting and Design

For a bold and colorful garden show, consider planting a celosia border; plant short celosia plants in the front, medium in the middle, and tall celosia in the back. Zinnias and marigolds make excellent planting partners as do ornamental edible vegetables. Celosias are tremendously long lasting in the vase as a cut flower and should be considered for all types of flower design; both the fresh and dried flower heads make quite a statement.

Try These

'Amigo Red' is an adorable compact variety, growing only 6 inches high, and is perfect for the container garden. A conversation piece in the garden is definitely Bombay Series, which is a variety that has strong colors and brainlike shapes. 'Fresh Look Yellow' is a gorgeous fluffy yellow flower. 'First Flame Orange' is a newer variety that has a dazzling orange fluff of a flower that is a show-off in the landscape.

Coleus

Solenostemon scutellarioides

Botanical Pronunciation
sol-en-oh-STEM-on skoot-el-lar-ee-OY-deez

Bloom Period and Seasonal Color
Blooms very late summer; foliage is colorful and varied

Mature Height × Spread
6 to 36 inches × 10 to 24 inches

For years, coleus were used exclusively as a vigorous shade annual, adored for their amazing variety of leaf colors and textures. New hybrids are particularly sun tolerant and have expanded the landscape design potential of coleus. While the leaves—which can be rounded, elongated, puckered, frilly, dissected, tiny, large, or any combination therein—are what makes coleus famous, if it's left to flower, it will be smothered with pollinators and hummingbirds. Coleus foliage colors are equally exciting, ranging from chartreuse to hot magenta to yellow to rust and every tint in between. It's excellent planted *en masse* for a wave of fabulous groundcover color in the landscape. Coleus are equally wonderful as filler foliage or a feature plant in container designs, making them a remarkably colorful garden statement plant.

When, Where, and How to Plant
Preferring fertile, well-drained soil, coleus need to be planted according to its sunlight preferences. Be sure to research the specific variety when purchasing seeds or plants. Start seeds indoors six weeks before the last frost date or sow seeds directly in the ground after the last danger of frost. Propagating coleus is simple and can be easily accomplished for overwintering indoors by taking tip cuttings in early. Cut a 3-inch section from a stem without a flower. Remove the lower leaves, leaving the top leaves intact, and place in a small pot with soil. Move the container to a warm location with bright light exposure and keep consistently moist. Cuttings develop roots within four to five weeks and can be transplanted for overwintering as a houseplant.

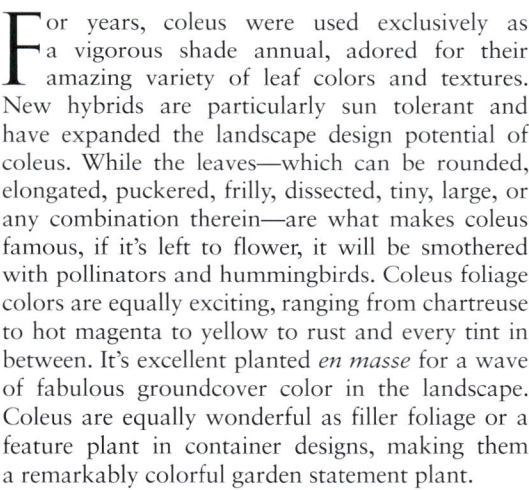

Growing Tips
Coleus prefers consistent watering and regular fertilization. Container plants like to be fertilized with an organic fertilizer every two weeks; ground plantings can go every four weeks.

Regional Advice and Care
To improve branching and a full habit, pinch off flowers. However, if you are trying to attract pollinators and hummingbirds, or want to collect seeds later in the season, be sure to leave the flowers. There are no serious insect or disease problems. Overwatering in shady conditions can sometimes encourage powdery mildew or root rot. These fungus issues can be treated with an organic fungicide.

Companion Planting and Design
Companion plants that work very well are ornamental edibles, sweet potato vine, begonias, fountain grass, and cannas. Each coleus has a unique growing habit—trailing, miniature, bushy, tall, sun loving, or shade loving—so companion planting is totally dependent on the size and nature of the specific coleus.

Try These
'Under the Sea® Bone Fish' has deeply dissected leaves with bold magenta and chartreuse lime colorations (see photo above). 'Luminesce' is an astounding neon pink color with a leaf that is sharply pointed. For a sun-loving variety, try 'Chocolate Mint Premium Sun', which has a leaf with a deep chocolate center surrounded by a bright green edge.

Dusty Miller

Senecio cineraria

Botanical Pronunciation
sen-NEESH-shee-oh sin-ner-RAIR-ee-uh

Other Name
Silverdust

Bloom Period and Seasonal Color
All season; silver-white foliage with yellow blooms in summer

Mature Height × Spread
6 to 24 inches × 12 to 24 inches

Dusty miller is named after its incredibly bright silver-white foliage. Its leaves make an amazing statement in the annual garden bed or window box, but its yellow flowers are an excellent pollinator attractor. Dusty miller is grown more for its leaf designs, which can be delicate and lacy or quite bold and wide depending upon the variety of plant. Typically this charming plant has a mounding habit and is remarkably heat- and drought-tolerant, with resistance to animal pests. Do not let its delicate look fool you; dusty miller is a tough little plant that can hold up to heavy wind and the first frosts in autumn relatively well. You can easily find the plants outlasting other annuals and performing into late October or early November.

When, Where, and How to Plant

For water-saving initiatives in your garden, you can plant dusty miller in xeric gardens with similarly drought-resistant plants. Dusty miller prefers full sun and while it will survive nicely in a drought-tolerant garden, it will also grow quite well mixed with grasses, perennials, or other annuals within a traditional garden bed that has soil amended with plenty of organic matter. Germinating from seed is easy. Do not cover seeds heavily with soil as the seeds are small and need light to germinate. Damping off can happen if the soil is kept too moist.

Growing Tips

Root rot is a complication often seen with this plant, as it loves dry conditions and can easily be

overwatered. Let the soil dry out between watering. It does not need feeding.

Regional Advice and Care

Pests are rare, but if you see insects on the leaves, simply spray with a soapy water mix. While dusty miller is known as an annual, I have seen the plant come back year after year. Simply cut off the plant at the ground level after it crumbles down from cold weather. Be patient in the spring as it is slow to start, but plants often return by June. It does not harm the plant if you cut it back to prevent it from crowding its neighbors.

Companion Planting and Design

When building an all-white themed garden bed, dusty miller helps by adding a striking white leaf tone in the mix. Excellent as a border edging, dusty miller looks fantastic in front of grasses and boldly colored annual flowers such as zinnias, celosia, and geranium. It's lovely planted in a mailbox garden where watering access might be limited. Dusty miller looks good when planted as an edger for a night garden because its silver foliage is easily seen in low light.

Try These

'Silverdust' is remarkably cold hardy. 'Cirrus' has fuzzy, elliptic, lobed leaves. 'New Look' has whiter leaves and is an excellent contribution to a floral arrangement.

Euphorbia

Euphorbia hypericifolia

Botanical Pronunciation
you-FOR-bee-uh hy-PEER-ih-see-FOE-lee-uh

Bloom Period and Seasonal Color
All season; white and blush blooms

Mature Height × Spread
8 to 12 inches × 20 to 28 inches

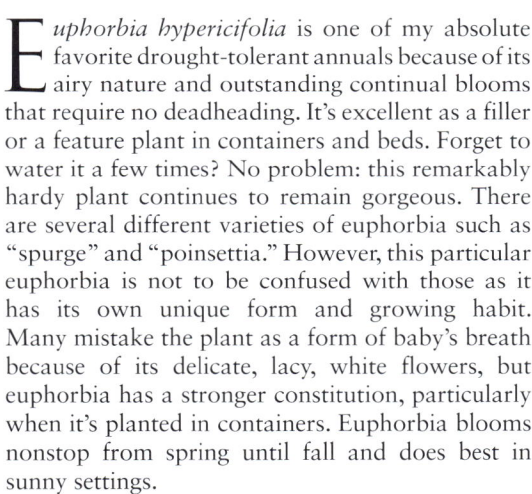

Euphorbia hypericifolia is one of my absolute favorite drought-tolerant annuals because of its airy nature and outstanding continual blooms that require no deadheading. It's excellent as a filler or a feature plant in containers and beds. Forget to water it a few times? No problem: this remarkably hardy plant continues to remain gorgeous. There are several different varieties of euphorbia such as "spurge" and "poinsettia." However, this particular euphorbia is not to be confused with those as it has its own unique form and growing habit. Many mistake the plant as a form of baby's breath because of its delicate, lacy, white flowers, but euphorbia has a stronger constitution, particularly when it's planted in containers. Euphorbia blooms nonstop from spring until fall and does best in sunny settings.

When, Where, and How to Plant
Frost- and cold-sensitive, euphorbia requires warmer growing conditions. Be sure to plant well after the last frost in well-drained soil that has been amended with plenty of organic matter. Wear gloves as all euphorbia have a sticky white sap that can cause skin irritation. Although euphorbias prefer sun, most will perform in shade but will be more leggy and less florific.

Growing Tips
Water well after planting until acclimated; however, do not overwater as the plant does well with dry conditions. Fertilizer is not strictly required although adding an organic fertilizer once or twice mid-season will not harm the plant.

Regional Advice and Care
Trim back or pinch plants to encourage branching at any time throughout the growing period. Make sure all tools are washed after trimming to remove sap. Pests should be sprayed with a soap and water mixture. At the end of the growing season, feel free to bring inside as a winter season houseplant.

Companion Planting and Design
Planting *Euphorbia hypericifolia* with other low-maintenance plants such as lantana and sweet potato vine in a container makes water conservation a snap. All-white gardens are enhanced with the frothy white mounds of flowers planted as a perennial filler or garden bed edger. Because of its full, mounded nature, *E. hypericifolia* looks stunning in a container partnered with calibrachoa and angelonia. When using *E. hypericifolia* as a cut flower in arrangements, it will be necessary to hold the stems in a flame for several seconds or dip stems in boiling water to prevent sap bleeding.

Try These
Tough varieties include 'Cool Breeze', which can get up to 28 inches wide, and 'Breathless™ White Euphorbia', which has a darker foliage variation. 'Breathless™ Blush Euphorbia' has leaves tinged with red and clear white flowers. Award winner 'Diamond Frost® Euphorbia' trails out to 24 inches and has a different Latin name, *Euphorbia graminea*, although it has nearly the identical form and look of *E. hypericifolia*.

Flowering Tobacco

Nicotiana alata

Botanical Pronunciation
nih-koe-shee-AY-nuh ah-LAH-tuh

Other Name
Jasmine tobacco

Bloom Period and Seasonal Color
Summer to fall; white, yellow, lime green, pink, and red flowers

Mature Height × Spread
12 to 48 inches × 12 to 24 inches

A scented flowering tobacco bloom can be a little bit of heaven; many varieties have a scent that is downright alluring and are more likely to have a stronger scent toward late evening and at night. Heirlooms often have a stronger scent, some cultivars are scentless, and a few newer hybrids have light scents. Each flower is a colorful, trumpet-shaped tube with star-shaped petals. Hummingbirds adore the plant during the day, and hummingbird moths will spend hours circling flowering tobacco in the evening. While it *is* a member of the tobacco family, it is not recommended for consumption; it is addictive when smoked or sniffed and poisonous if eaten. Some cultivars can reach up to 4 feet tall and are narrow, so fit in most compact gardens quite nicely.

When, Where, and How to Plant
Nicotiana grows best in a sunny spot but prefers afternoon shade during the hot season. Soil should be well drained, rich organically, and consistently moist. Start seeds indoors 4 to 6 weeks before the last frost or plant directly on to the soil. Seeds are incredibly tiny, so try mixing the seed with sand for easier spreading. Press seeds lightly into the seed-starting mix and do not cover them as they require light to germinate.

Growing Tips
Water at the base of the plant to prevent powdery mildew; container plants typically require more watering. Mulching your plants will help hold the moisture around the base of the plant during hot weather.

Regional Advice and Care
Newer hybrid varieties are self-cleaning and require no deadheading. Although relatively pest-free, should spider mites or aphids settle on the plants, spray with insecticidal soap. Aphids can be dislodged with a spray of water, but be careful not to break the stems or leaves. Although rare, flowering tobacco is sometimes susceptible to tobacco mosaic virus or downy mildew (*Peronospora tabaci*). Signs include ringspots on leaves or yellowed crinkled growth; pull these diseased plants from the garden and inoculate the soil with an amendment that has chelated iron. Many varieties self-seed; supervise this to make sure the plant does not invade.

Companion Planting and Design
Night gardens and evening paths are enhanced when filled with fragrant varieties of flowering tobacco. Shorter varieties work well in containers, along borders, and in mass plantings. Taller varieties do well at the back of an annual bed or mixed into an informal cottage garden. Plant scented varieties in window boxes where their evening scent can drift into your home at night.

Try These
'Nicki Red' is a short variety with a bold color that has good weather tolerance and nonstop flowering. 'Saratoga' is very short, blooms early in the season, and has a light evening scent. 'Eau de Cologne Mixed' has an amazing scent, mixed bright colors, and grows to be around 2 feet tall.

Geranium

Pelargonium × hortorum

Botanical Pronunciation
pell-lar-GO-nee-um hor-TOR-rum

Other Name
House geranium

Bloom Period and Seasonal Color
Spring to fall; red, white, lavender, salmon, orange, pink, striped, and bicolor flowers

Mature Height × Spread
5 to 36 inches × 12 to 36 inches

House geraniums (also called zonal geraniums) have had a reputation in the garden world as being old-fashioned. Yet, with new cultivars that include miniature and dwarf varieties, some with stripes and bicolor color shades, I have found the geranium to be filled with new excitement for the window box and garden bed. Scented geraniums are essentially house geraniums grown for their extremely fragrant leaves. They are magnificent featured next to busy walkways. Scents are split among seven prime categories: rose, lemon, mint, fruit and nut, spice, pungent, and oak-leaved. Sitting on a patio next to a rose-scented geranium can leave one feeling as if he or she is laying in a bed of roses. The scented leaves are excellent tucked into a modern day tussy-mussy.

When, Where, and How to Plant
Plant this flower where it will get at least ten hours of sun per day, after the last frost, either from seed or plant, in a rich, well-drained soil. It needs air circulation, so don't crowd the plants.

Growing Tips
House geraniums enjoy a light mulch cover to cool the root zone and help hold water. Do not overwater; house geraniums are fairly drought tolerant and need to dry out between watering or they can suffer from root rot. Feed a water-soluble organic fertilizer every few weeks. But do not overfertilize or you will have heavy leaf production and fewer flowers.

Regional Advice and Care
Deadheading keeps the plant in bloom. House geraniums can be sensitive to several fungal diseases such as black leg, blight, root and stem rots, rust, and botrytis blight. These can be controlled by preventative foliar applications of an organic fungicide. Pests include mites, mealybugs, caterpillars, aphids, and Japanese beetles. Handpick beetles and larger pests, and use a soapy water solution for the other types of common pests.

Companion Planting and Design
House geraniums are classic container and window box plants. For a bold container combination, try mixing a bright orange house geranium with purple petunias, chartreuse sweet potato vine, and white *Euphorbia hypericifolia*. Miniature geraniums are great border plants and look fabulous with other drought-tolerant plants such as zinnia and salvia.

Try These
There are endless varieties of house geraniums. Delightful 5-inch miniatures like the red 'Caligula' or orange 'Coddenham' offer an interesting look as a path edger. For a taller burst of bright orange color try 'Sunrise Orange Geranium Zonal'. 'Allure Light Pink' has a loose, pale pink flower with a memorable hot pink blotch in the middle. 'Attar of Roses' is a delightful rose-scented geranium. 'Chocolate Mint' smells sweet and chocolaty, just as its name describes.

Gerbera

Gerbera jamesonii

Botanical Pronunciation
GUR-bur-uh juh-may-SUN-ee-eye

Other Name
Transvaal daisy

Bloom Period and Seasonal Color
Spring and fall; red, pink, yellow, orange, salmon, and white flowers

Mature Height × Spread
6 to 24 inches × 12 to 24 inches

The National Garden Bureau awarded the gerbera daisy its Annual of the Year award because the plant is an easy-to-grow, colorful annual that has gorgeous, long-lasting blooms. Preferring cooler evenings, gerbera daisies perform best in the spring and the fall and must have heat relief in the mid-summer, such as afternoon shade, or they wilt. Plants come in dozens of eye-catching color variations from pale to bold shades. Flowers have velvety petals, large eyes, and rest on thick, leafless stems above the plant's crown. Marvelous as a cut flower, gerbera daisies last nearly two weeks if freshly cut under water. To avoid early wilt on the cut flowers, do not display gerbera daisies near ripening fruits or vegetables because the gas they emit during ripening can affect the flowers.

When, Where, and How to Plant

Gerbera daisies prefer extremely well-drained soil, are tolerant of sandy soil, and do best when planted in full sun after the last frost. Seeds need to be planted on top of the soil as they require light to germinate. Plant at least 12 weeks before last frost if starting indoors. When purchasing plants, make sure they have not been overwatered or have rot; search for healthy plants for better success.

Growing Tips

Do not overwater as gerberas prefer drying out between waterings. Add a water-soluble organic fertilizer frequently, at least every few weeks.

Regional Advice and Care

Deadheading keeps the plant continually blooming. Gerbera are fairly trouble-free, but they can be sensitive to several fungal diseases including blackspot, crown rot, and root rot, mostly due to overwatering and poor planting locations. Encourage space and good air circulation, and remove dead leaves quickly to help prevent fungal problems. Spray aphids off and treat other pests with a soapy water spray.

Companion Planting and Design

Planting in containers and window boxes with green trailing plants such as ivy or small-flowered spillers such as bacopa keep the eye focused on the bold design and shape of the gerbera daisy. Flower heads can range in size from 2½ inches to 5 inches wide, so companion placement depends on the size of the plant. They are excellent with ornamental edible greens such as blood beets, lettuces, and lacinto kale. Boldly colored zinnias make great cut-flower companions in a vase.

Try These

'Cross Road' is astounding with a huge yellow flower head and a second inner double layer of red petals. Gerrondo series have giant flower heads filled with so many petals they almost resemble a mum; it's excellent as a cut flower. Warm-colored gardens look fantastic with 'Sombrero', a bold red-flowered variety.

Kale

Brassica oleracea var. *acephela*

Botanical Pronunciation
BRA-sih-kah oler-aye-CEE-ah

Bloom Period and Seasonal Color
All season; blue, gray, green, burgundy, bronze, and purple leaves

Mature Height × Spread
12 to 72 inches × 12 to 36 inches

Kale is a surprisingly versatile and gorgeous ornamental for annual containers and garden beds, with the added benefit of being edible. Leaf colors range from green to blue to red to purple and combine well with bold annual flowers. Size varies by species, but some plants can grow up to 6 feet tall. Leaves also have various shapes that can be curly, flat-headed, tall, short, stiff, or floppy. Kale stands up well to dry conditions and performs like a champion in cold conditions; often a couple of frosts leave the plant tasting sweeter. Beyond making a gorgeous statement in your garden, kale is also a nutritional powerhouse that contains calcium; iron; vitamins A, C, and K; minerals; phytonutrients; and antioxidants.

When, Where, and How to Plant
While kale is known as a cool-season vegetable for early season (April) or late season (July to August) planting, it also does quite well all season long as an ornamental plant. Grow it from seeds or transplants in well-drained soil that is richly amended with rotted manure or compost for strong growth. Transplants can be planted three to four weeks before your last frost-free date. Seeds are planted ¼- to ¾-inch deep and require five to six weeks to reach a good planting size.

Growing Tips
Kale belongs to the Brassica (cabbage) family, and crop rotation is strongly recommended. Do not grow it in the same soil as other Brassica family members for at least three seasons. Water at the base of the plant to prevent fungal issues on the leaves. Do not overwater.

Regional Advice and Care
Pests can include aphids, imported cabbage worms, cabbage looper, diamondback moths, and flea beetles. Treat the pests organically by spraying or picking them off. Spray with soapy water depending upon the pest. Control fungus issues with foliar applications of an organic fungicide. Harvest very young leaves for salads. Remove the larger, outer, more mature leaves for cooked greens.

Companion Planting and Design
Kale works very well in the fall when planted in a cool-season mixed bed of snapdragon, Swiss chard, aster, and chrysanthemum. Gerbera daisies and sweet potato vine look wonderful in window boxes with a short variety of kale. Kale seems to love shade and does wonderfully mixed with coleus in shade containers and beds.

Try These
'Italian Lacinato Nero Toscana Organic', also known as Dinosaur Kale, is my favorite kale variety. It looks as if the plant comes from a prehistoric world, adding a tremendous amount of interest to a container garden. 'Kale Dwarf Blue Curled Organic' is a diminutive variety of kale with bold blue leaves. 'Winterbor' is lower to the ground and quite green, and 'Flowering Kale' features a center leaf section that is a bright white or pink with purple outer leaves.

Lantana

Lantana camara

Botanical Pronunciation
lan-TA-na ca-MA-ra

Bloom Period and Seasonal Color
All season; yellow, red, orange, pink, white, and mixed flowers

Mature Height × Spread
24 inches × 24 inches

Lantana is a drought-tolerant fragrant plant with a branching habit that is known to be an invasive perennial in the southern states. Here, however, lantana is a well-controlled window box, container, and bedding plant with an intense love of the hot summer. It is adored by butterflies, hummingbirds, and hummingbird moths. Lantana has the most amazing clusters of intensely colored showy flowers that are captivating in the garden. While beneficial insects love this plant, its one drawback is that it is quite toxic to dogs, cats, and humans if eaten. Lantana prefers full direct sun and can survive both outdoors and indoors. However, it will not flower as well if it's placed in less sunny conditions.

When, Where, and How to Plant

Frost and cold sensitive, lantana not only requires warmer growing conditions, it thrives in hot, dry spots in your garden. Be sure to plant in a very well-drained soil that has been amended with plenty of organic matter, and mulch well. Lantana prefers acidic soils but really does quite well in most soil types if it is well drained. Mix oak leaves in with your planting bed to help raise the acidity of your soil.

Growing Tips

Water well after planning until lantana is acclimated; however, do not overwater as the plant does better with dry conditions. Let it dry between watering. Fertilizer is not strictly required although adding an organic fertilizer once or twice mid-season will not harm the plant. Trim back or pinch plants to encourage branching at any time throughout the growing period, although deadheading is not required.

Regional Advice and Care

Cut back the lantana if it grows out of bounds or needs refreshing. Whiteflies can attack this plant. Adult whiteflies can be treated by spraying with soapy water or garlic oil.

Companion Planting and Design

Due to its toxicity when eaten, it is advisable to keep this plant well away from play areas for children and pets. Plant lantana with drought-tolerant companion plants such as euphorbia, English lavender, and dusty miller in a container or window box. It works as an excellent low-maintenance groundcover and can be spectacular featured along a walkway. Mix white lantana with white angelonia for a memorable all-white container planting. Lantana can be a wonderful feature in rock gardens, particularly as a repeating, drifting mound flowing around the garden's larger accent plants such as Russian sage.

Try These

'Bandana® Cherry' is a gorgeous, bold, berry-colored flower cluster with a bright yellow center cluster of blooms. 'Little Lucky Red' is a delightfully small plant reaching a height of 10 to 12 inches, with powerfully bold red, orange, and yellow fading in its color structure. 'Landmark White' is an award winner with a pure white flower at the edge of the cluster, leading to a very creamy ivory in the center.

Lobelia

Lobelia erinus

Botanical Pronunciation
loe-BEEL-yuh ur-EYE-nus

Other Name
Edging lobelia

Bloom Period and Seasonal Color
Spring to frost; white, pink, rose, violet, and blue flowers

Mature Height × Spread
4 to 12 inches × 6 to 18 inches

Few flowers have the intense blue that several of the lobelia varieties provide. With small green leaves that have a bronzy purple shade, a trailing habit, and flowers that are ½ inch or less in diameter, these little plants can make a big color show in your garden. Preferring cool weather, lobelia is known for spectacular impact in early summer, particularly when planted *en masse* along sidewalks and borders as edging. Once the temperatures hit 80 degrees, the plants will survive, but flowering will slow. If the plant is maintained, it will reflower again when temperatures cool down in the fall. Cascading types of lobelia are most impactful flowing from pots and window boxes with spectacular color results.

When, Where, and How to Plant
Although lobelia prefers cool conditions, it is killed by a heavy frost, and should be planted from seed in spring and summer after the last frost. Place lobelia in a sunny location with good drainage, although it will adapt to part sun. Seeds prefer light to germinate, so it is best to sow seeds on the top of soil, then water gently until it's rooted to prevent seeds from washing away; or start indoors four weeks before planting outside. Plants can be placed directly in soil and watered in well.

Growing Tips
Do not keep the roots in constant water as lobelia does not like wet feet, but do water quite frequently, particularly once summer temperatures get above 80 degrees, as the plants prefer cool roots and consistent moisture. Let the soil dry out between waterings. Mulch after planting, then fertilize once per month with a liquid organic fertilizer to see stronger plant performance. If plants get leggy or appear to die back because of heat, simply shear back their growth with clippers.

Regional Advice and Care
Deadheading is not needed. If you are concerned about performance during high heat weather, try planting some of the newer lobelia that has been developed to combat hot conditions. Plants grown in shadier conditions might be prone to powdery mildew, which can be treated with an organic fungicide.

Companion Planting and Design
Lobelia is easy to grow, and the plants make a fantastic spiller in spring containers. Try combining lobelia, pansies, and lettuce together for a sweet little container combination. Good companion plants include roses and geraniums. Lobelia is beautiful as an edger along sidewalks and paths when planted *en masse*.

Try These
For an award-winning, soft blue lobelia, try 'Laguna™ Sky Blue'. 'Lucia Dark Blue' is a deep blue with exceptional heat tolerance and a trailing habit. 'Riviera Midnight Blue' has deep purple flowers. 'Regatta Rose' has magenta flowers with a white eye. 'Magadi Compact White' is a mounding variety with an intensely white flower.

Marigold

Tagetes spp.

Botanical Pronunciation
tuh-JEE-teez

Bloom Period and Seasonal Color
Spring to fall; cream, yellow, gold, orange, and orange-red flowers

Mature Height × Spread
6 to 42 inches × 8 to 24 inches

Marigolds have become the reliable gold standard annual plant for gardens across the U.S. because this plant is nearly fail-proof. With bold colors and a hardy personality, marigolds contribute greatly to a drought-tolerant garden bed. Certain marigold varieties have a strong scent that does not deter insect pests but does seem to deter animal pests. I have used marigolds consistently around my unfenced front lawn vegetable garden, and rabbits have not touched my cabbages in years. Some modern hybrids do not have that pungent marigold scent, so if you want to deter animal pests, purchase the varieties that have a stronger smell. Marigolds are edible; their petals look lovely in a summer salad or as decorations on a cake.

When, Where, and How to Plant
Plant this flower in the spring after the last frost, either from seed or transplants. Give it a spot in a rich, well-drained soil with compost or manure mixed in for better root development. While this plant will do well in sun or shade, it will perform more reliably if you plant it in sun to part sun. Sow seeds eight weeks before the last frost, and plant very lightly in soil as the seeds are quite tiny.

Growing Tips
Marigolds will do well on their own but enjoy an organic fertilizer once every four weeks or so, particularly if planted in a container. While marigolds are known to be drought tolerant, they still need consistent water. Be sure to water at the base of the plant, and allow the soil to dry out between waterings. However, while consistent watering is important, overwatering will create root disease and stem rot problems.

Regional Advice and Care
Deadheading is not typically needed, particularly with newer hybrids, but flower beds look better if you keep the marigolds cleaned. Pinch plants to promote more flowering and branching. Aphids are best treated by a strong blast of water from a garden hose or spraying the bugs with soapy water.

Companion Planting and Design
Marigolds often form the backbone of plantings because of their adaptability. Use them freely in borders, edging, containers, and window boxes. Marigolds look fantastic planted with celosia and dusty millers in garden beds and containers. For a lovely contrasting container combination, pair a deep purple angelonia with a bold orange marigold.

Try These
'Zenith Red' is 14 to 16 inches tall and has a huge 4-inch flower head. 'Lofty Lady' is a bold yellow that stands 4 feet high, making a great back-of-the-border statement. 'Taishan' marigolds are dwarf African marigolds that come in yellow, gold, and orange and are nonstop, self-cleaning performers in the garden. African marigold 'Vanilla' is an off-white variety. French marigold 'Durango™ Bee' has a gorgeous bicolor flower petal, orange-red inside, with a yellow exterior.

Moss Rose

Portulaca grandiflora

Botanical Pronunciation
por-tew-LAHK-uh grand-ih-FLOR-uh

Other Name
Rose moss

Bloom Period and Seasonal Color
Summer; white, yellow, peach, orange, red, magenta, pink, purple, lilac, and bicolor flowers

Mature Height × Spread
4 to 8 inches × 18 inches

Moss rose is a remarkably easy-to-grow succulent with gorgeous roselike flowers that many of us remember from our grandmother's gardens. When other plants wilt because of hot and dry conditions, these plants flourish and flower nonstop. Moss rose loves poor, quick-draining, gravelly soil and full sun. If exposed to an abundance of shade, some varieties of the moss rose flower will remain closed. This plant has small, sparse, fleshy leaves that store water, allowing the plant to survive and perform during dry periods. Moss rose makes a fantastic cut flower and looks delightful displayed in little bud vases. With continuous blooming through summer, this plant makes an excellent addition to any sunny garden bed or container.

When, Where, and How to Plant

Plants prefer warm weather and average to poor soils that are loose, gravelly, sandy, or loamy. Be sure soil composition is well draining. Sow seeds indoors four weeks before the last frost or sow seeds early in the season, covering lightly with ⅛ inch of organic seed-starting soil. Moss roses grow nearly prostrate as a mat of fleshy leaves with stems topped by flowers, so space plants 1 to 2 feet apart so they are able to spread.

Growing Tips

Water well after planting until it's acclimated; however, do not overwater as the plant suffers from fungal diseases such as stem and root rot if it's watered too much. Fertilizer is not recommended.

Regional Advice and Care

Trim back or pinch plants to increase air circulation and neaten up a sprawling moss rose at any time throughout the growing period. Moss rose frequently reseeds and self-sows around the garden but is not considered invasive as it is easily removed if there is an issue. Plants are incredibly cold sensitive and will immediately brown at any signs of frost; be sure to cover your plantings when a frost is expected in order to extend the growing season on into fall.

Companion Planting and Design

Seed moss roses in difficult growing spots as a filler plant. It's excellent when grown in crevices between stones in and along paths; it will even grow in the cracks of a wall. Because the flowers of the moss rose are edible, this plant makes a wonderful companion with herbs and nasturtium. Moss rose looks great in containers and window boxes with zinnia and sweet potato vine. Other drought-tolerant planting partners include dusty miller and celosia.

Try These

'Happy Hour Peppermint' has a mounded habit and amazing striped, pink-and-white petals. 'Sundial White' moss rose is a fabulous white bloom with a yellow eye. 'Happy Trails Mixture' is a brilliantly bold mix of colors with trailing branches up to 18 inches long. 'Color Carousel' mix has double blooms and rainbow colors. 'Sundial Chiffon' has the palest pink flowers with a golden eye that truly resembles a rose.

Nasturtium

Tropaeolum majus

Botanical Pronunciation
TROPE-ee-oh-lum MAY-jus

Bloom Period and Seasonal Color Spring to summer; deep red, orange, and yellow flowers; variegated leaves offer three-season interest

Mature Height × Spread 1 to 3 feet × 1 ½ to 10 feet; trailing varieties can be 4 feet long and climbing varieties climb over 10 feet

Nasturtiums are a fantastic, carefree ornamental (and edible) annual that thrives on neglect and prefers spring and summer growing conditions. Once they start blooming, they bloom all season long until the first frost. They are surprisingly easy to grow, come in many different varieties and sizes, and offer a bold punch of color in containers and bedding plantings. Mounding varieties are excellent as edging plants and function as superb fillers in annual and perennial beds. Planting nasturtiums as drifters along straight walkways softens the edges of the pathway, creating an attractive frame for a garden view. Flowers are favored by pollinators and offer people a delightful peppery taste in salads, cocktails, and desserts.

When, Where, and How to Plant
Plant nasturtiums from seed in spring, after the last frost, to summer into containers or beds. Nasturtiums do not like to be transplanted and will function best when grown from seed in soil that is lean (not overly fertile) and well drained. Heavy or rich soil produces excess leaf and no flowers. A part shade location produces fewer flowers as nasturtiums prefer full sun. However, they will survive well in part shade. Scratch each seed (to nick the seed coat) and soak it overnight in water before planting. Seeds germinate in darkness, so each seed must be covered with soil approximately ½-inch deep. Sow seed every 6 to 12 inches.

Growing Tips
Start the plant off right by watering regularly for the first week after planting. After the initial week, water as you would the other annuals in your garden. Do not fertilize.

Regional Advice and Care
Deadheading is not typically needed. Nasturtiums are prone to aphids, which can be removed with a strong blast of water from a garden hose. Additionally, flea beetles, slugs, and cabbage worms seem to love the spicy taste of the leaf. These are best treated by handpicking or spraying the pests with soapy water.

Companion Planting and Design
In landscape design, nasturtiums are great trap crop companion plants to roses and vegetables because of their aphid-attracting abilities. They naturally keep the pests off the companion plants. Use bushy varieties of nasturtiums as a filler between perennials. Trailing varieties are absolutely gorgeous tumbling over walls and patio edging. Companion plants include roses, geraniums, and edible ornamental vegetables, such as kale, cabbages, and Swiss chard.

Try These
My favorite nasturtium is 'Alaska Variegated Heirloom' because of its captivating variegated leaf that features a calico of white, pale green, and dark green color combinations. 'Mahogany' has intense, deep red flowers that make a beautiful show as a culinary flower. 'Empress of India' is the perfect hummingbird plant and attracts the little birds in droves.

New Guinea Impatiens

Impatiens hawkeri

Botanical Pronunciation
im-PAY-shunz HAWK-ur-eye

Bloom Period and Seasonal Color
Summer; white, pink, red, salmon, orange, yellow, mauve, and violet flowers; colorful foliage

Mature Height × Spread
12 to 24 inches × 12 to 24 inches

New Guinea impatiens are native to New Guinea, an island north of the continent of Australia. They differ from the traditional elfin impatiens, *I. walleriana*, in several ways. Typically, New Guinea impatiens are started from vegetative cuttings and are challenging to propagate from seed, while traditional impatiens are easily grown from seed. Downy mildew, an invasive fungal pathogen, has attacked a strong percentage of our regional traditional elfin impatiens. New Guinea seems relatively unaffected by the disease, so it functions as a great plant substitute to *I. walleriana* as the growing requirements are quite similar for each plant. New Guinea impatiens are also known for their foliage, which can be even more impressive than the plant's beautiful flowers in a container or garden bed.

When, Where, and How to Plant
New Guinea impatiens will perform their best in locations that get morning sun and afternoon shade, although New Guinea impatiens prefer shade or part shade whenever possible. Plants that have too much sun exposure will not bloom as well as shaded plants. They require moist, well-drained, fertile soils. While it is possible to grow from seed, it is difficult to get them started, so I prefer purchasing plants at a nursery or garden center. Plant around two weeks after the last frost.

Growing Tips
Fertilize every two weeks with an organic, water-soluble fertilizer or incorporate an organic slow-release fertilizer into the soil prior to planting. New Guinea impatiens require evenly moist soil. If it is too wet, plants are prone to root rot. If it is too dry, plants wilt dreadfully. Stress from drought will force the flower buds to drop and plants to produce fewer flowers, and you will notice browning of leaf margins and leaf drop as well. So keep up the watering.

Regional Advice and Care
Prone to aphids, which can be removed with a strong blast of water from a garden hose, New Guinea impatiens also suffer from caterpillars and mites. Treat by handpicking or spraying the pests with soapy water. Overwatering in shady conditions can sometimes encourage powdery mildew or root rot. These fungus issues can be treated with an organic fungicide.

Companion Planting and Design
Good companions include shade-loving, moisture-loving plants such as ferns, hostas, and coleus. Ornamental edibles such as leafy kale, red beet greens, and lettuces grow well with New Guinea impatiens as well. Torenia or dragon wing begonia combined with sweet potato vine make excellent container partners.

Try These
An easy-to-grow, award-winning variety that has a gob-stopping bicolor flower is 'Infinity® Blushing Crimson'. For a mounded habit and large, eye-catching, striped orange bloom, try 'Celebrette Orange Stripe'. 'Sonic Sweet Purple '06' has a deep burgundy, sometimes purple leaf. All the New Guinea impatiens from the Painted Paradise® series have incredible tri-color leaves that are as gorgeous as their flowers.

Pansy

Viola × wittrockiana

Botanical Pronunciation
vye-OH-luh wit-rock-kee-AY-nuh

Bloom Period and Seasonal Color
Spring to fall; yellow, orange, peach, rust, red, lilac, purple, blue, blotch, bicolor, and black flowers

Mature Height × Spread
4 to 9 inches × 6 to 16 inches

When I think of the pansy, I think of the happy cool-weather flower that is both a celebration of spring's and fall's changing seasons. Pansies are a group of large-flowered hybrid plants cultivated as garden flowers; however, pansies are derived from a *Viola* species. Their nodding faces are often the welcome sign that spring has finally made it to our Midwestern gardens. From the tiny purple Johnny jump-ups my grandmother first introduced to me as a little girl to the large 3-inch golden yellow blooms of a giant pansy, these flowers are a welcomed flower explosion for the container and garden bed. Hardy varieties can be planted in early fall, and with adequate protection and a mild winter, can be revived to ride out the spring weather until summer's heat hits.

When, Where, and How to Plant

Pansies will grow in a wide variety of soils but prefer soil that is well drained and rich in organic matter such as rotted manure and compost. Sow or plant directly in soil from spring to early summer after temperatures consistently reach at least 68 degrees (both spring and fall). While the flowers prefer direct sunlight, once the heat comes out the plants wilt, so it is better to plant in part sun or perhaps a location where the plant will have shade in the heat of the late day.

Growing Tips

Water seeds gently when they're first planted so they will not wash away. Fertilizer is rarely needed, although adding an organic fertilizer when initially starting the plants can assist spring growth.

Regional Advice and Care

Be sure to deadhead the blooms to keep the plants continually flowering. Cut back overgrowth. Aphids are best treated by a strong blast of water from a garden hose. Slugs and earwigs must be trapped. To control earwigs, roll up a sheet of newspaper and lay it out at night. Water the newspaper. In the morning, earwigs will be trapped inside; throw newspaper in the garbage. Plants can be prone to powdery mildew, which can be treated with an organic fungicide.

Companion Planting and Design

Fall planting ideas include combining with flowering kale, chrysanthemums, heuchera, and hostas. Spring ideas include planting pansies with muscari and squill or, for a later bulb combination display, late bulbs like daffodil and allium. Additionally, pansies can be paired with alyssum, dianthus, and osteospermum. Because they are edible, pansies combine well with lettuces, parsley, and mint in containers.

Try These

'Fizzy Lemonberry' is a showy, double-ruffled yellow, lavender, and deep purple cool-season variety. 'Bowles' Black Pansy' has blooms so dark purple they appear to be black. 'Purple Rain' is an incredibly cold-hardy, deep purple flowering plant that reaches 18 inches in height, with a cascading habit. 'Big Shot' pansies have giant, 3-inch blooms with a variety of colors that have dark inner faces and bold exterior colors.

Petunia

Petunia × hybrida

Botanical Pronunciation
peh-TOON-yuh

Bloom Period and Seasonal Color
Spring to fall; red, white, yellow, orange, lavender, pink, purple, black, striped, and bicolor flowers

Mature Height × Spread
6 to 15 inches × 8 to 36 inches

As one of the most popular and easy-to-grow annuals, petunias are America's flower sweetheart. They have wide, trumpet-shaped flowers and branching foliage that is hairy and a bit sticky. There is amazing variety within the petunia family: single, double, and semi-double blooms; ruffled or smooth petals; veined, striped, blotched, or solid colors; and mounding and cascading habits. Grandiflora petunias typically grow to 10 or 12 inches high and have large 4- to 5-inch wavy blossoms. These flowers need deadheading and do not do well in heavy rain. Multiflora petunias are more compact, have 2-inch blooms, and hold up better to the weather. Spreading type petunias called milliflora are self-cleaning and quite prolific bloomers. These petunia series include 'Wave', 'Supertunia', 'Cascadia', and 'Surfinia'.

When, Where, and How to Plant

Plant this flower in sun, at least ten hours per day, after the last frost either from seed or plant, providing a rich, well-drained soil. Petunias prefer a little afternoon shade, if possible, and they are heavy feeders. Mix chelated iron in the soil when planting to help keep the plant green and producing.

Growing Tips

Incorporate an organic slow-release fertilizer into the soil to feed over the season. Petunias can suffer from root rot if overwatered, so they need excellent soil drainage. Water regularly, however, letting the top of the soil become dry to the touch before repeating. If you wait too long to water, the plant will wilt. Container plants typically require more watering. Cloudy days with wetter weather will cause delayed plant flowering.

Regional Advice and Care

Deadheading is not needed for self-cleaning varieties; however, pinching or shearing stems back midsummer will stimulate growth. Aphids are best treated by a strong blast of water from a garden hose or spraying the bugs with soapy water. Pythium, powdery mildew, and other fungus issues can occur with heavy rain or shadier conditions. Treat with an organic fungicide.

Companion Planting and Design

Petunias perform well in hanging baskets, window boxes, and containers. Spreading petunias do particularly well planted *en masse* in garden beds. Partners include euphorbia, angelonia, calibrachoa, geranium, grasses, sweet potato vine, and mixed varieties of petunia. Creating color-themed containers is easy with petunias: all-black, all-pink, or all-white containers can provide a striking display.

Try These

I prefer the modern spreading/trailing types of petunias that stand up to rain and do not require deadheading, such as 'Supertunia® Pretty Much Picasso®', which has unique purple flowers lined with lime green. 'Double Wave™ White Spreading Double Petunia' is an eye-catching variety with trailing double petunias. 'Surfinia® Trailing Petunia Purple Picotee' has purple flowers with white edges. 'Mini Me™ Pink Velvet Petunia' has tiny flowers. 'Phantom' shows off a velvety black base color with a distinctive yellow star pattern on each flower face.

Pineapple Sage

Salvia elegans

Botanical Pronunciation
sal-vee-UH EL-ih-ganz

Bloom Period and Seasonal Color
Fall; red flowers above scented foliage

Mature Height × Spread
48 inches × 24 inches

Named for its amazing pineapple-scented foliage, pineapple sage grows as a quiet, tall, vase-shaped, green filler plant at the back of a border or drought-tolerant garden bed. In late September or October, its cardinal-red panicles explode forth and give hummingbirds and butterflies their last sup of nectar before their fall migration south. Pineapple sage leaves can be clipped throughout the season to use in summer beverages such as herbal teas or cocktails. Make it into flavored simple syrup, sweet herb vinegar, muddle it with lime juice, or add chopped leaves to fruit salad. Set Victorian-style tussy-mussies out for afternoon tea parties to sweeten the smell of your dining area or patio. Its edible 3-inch-long red flowers are gorgeous outdoors or on salads.

When, Where, and How to Plant

Pineapple sage prefers a place in full sun where the soil is well drained but moist and rich enough to support its swift growth. Space plants 18 to 20 inches apart. Be sure to put this plant at the back of the border or planting space as it can easily shade other plants with its tall stature. Fertilize at planting with organic, timed-released granules. If overwintering is desired, trim back the plant, dig it up after the first frost, pot in containers, and place in a sunny window or greenhouse until replanting next spring.

Growing Tips

Relatively carefree pineapple sage needs no particular attention after it's planted. Water well until it's acclimated in its planting hole; however, do not overwater as the plant does better in well-drained conditions. Let soil dry between waterings.

Regional Advice and Care

Deadheading is not needed. Trimming the plant will not harm it, but may delay flowering. Plants grown in shadier conditions might be prone to powdery mildew, which can be treated with an organic fungicide. Pests can include aphids and caterpillars. Treat the pests organically by spraying with soapy water or picking them off.

Companion Planting and Design

Pineapple sage performs beautifully when blended into a native or drought-tolerant garden. It works as a gorgeous green backdrop for the hummingbird flower border. Herb gardens are often filled with shorter growing herbs; try placing a bird bath at the back of the garden with pineapple sage surrounding it in order to give height to the herb bed. Plant a row of pineapple sage as a side edger to vegetable or perennial beds, and the plant will function as a dividing wall.

Try These

Standard pineapple sage is the tallest of the varieties. Newer varieties are shorter and grown for scent and color variations. 'Golden Delicious' is a 24-inch-tall, pineapple-scented, yellow-foliaged, heat-tolerant variety with fire-engine-red flowers. 'Tangerine' smells citrusy, and 'Honey Melon' is the longest bloomer. Both flower earlier than other varieties but stand only 24 inches tall.

Purple Basil

Ocimum basilicum purpureum

Botanical Pronunciation
OH-see-mum bah-SIL-ih-kum per-per-EE-um

Bloom Period and Seasonal Color
All season; burgundy, bronze, and purple leaves

Mature Height × Spread
12 to 24 inches × 12 to 24 inches

Purple basil is a colorful addition to any flower or herb garden, particularly as a filler or edger. With a strong, almost spicy aroma, purple basil can contribute to your garden with aroma as well as its bold foliage. An additional benefit is that it is useful seasoning in Italian, Greek, Mexican, and tomato dishes. Purple basil can be used in any recipe that calls for sweet basil, although the flavor is more intense than traditional sweet basil. Amazing purple foliage looks attractive in cut flower arrangements. Beyond making a gorgeous statement in your garden, purple basil is also a nutritional powerhouse with vitamins A, C, K, B6, iron, calcium, potassium, and tryptophan.

When, Where, and How to Plant
Purple basil prefers a sunny location that gets at least six hours of sun per day. Grow from seeds or transplants in well-drained soil that is richly amended with rotted manure or compost. To start from seed, wait until two weeks after your last frost, and then place seeds onto prepared soil and cover with ⅛ inch of soil.

Growing Tips
In late summer heat and drought, purple basil can become slightly bitter and lose some of its color. Overfertilization can result in lots of leaf with lesser flavor. To encourage bushy growth, prune back the leaves every two or three weeks and remove flower buds immediately upon their appearance. When watering purple basil, always water at the base of a plant to prevent fungal issues on the leaves.

Regional Advice and Care
Store fresh basil sprigs in a glass of fresh, cool water on the counter, out of direct sunlight. To freeze basil, chop the leaves and place them in an ice cube tray, then drizzle olive oil over the tops of the leaves until you have a full tray. Freeze. Use the basil olive oil cube for flavorings in sauces and stews. Treat fusarium wilt and other fungus issues with foliar applications of an organic fungicide.

Companion Planting and Design
Purple basil looks fantastic as an ornamental edible when combined in containers with purple-flowering annuals such as a spreading petunia, angelonia, and sweet potato vine. Window boxes filled with purple basil, parsley, and white gerbera daisies are simply breathtaking. Use purple basil stems in cut flower arrangements that include zinnia and celosia for a bold color statement.

Try These
'Purple Ruffles' is a deep purple with a surprising ruffle design to the leaf, which makes a strong statement in a container. 'Osmin Purple' has a sweeter flavor with a fruity scent. 'Purple Dark Opal' has an intense purple leaf, fruity taste, strong flavor, and is good for drying. 'Italian Violetto' is a deep red-purple with purple stems and glossy leaves on full bushy plants; it has a powerfully sweet scent and a slight clove flavor.

Salvia

Salvia splendens

Botanical Pronunciation
SAL-vee-uh splen-DENZ

Other Name
Scarlet sage

Bloom Period and Seasonal Color
Summer to fall; red, salmon, yellow, pink, burgundy, purple, and white flowers

Mature Height × Spread
6 to 36 inches × 10 to 24 inches

Traditionally, salvia's upright habit and drought-tolerant nature make it a great low-maintenance annual. Salvia forms clumps and typically grows 1 to 2 feet tall on stiff stems. What makes it so captivating is the flower—a long, bright tube of color up to 2 inches long, which blooms from summer to fall. Hybridization has expanded the color selection greatly, and they are available in a variety of shades. Because of their strong stems and long-lasting blooms, they make an excellent choice for cut flower arrangements. Hummingbirds *love* salvia as do many beneficial insects. Salvia's foliage has a pleasant fragrance, which makes it a nice flower to plant *en masse*.

When, Where, and How to Plant

Salvias can be found from early summer at garden centers across the state, and they can also be grown from seed. Plant two weeks after the last frost in a full sun location with a bed amended with a heavy level of organic matter. They require six to eight hours of direct sun per day in order to produce an abundance of flower spikes. White- and light-colored flower spikes can become sunburned and brown at the tips if placed in an excessively hot and dry spot with direct sun for an entire day. Therefore, paler flowers might do better sited in part sun conditions.

Growing Tips

Water well until established, but do not overwater as salvias can suffer root rot from overwatering.

Once established in the garden, this plant will require very minimal care. Fertilize by adding an organic granular fertilizer to the soil or by feeding a water-soluble organic fertilizer every four weeks.

Regional Advice and Care

Remove spent flower heads to keep the plants continually blooming and looking good. Treat aphids with a strong blast of water from a garden hose or by spraying the bugs with soapy water. Plants grown in shadier conditions might be prone to powdery mildew; water at the base of a plant to help prevent fungal issues.

Companion Planting and Design

Salvia's upright habit makes it the perfect companion plant for cascading plants such as petunia, calibrachoa, or sweet potato vine, either in containers or sprawling across borders and garden beds. They are gorgeous in front of ornamental edibles, fountain grass, celosia, and zinnia. For a red, white, and blue combination, try planting blue lobelia, red salvia, and white alyssum together.

Try These

'Lighthouse Purple' is tall and will reach a height of 24 to 30 inches and width over 12 inches. 'Vista Red and White' has striped red-and-white florets. It is a full flower with well-packed flower spikes. The 'Firecracker' series has multiple colors to choose from, blooms incessantly, and has a dwarf habit.

Snapdragon

Antirrhinum majus

Botanical Pronunciation
an-tur-RYE-num MAY-jus

Other Name
Snaps

Bloom Period and Seasonal Color
Spring to fall; yellow, orchid, rose, magenta, orange, white, red, burgundy, and bicolor flowers

Mature Height × Spread
6 to 48 inches × 6 to 24 inches

Snapdragon blooms are said to resemble a dragon's mouth opening and closing, but my daughters and I have always called snapdragons "opera singers" because of the way that a snap's "mouth" seems to resemble a singer's when the flower mouth opens and closes when you squeeze its sides. Perhaps you will be as captivated as we are with the snapdragon's gorgeous upright blossoms. Snapdragons produce upright racemes of two-lipped blooms with spreading, rounded lobes in a vast array of attractive colors. These vivid flowers flourish summer through autumn. Snapdragons have a lovely fragrance and are an excellent choice for cut flower arrangements due to their wide variety of colors. Hummingbirds need an open snap flower variety that resembles a butterfly in order to sip its nectar.

When, Where, and How to Plant

Snapdragons can be found in spring at garden centers and can also be grown from seed. Plant two weeks after last frost in a full sun location in a bed amended with a heavy level of organic matter. They will perform in part sun but definitely require six to eight hours of direct sun per day in order to produce florific plants. Propagate by seed by starting indoors six to eight weeks before the last frost. The seeds need light to germinate, so plant them on top of the soil. These are excellent spring and fall plants, tolerating some frost and growing best in cool weather.

Growing Tips

Snapdragons are known to be fairly drought tolerant, but they still need consistent water. Water at the base of a plant and allow the soil to dry out between waterings. Watering at the base of the plant instead of overhead watering can keep the snapdragon foliage from becoming wet, which encourages fungal disease. After plants become established, water about 1 inch per week. Mulch the snapdragon bed to help hold moisture in.

Regional Advice and Care

Encourage branching by deadheading regularly; pinch back stems when plants are approximately 3 to 4 inches tall. Some tall varieties might need staking, or mix with other plants that will help support the snapdragons. Spray aphids off plants with a strong blast of water from a garden hose or spray the bugs with soapy water. Fungus can be controlled with an organic fungicide.

Companion Planting and Design

Snapdragon's upright habit and colorful flowers make it the perfect companion plant for cascading plants such as the petunia, calibrachoa, or sweet potato vine. Spring plantings that include lobelia, lettuces, and baby blue eyes make a lovely container combination.

Try These

For cut flowers, the Rocket series is a great choice. 'Apollo Cinnamon Cutflower' is a unique bronzy red color with open snaps that enable hummingbirds to sup. 'Tried & True™ Trailing Snapdragons Fruit Salad™, series have long-lasting blooms on trailing stems. 'Twinny Mix' has a doubled, open butterfly form.

Sunflower

Helianthus annuus

Botanical Pronunciation
hee-lee-AN-thus AN-yew-us

Bloom Period and Seasonal Color
Summer; white, yellow, gold, red, orange, and brown flowers

Mature Height × Spread
1 to 24 feet × 2 to 5 feet

Children love sunflowers because they are so easy to grow from seed. Toss seeds into the ground, give them a little love, and before you know it you will have amazing smiling flower faces standing in your garden. Modern dwarf hybrids come in shorter varieties while tall varieties bring a completely unique look to a native garden, vegetable garden, or border. Sunflower seeds and leaves emit a substance that inhibits the growth of some plants such as potatoes and pole beans. Where sunflower seeds are used as bird feed, toxins from the seed hulls will kill the grass below. These toxins are harmless to humans and animals, and the seed can be collected to feed birds or your family.

When, Where, and How to Plant

Plant directly in the soil from seed after the last frost. Be sure to place in a sunny spot. Sunflowers will do well in most soils, but providing a rich, well-drained soil with compost mixed in will help its establishment. Protect tall varieties from the wind to prevent breakage.

Growing Tips

Because sunflowers are so tall, their roots spread and hold the soil well; this makes them fairly adaptable to drought. However, it is best to water regularly throughout their flower growth periods, which are about eighteen days before and after flowering. In order to encourage root growth, it is better to water the plant deeply once per week, rather than shallowly several times per week.

Regional Advice and Care

Some sunflowers need staking. Branches are fairly brittle and the stem has hairy spikes, so to stake or reposition the plant in any way, wear gloves. Tie the plants loosely to stakes with a soft material. If you are growing sunflowers to harvest seeds for food, keep in mind that upon ripening, squirrels and birds will eat the seeds right off the plant. Consider netting the heads to prevent pesky thieves in the garden.

Companion Planting and Design

Sunflowers' bright colors partner well with other boldly colored drought-tolerant annuals such as celosia and tall zinnias. White varieties make excellent contributors to an evening or night garden as they are easily seen with moonlight. Bushy, midsized sunflowers look brilliant behind a row of purple Russian sage or grasses. Large containers are lovely when filled with dwarf sunflowers surrounded by bacopa and white petunias.

Try These

'Moonshadow' has white flowers with a large black center; it's pollen-free and multibranching. 'Pacino Lemon' is one of the smallest varieties, growing between 12 to 18 inches high with a 4-inch flower head. 'Sunzilla' can grow up to 24 feet, although it's more likely to grow 14 to 16 feet. For a dramatic 6-foot-tall accent in native and drought-tolerant beds, try 'Moulin Rouge'; it is a true red with no hint of gold on multibranching plants.

Sweet Potato Vine

Ipomoea batatas

Botanical Pronunciation
ip-oh-MEE-uh bat-TAT-ahs

Bloom Period and Seasonal Color
Spring to fall; bronze, black, chartreuse, green, purple, and bicolor foliage

Mature Height × Spread
8 to 15 inches × trailing to 60 inches

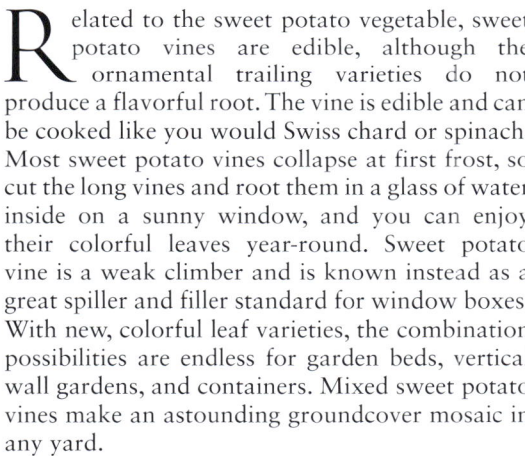

Related to the sweet potato vegetable, sweet potato vines are edible, although the ornamental trailing varieties do not produce a flavorful root. The vine is edible and can be cooked like you would Swiss chard or spinach. Most sweet potato vines collapse at first frost, so cut the long vines and root them in a glass of water inside on a sunny window, and you can enjoy their colorful leaves year-round. Sweet potato vine is a weak climber and is known instead as a great spiller and filler standard for window boxes. With new, colorful leaf varieties, the combination possibilities are endless for garden beds, vertical wall gardens, and containers. Mixed sweet potato vines make an astounding groundcover mosaic in any yard.

When, Where, and How to Plant

While most plant labels for the sweet potato vine say to plant in full sun, the vine will also do well in shadier light exposures, growing more length in full sun situations. Amend soil with a heavy amount of organic content such as compost or rotted manure. Sweet potato vine prefers a well-drained soil. Mix chelated iron in the soil when planting to help keep the color strong and producing.

Growing Tips

Incorporate an organic, slow-release fertilizer into the soil when planting or use an organic water-soluble fertilizer every few weeks throughout spring and summer. Ornamental sweet potato vine is generally carefree and exceptionally heat tolerant. However, they can suffer from root rot if overwatered, so the soil needs to dry out between waterings. Although it is fairly drought tolerant, if you wait too long to water the plant, it will wilt. Container plants typically require more watering than ground-planted vines.

Regional Advice and Care

Sweet potato tubers can be dug up in the fall and overwintered in a cool, dark, place. Deer, rabbits, and voles love sweet potato vine. Additional pests include beetles; handpick to remove. Spray aphids with soapy water or use a strong blast of water from a garden hose to remove them.

Companion Planting and Design

Sweet potato vines perform well when planted *en masse* in borders and garden beds. They drape beautifully over hanging baskets, window boxes, and containers. Planting partners include euphorbia, angelonia, calibrachoa, geranium, grasses, zinnia, and mixed varieties of petunia. Building walls of draping color over balconies is quite easy to do.

Try These

'Blackie' has deep purple, almost black foliage that is shaped like a hand. 'Marguerite' brings bold chartreuse green colors to brighten up shadier areas. 'Sweet Caroline Sweetheart Red' has adorable little heart-shaped leaves with a bronzy red tone. 'Illusion® Emerald Lace' is a bright green plant with a more upright habit with less trailing stems; it goes well with more trailing varieties of flowers. 'Tricolor' has ivylike green, white, and pink leaves that trail up to 36 inches.

Swiss Chard

Beta vulgaris ssp. *cicla*

Botanical Pronunciation
BAY-tah VOOL-gah-rus SIK-la

Other Name
Chard

Bloom Period and Seasonal Color
All season; green or burgundy leaves; stems that can be red, yellow, orange, white, or magenta

Mature Height × Spread
10 to 30 inches × 10 to 30 inches

Swiss chard is a marvelous ornamental edible with amazingly glossy, crinkly leaves and colorful stems or petioles. It is a leafy green from the beet family that has the unique quality of being both heat- and cold-tolerant. These plants have made a gorgeous statement in my front lawn vegetable garden for many years, and when planted in extra-fertile soil they can easily grow over their 30-inch size expectation. When used for ornamental purposes, harvest by picking leaves from the outside of each plant as new leaves come up through the crown. When plants are completely cut down early in the season, they will return with a passion for a second harvest. Vitamins and minerals found in chard include iron; vitamins A, C, K; and potassium.

When, Where, and How to Plant
Swiss chard can be planted in spring for summer interest or planted in early fall for a fall display. Grow from seeds or transplants in well-drained soil that is richly amended with rotted manure or compost for sturdy growth. Transplants can be planted three to four weeks before the last frost-free date. Seeds are planted ¼- to ¾-inch deep and require five to six weeks to reach a good planting size.

Growing Tips
Swiss chard likes consistent watering. Mulching the area around Swiss chard enables better moisture retention and protects against weeds.

Regional Advice and Care
If Swiss chard bolts (goes to seed), cut off the flowering stem at the base of the plant; the flower can get quite tall but is not attractive. Cut stems off at the base of the plant in fall, and you might be surprised by returning plants in spring. Plants are typically problem-free but can be attacked by mites, aphids, and caterpillars. Treat the pests organically by picking them off or spraying with soapy water. Swiss chard can get cercospora leaf spot, a disease that disfigures the leaves with ash-gray spots that have purple edges, or fungal issues. Control fungus with foliar applications of an organic fungicide.

Companion Planting and Design
Swiss chard looks pretty in the fall when planted in a cool-season mixed bed of snapdragon, kale, asters, and chrysanthemums. Calibrachoa and sweet potato vine look wonderful with Swiss chard in window boxes and containers. White-stemmed Swiss chard looks fantastic in an all-white garden. Use these plants in a formal flower garden or mixed in clumps within a cottage garden with equal beauty.

Try These
'Fordhook Giant' is a cold-hardy variety loved for its crisp leaves and white ribs. 'Bright Lights' has stem colors that include red, gold, yellow, magenta, and orange. 'Red & White Mix Organic' has bold red and clear white stems and looks great combined with red and white snapdragons. 'Peppermint' has two-toned stems. 'Golden Swiss Chard Organic' has golden stems.

Zinnia

Zinnia elegans

Botanical Pronunciation
ZIN-ee-uh ELL-ih-ganz

Bloom Period and Seasonal Color
Spring to fall; white, yellow, orange, red, rose, magenta, green, orange, purple, striped, speckled, bicolor, and tricolor flowers

Mature Height × Spread
6 to 36 inches × 6 to 18 inches

When I was a young girl growing up on our farm, my grandmother used to have a cutting garden filled with tall rows of zinnias with huge, dahlia-like blooms. She would cut the flowers and place them in dazzling arrangements all throughout her house. Those memories have forever emblazoned the zinnia in my mind as one of the most stunning annuals ever. Flowers come in every imaginable color except true blue, and the speckled and tricolor varieties simply shock you with their beauty. Blooms are sturdy and rarely need staking, and they attract butterflies in droves. Flower heads can be singles or doubles, and range from ½-inch in size all the way to 6 inches wide, depending upon the variety.

When, Where, and How to Plant

Plant this flower in the spring, adding compost or manure to provide a rich, well-drained soil, and giving the plants lots of room to grow. Zinnias will produce more blooms in full sunshine. While bedding zinnias from the nursery can readily succeed, depending upon the variety, double flowering zinnias will occasionally revert back to a single flowering plant if they are moved and transplanted too young. Sowing zinnia seeds directly into the garden after all danger of frost has passed is preferable.

Growing Tips

Zinnias prefer a dry and well-drained soil, so be sure to water at the base of the plant and allow the soil to dry out between waterings. Fertilize with an organic fertilizer every few weeks.

Regional Advice and Care

Deadhead zinnias regularly to keep their nonstop performance going. Zinnias are plagued by powdery mildew, so maintaining good air circulation around them, watering the plants at the roots, and choosing mildew-resistant varieties will help prevent further damage. Additionally, you can control fungus with foliar applications of an organic fungicide. Beetles can be handpicked and aphids are best treated with a strong blast of water from a garden hose or by spraying the bugs with soapy water.

Companion Planting and Design

Zinnias are gorgeous planted in clumps of bold color in front of perennials. Dwarf zinnias planted *en masse* are fantastic pathway edgers. Use zinnias in borders, edging, containers, and window boxes. For a bold impact, plant zinnias with marigolds, celosia, and dusty millers in garden beds and containers. Tall zinnias add a surprising shot of color at the back of cottage garden beds.

Try These

'Profusion White Hybrid' is a shorter variety that has won awards for its astounding disease and mildew resistance. Benarys Giant series has huge 5-inch blooms and can reach over 40 inches tall. 'Super Cactus Lilac Emperor' has astounding purple blooms that are fully 5 inches across with unusual, needlelike petals. 'Envy' is a chartreuse green variety that stands 24 to 30 inches tall and has 3-inch blooms.

BULBS
FOR INDIANA

ulbs teach gardeners patience. Most bulbs are planted in the cool fall as withered-looking brown clumps and burst forth months later in a remarkable show of joy and happiness. Waiting through the winter for hardy bulbs to grow is excruciating; it seems to take forever. When the flowers finally arrive, you know the time you spent muddying your knees in the fall was more than worth it.

What Are Bulbs?

In this chapter, the term "bulb" is used rather loosely. Also included are rhizomes, tubers, and corms, which are often lumped into the bulb category. *Rhizomes* are hard

Purple crocus makes an amazing show and is one of the earliest blooming bulbs to greet visitors to the garden, sometimes arriving while snow is still on the ground. Here the crocus is blooming together with aconite.

stems that, when planted underground like a bulb, produce roots and shoots sent out from nodes. They grow horizontally beneath the surface of the soil and can sprout anyplace along the area of the stem. *Tubers* have leathery skin and eyes that produce fresh plant growth. Potatoes are tubers, but so are many varieties of flowers. *Corms* look a lot like bulbs, but they do not grow layers and instead have a base for a flower stem that is solid. Corms are also known as *bulbo-tubers* and each corm is really a swollen plant stem resting below the surface of the soil.

True bulbs grow in layers like an onion and are held together with a basal plate where the physical roots form and grow. Hardy bulbs are dormant in the winter and emerge in the spring with plant stems and flowers. Each plant's flower lives for a short time and then shrivels, leaving the leaf matter and seed stem. Eventually the leaf matter shrivels as well, and then the process starts all over again. Tender bulbs are not hardy in the Midwest and must be dug up annually and replanted.

How to Plant Bulbs

By and large, planning your landscape with bulbs means understanding the nature of the individual bulb you are planting. For example, some varieties of daffodils are tall and some are short; you want to plant the bulbs with an understanding of which plant can be easily seen in its growing period so you can plan your daffodil planting accordingly. If you plant a tiny daffodil at the back of the garden bed beneath all the taller growing tulips, you will never see the daffodil you worked so diligently to plant.

Most bulbs love a site with well-drained soil filled with organic matter. Appropriate sunlight is a must too. Bulbs like phosphorus, and if soil tests show your soil is phosphorus-deficient, you will have to add some together with any other soil amendments needed. Be sure you understand which way the plant grows so that you put the base of the bulb at the bottom of a planting hole and top of the bulb pointing up. As a general rule, dig a hole three times deeper than the circumference of the bulb. In other words, if the bulb is 2 inches around, plant the bulb 6 inches deep. If it is 3 inches around, plant the bulb 9 inches deep, and so on. Add organic bulb fertilizer in the planting hole if you like, and top off the planting with a nice shovelful of compost.

Once the bulb flowers on a hardy bulb, I typically cut the seed stem off and let the leafy matter remain for the rest of the season so that the bulbs will receive and store nutrients to help them perform again the following year. Dig tender bulbs and store them inside until next season; plant them again in the spring.

Bulbs add beautiful seasonal interest. If a landscape is planned well with consecutive plantings, it can offer a very long display of blooming flowers. Planting bulbs in between perennials and shrubs adds a punch of color. Additionally, naturalized plantings of bulbs can shower your garden with large drifts and waves of beauty.

Allium

Allium spp.

Botanical Pronunciation
AL-ee-um

Bloom Period and Seasonal Color
Spring to early summer; purple, yellow, pink, and white flowers

Mature Height × Spread
12 to 48 inches × 4 to 18 inches

*A*llium is the Latin word for garlic, and if you crush an allium flower, you can smell the telltale oniony-garlic scent. Ornamental allium bulbs can lend an impactful and otherworldly look to the garden with their naked heads bobbing atop leafless stems. Available in a wide palette of colors, bloom times, heights, and flower shapes, alliums are super easy to grow. My favorites are the tall varieties, and while the tallest are supposed to grow to 4 feet, I have seen the 'White Giant' stretch closer to 5 feet when it's planted in fertile soil. They make perfect cut flowers and dry well, so alliums are great in wreaths and table displays. Alliums are sturdy plants and relatively resistant to deer, voles, chipmunks, and rabbits.

When, Where, and How to Plant

Plant this bulb in the fall after the first frost in a rich, well-drained soil with compost added. Alliums will produce more blooms in a drier spot with full sunshine. Mix organic bulb fertilizer in the planting holes. Large bulbs can be planted at a depth of 6 inches, and smaller bulbs should be planted 3 to 5 inches below the soil surface with the pointy end facing up.

Growing Tips

Once planted, do not water alliums unless conditions are that of extreme drought; alliums like dry conditions and do not like standing water. Boggy sites will cause the bulbs to rot.

Regional Advice and Care

If the allium appears to be producing two or three flowered stems with slightly smaller flowers in the spring, it is time to divide them. Alliums multiply by creating tiny bulblets that are attached to the primary bulb. Every few years, dig up the bulbs in the fall and split off the bulblets, replanting those in a different location. They take about two to three years to produce blossoms on their own. If you use allium in cut flower arrangements, be sure to cut the stem only; the foliage is needed to help the plant continue putting energy into the bulb for next season.

Companion Planting and Design

Smart companion plantings will hide allium's yellowing foliage once the flowers die back. Perennial selections such as daylilies, hakonechloa, nepeta, and wild geraniums make excellent companion plants. Irises make great blooming partners with the allium as they both bloom at the last of spring and first of summer.

Try These

'Globemaster' stands 24 to 36 inches tall, has 10-inch balls of aster-violet florets, and easily withstands wind gusts and drenching rains. 'Star of Persia' has starry amethyst florets on 12-inch flowering heads. 'White Giant' has 6- to 8-inch heads of white and stands 48 inches tall. 'Azureum' reaches 24 inches high and has a true blue 1½-inch flower head. 'Karataviense' is a low-growing variety known for its attractive leaves that has a 3-inch white head.

Caladium

Caladium spp.

Botanical Pronunciation
kah-LEY-dee-uhm

Bloom Period and Seasonal Color
Summer; green, chartreuse, white, rose, pink, red, splotched, and striped leaves

Mature Height × Spread
12 to 48 inches × 4 to 18 inches

Caladiums are tubers that are grown for their colorful tropical (but very cold sensitive) foliage. With prominently colored midribs and contrasting margins, dozens of designs, and many color combinations, caladium foliage makes an amazing statement in the garden. When the sun hits the leaves of a caladium, it looks like a stained glass work of art. Strap- or lance-leaved types have a more compact habit, standing 12 inches or shorter with smaller, thick, elongated leaves on short petioles. Fancy-leaved plants grow 12 to 30 inches tall and have heart- or partly heart-shaped leaves with long petioles. Find caladiums at nurseries or by mail order in pots or as dormant tubers. All parts are poisonous and should not be planted where pets or children can reach them.

When, Where, and How to Plant
Start a good quality, firm, and knobby tuber indoors in a container eight weeks before the last frost, placing the bumpy parts, or eyes, facing up. Caladiums will not start growing without a long period of heat that tops 70 to 75 degrees both during the day and night. If the area where the plant is being started is cooler, consider heating the bottom of the containers to kick-start the growing process. After all danger of frost is over, move the plants outdoors to a shade to part sun area. Plant the tuber in a rich, well-drained soil, 1½ to 2 inches deep.

Growing Tips
Caladiums *love* water and need to stay regularly moist. Mulch once they're planted in the ground.

Humidity is good for the plant; however, excessive water can cause rot. Considered light feeders, caladiums will green up and lose some of their interesting color, or suffer burnt leaves, if overfertilized. Use an organic fertilizer at planting, then fertilize only if needed later in the season.

Regional Advice and Care
Dig caladiums before the first frost, dry the tubers and store them in a cool, dry location to overwinter. Caladiums enjoy a winter dormancy of at least eight weeks before starting their growth cycle again. If a caladium is located in full sun, it is likely to get sunburned leaves.

Companion Planting and Design
Companion plants for garden beds include shade lovers such as hostas, ferns, heuchera, and brunnera. For a fantastic shade container or window box, mix Dragon Wing begonia, coleus, and sweet potato vine together with caladium. White varieties are excellent for evening or night gardens.

Try These
'Red Flash' has a bold red leaf with green borders. 'Moonlight' is a delicate white caladium with a minute green coloration outlining the leaf. 'Raspberry Moon' has a distinctive look with off-white and green layered with bright blotches of neon pink. 'Blizzard' is brilliant white with green veining. 'Siam Moon' is a tall variety from Thailand with black stems, hot pink leaves, and unusual deep green veining.

Canna

Canna spp.

Botanical Pronunciation
KAY-nah

Bloom Period and Seasonal Color
Summer; red, yellow, salmon, orange, pink, and white flowers

Mature Height × Spread
1½ to 15 feet × 1 to 3 feet

Cannas are unlike almost any other flower and make a remarkable statement in your garden. They have fleshy roots that are rhizomatous. These rhizomes produce erect stalks with broad, long leaves, and flower stalks that rise in the center. Traditionally admired for their height and large, showy flowers, more recent hybrids have developed spectacular foliage that can come in green, bronze, blue, purple, striped, and multicolored hues. Surprisingly versatile, cannas can survive drought quite well and can also live in boggy situations. Canna rhizomes are edible too. Mash into a pulp, remove the fiber, and dry the remaining starch to make it into flour. You can also eat the roots raw or treat them like potatoes and bake or boil them. Leaves can be used like banana leaves to wrap foods for steaming.

When, Where, and How to Plant

Canna is a heat lover and needs to be planted in an organically enriched soil well after the first frost. Amend soil with rotted manure or compost and plant rhizomes horizontally in a 4- to 6-inch-deep trench, spacing them approximately 2 feet apart. For earlier flowers, start four weeks before the last frost in a planted pot indoors with a sunny and warm exposure. Wind protection will help keep the leaves from being ripped during windy storms.

Growing Tips

Cannas love water and like to stay regularly moist but will grow if you let the area dry between waterings as well. Mulch well to help retain moisture. They flower best when fertilized monthly with an organic fertilizer.

Regional Advice and Care

While some hybrids are self-cleaning, the majority of cannas do better if they are deadheaded regularly. To save money, reuse your canna rhizomes every season. When canna leaves begin to die back, cut off foliage to about 4 inches, dig up the rhizomes and let dry in a protected area for a few days. Store the rhizomes in a cool dry place (45 to 50 degrees) over the winter; do not let them completely dry out. Divide the rhizome shoots in the spring and replant after danger of all frost is past.

Companion Planting and Design

Astounding planted in a bed *en masse*, cannas also look good at the back of garden beds and borders. Shorter cultivars look dazzling in containers thickly planted with sweet potato vine and calibrachoa or petunia. Black-leaved varieties look stunning in white-and-black themed garden beds. Cannas are perfect as a summer privacy fence or garden divider when planted in a straight row.

Try These

With amazing white blooms, 'New White' is a complete stunner in the garden. 'Blueberry Sparkler' has pink self-cleaning flowers and a mixed purple-blue leaf. 'Maui Punch' has a spectacular yellow-and-orange speckled flower. 'Purple Haze Flower Power™' has deep purple leaves, an orange flower, and was a favorite for my hummingbirds. The Tropicanna® series has breathtaking striped and multicolored foliage. 'Australia' has black leaves.

Crocus

Crocus spp.

Botanical Pronunciation
CROW-kus

Bloom Period and Seasonal Color
Spring and fall; purple, blue, yellow, pink, white, and striped flowers

Mature Height × Spread
2 to 6 inches × 2 inches

rocus is one of the earliest flowers to pop up in spring, sometimes when there is still snow on the ground! Most varieties grow quite well down to Zone 4. There are spring-blooming crocus that have grasslike leaves and autumn crocus that appears to have no foliage at all. All varieties have sweet, up-facing, cup-shaped blooms that captivate passersby. Fall crocus, also called saffron crocus, has a flower with several bright red-orange threads, or stigmas. These threads are an edible, delicious, and colorful seasoning. 'Saffron' can be grown in Zone 5 if extremely protected.

When, Where, and How to Plant
Crocuses enjoy a well-drained bed. Plant in a sunny spot because these easy bulbs only open fully when sun touches the flower. Place the crocuses approximately 2 to 4 inches deep and 3 to 5 inches apart. Spring-blooming crocuses should be planted in fall after the first frost. Fall-blooming varieties should be planted in spring. Plant crocus corms in groups or clusters rather than spacing them in a single line because individual flowers are difficult to see when planted alone. Plant groups of twelve or more in small clusters for the best effect.

Growing Tips
Plant well away from water-loving plants as crocus prefers it dry. Mix organic bulb fertilizer in the planting holes.

Regional Advice and Care
Leave foliage on the plants until it turns brown and withers in order to help put energy back into the corm. While deer and rabbit seem to leave the bulbs alone, voles, squirrels, and mice may dig up and eat the corms. If this is a concern, plant crocus bulbs in buried wire cages.

Companion Planting and Design
Crocus is fabulous planted under low-growing groundcovers such as *Ajuga* 'Chocolate Chip' or *Campanula* 'Blue Clips'. Plant *en masse* beneath grass, but hold off on mowing in spring until the foliage of the crocus dies back. Mix with other extra-early blooming bulbs such as glory-of-the-snow or daffodil varieties such as 'February Gold' or 'Tête-à-Tête' in garden beds. Bring spring to your home early by forcing crocus in a sunny window in winter vases or baskets.

Try These
Crocus sativus, or the saffron crocus, naturalizes well and can contribute greatly to your spice cabinet as well as your garden; it's best in Zone 6. 'Cloth of Gold' has blooms of bright yellow with dark mahogany stripes on the outer petals. 'Blue Pearl' is a translucent true blue. 'Pickwick' has a purple-and-white striped flower. 'Jeanne D'Arc Giant' is a gorgeous white flower. 'Yellow Mammoth' has huge yellow blooms. 'Cassiope' is an autumn-blooming crocus with light blue-violet flowers and a yellow throat.

Daffodil

Narcissus spp.

Botanical Pronunciation
nar-SISS-us

Other Name
Jonquil

Bloom Period and Seasonal Color
Spring; yellow, white, pink, peach, and orange flowers

Mature Height × Spread
2 to 24 inches × 2 to 6 inches

Daffodils are available in thousands of varieties and are tough, prolific bulbs that come back year after year. Deer and other animal pests do not like daffodils (which are members of the onion family). That makes them an excellent selection for mass naturalized plantings on properties in the country or near forest preserves. Daffodils flowers symbolize friendship and are often given in spring to celebrate new life. New hybrids and varieties have enlivened the traditional yellow flower with the ring of flat petals surrounding a long trumpet cup that we know as the daffodil. White, yellow, pink, and orange varieties with single, double, or split cups offer gardeners amazing selections. There are early-, middle-, and late-spring blooming varieties to choose from as well.

When, Where, and How to Plant

Daffodils like to be planted in a fertile, amended soil in a well-drained bed. Plant about 2 weeks before the ground freezes hard, usually after the first frost. Mix organic bulb fertilizer in the planting holes, but do not overfertilize as that can overproduce green stems and lessen flower development. Plant bulbs two to five times their own depth, the pointy end facing the sky, preferably in full sun (though part sun will do).

Growing Tips

Most daffodils are drought tolerant; however, if there is an extreme drought in spring, they will need to be watered on occasion.

Regional Advice and Care

Deadhead the gnarly dried flower heads to prevent seed setting, but leave foliage on the plants until it turns brown and withers in order to encourage the energy for future growth to go back to the bulb. Arrange cut daffodils alone in a vase or soak for twenty-four hours without cutting the stem again before mixing with other flowers; their stems secrete a fluid that encourages other flowers to wilt.

Companion Planting and Design

Yellow and white daffodils make marvelous naturalized scenes in the landscape when planted *en masse*. Combining them with Dutch iris, Siberian squills, and hyacinths in containers and planting beds will produce handsome color-filled displays. To create a spring bed of rosy red and white, try planting 'Thalia' daffodil, which has fragrant white blossoms, with 'Christmas Marvel', a rose-colored tulip. For a red, white, and blue combination, try white daffodils, blue hyacinths, and bright red tulips. Miniature white and pink daffodils look adorable with the diminutive pink muscari. Orange varieties bring a bold contrast when planted with purple-hued partners.

Try These

'Centannees Split Cup' is a type of butterfly daffodil with bright orange, broad, flat, split cups against an off-white back petal. 'Salome pink' has a white petal and pink cup that's edged yellow. 'Tête-à-tête' is one of the tiniest and earliest blooming daffodils. 'Acropolis double' is a white variety with a strong hint of coral orange in the center of the flower and functions well as a naturalizing daffodil.

Dutch Iris

Iris reticulata

Botanical Pronunciation
EYE-riss reh-tik-yew-LAY-tah

Other Name
Netted iris

Bloom Period and Seasonal Color
Early spring; blue, indigo, violet, white, yellow, bicolor, and striped flowers

Mature Height × Spread
3 to 6 inches × 2 inches

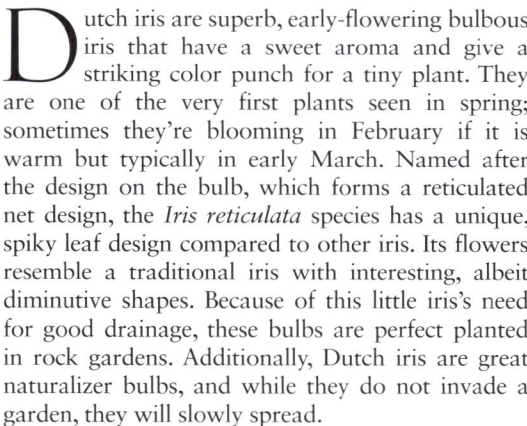

Dutch iris are superb, early-flowering bulbous iris that have a sweet aroma and give a striking color punch for a tiny plant. They are one of the very first plants seen in spring; sometimes they're blooming in February if it is warm but typically in early March. Named after the design on the bulb, which forms a reticulated net design, the *Iris reticulata* species has a unique, spiky leaf design compared to other iris. Its flowers resemble a traditional iris with interesting, albeit diminutive shapes. Because of this little iris's need for good drainage, these bulbs are perfect planted in rock gardens. Additionally, Dutch iris are great naturalizer bulbs, and while they do not invade a garden, they will slowly spread.

When, Where, and How to Plant

Dutch iris like to be placed in *very* well-drained (even rocky) beds, in fertile soil that has organic bulb fertilizer mixed in with the planting holes. Plant Dutch iris bulbs 3 to 4 inches deep, spaced 3 to 4 inches apart. This plant can also be grown as an annual; plant new bulbs each fall for desired color and design changes.

Growing Tips

To ensure consistent flowering from year to year, be sure to fertilize annually after the flowers fade.

Regional Advice and Care

Deadhead the dried flower heads, but leave the foliage on the plants until it turns brown and withers in order to encourage the energy for future growth to go back to the bulb. Creative companion planting will hide the foliage. Bulbs propagate by bulblets growing off the original bulb after blooming. Each new bulblet requires several years to mature, and they will generally spread on their own without assistance. However, if you notice the original flower declining, dig the bulbs up, separate the bulblets, and replant.

Companion Planting and Design

Use Dutch iris as a cutting flower; their tiny nature makes them suitable for tiny bud vases. Flowers pop out in early spring at about the same moment as snowdrops, glory-of-the-snow, and the early crocuses, so they make excellent planting partners. Grape hyacinth and fritillaria also make perfect partners with the Dutch iris, particularly in container designs. Dutch iris bulbs naturalize and they look wonderful planted *en masse* around hostas. By the time the iris bulb is done blooming, the hostas have grown over the browning foliage.

Try These

For a delightfully fragrant variety, try 'Cantab', a stunning flax blue flower with a yellow center. 'J.S. Dijt' is a deep purple. 'George' has a deep purple, but it leans toward a violet-purple shade. For a deep royal blue, try 'Harmony'; the blue falls (petals) are topped with a white-edged yellow blotch. 'Katherine Hodgkin' is a very large, white, longer-lasting bloom, with intense Delft blue striping throughout the flowers and a spot of yellow at the base of the petals.

Gladiolus

Gladiolus spp.

Botanical Pronunciation
glah-dee-OH-luss

Other Name
Glads

Bloom Period and Seasonal Color
Summer; every color of the rainbow as well as bicolors and multicolors

Mature Height × Spread
2 to 5 feet × 1 to 2 feet

Tall, statuesque, and colorful are just a few words to describe a gladiolus flower, which is grown from a corm. Carrying a bunch of freshly cut glads in from my grandmother's garden is one of my earliest memories. I was a tiny girl, and the flowers completely overwhelmed me with their intense color and absolutely giant stems that were nearly as tall as I was at the time. There are dwarf forms that are shorter in stature, but the large-flowered glads are certainly the most majestic as cut flowers in a vase. Cutting gardens can support long rows of gladioli resting along string supports to support their height. In a traditional garden bed, grouping glads together looks very attractive and helps keep them supported without a stake.

When, Where, and How to Plant

Glads prefer a sandy loam soil. If you have clayey or rocky soil, amend your beds with rotted manure or compost to loosen and enrich the soil. Plant the gladioli in a sunny spot, mixing organic bulb fertilizer in the planting holes, after the last frost. Dig holes that are approximately 6 to 7 inches deep and around 6 to 8 inches apart, placing the corm in the planting hole with the pointy side facing up. While straight rows are great for cutting gardens, plant glads in groups or clusters of twelve or more for best effect in mixed garden beds.

Growing Tips

While gladioli can be surprisingly drought tolerant, they appreciate consistent water and mulch. Moderate watering will encourage a strong plant, while excessive watering will cause corm rot.

Regional Advice and Care

Leave foliage on plants until it withers in order to put energy back into producing corms. Each summer, the elderly "mother corm" will be dried up at the end of the season, but the new corms will be attached to the mother. Dig up corms in fall and store them in the vegetable drawer of a refrigerator or other cool (but not freezing) place. Aphids are best treated with a strong blast of water. Handpick or spray other pests with soapy water. Corm rot, powdery mildew, and other fungus issues can be treated with an organic fungicide.

Companion Planting and Design

Cut flower spikes at a slant, leaving at least five leaves on the plant to support new corm growth, and immediately place the flowers in water; laying them down will make the tips become curved permanently. Planting bold red glads in groups around your garden will attract hummingbirds. Perennial and cottage gardens look good planted with two or three repeating colors in groups.

Try These

'White Prosperity' is a beacon in the garden with a 60-inch height and all white flowers. 'Black Jack' has black edges, deep red centers, and is about 47 inches tall. 'Costa' is an amazing royal blue fading to white with a ruffled flower. 'Zizanie' is only 12 to 24 inches tall but has astonishing red-and-white striped/splotched flower petals.

Hyacinth

Hyacinthus orientalis

Botanical Pronunciation
hye-uh-SIN-thuss or-ee-un-TAY-liss

Other Name
Dutch hyacinth

Bloom Period and Seasonal Color
Spring; all colors including black, striped, and bicolors

Mature Height × Spread
2 to 12 inches × 4 inches

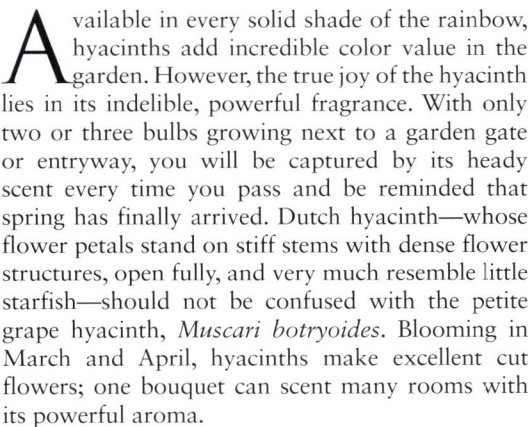

Available in every solid shade of the rainbow, hyacinths add incredible color value in the garden. However, the true joy of the hyacinth lies in its indelible, powerful fragrance. With only two or three bulbs growing next to a garden gate or entryway, you will be captured by its heady scent every time you pass and be reminded that spring has finally arrived. Dutch hyacinth—whose flower petals stand on stiff stems with dense flower structures, open fully, and very much resemble little starfish—should not be confused with the petite grape hyacinth, *Muscari botryoides*. Blooming in March and April, hyacinths make excellent cut flowers; one bouquet can scent many rooms with its powerful aroma.

When, Where, and How to Plant

Hyacinths love full sun, but they will tolerate light shade. Plant your hyacinth bulbs about six to eight weeks before the first hard frost in the fall. Hyacinths like fertile, organically amended soil in a well-drained bed. Dig a hole 6 to 8 inches deep, and space the bulbs 4 to 6 inches apart. Then set the bulb, pointy end facing up, in the hole and cover with soil.

Growing Tips

Most hyacinths are drought tolerant; however, if there is an extreme drought in the spring or fall, they will need to be watered on occasion. Excessive fertilizer is not required; an annual application of rotted manure or compost will do.

Regional Advice and Care

After the hyacinths bloom in spring, allow the plants to grow until their foliage dies. They need time after blooming to store energy in the bulbs for next season. To remove the withered plant, snip it off at the base with clippers or twist the leaves while pulling lightly, but do not pull up the bulb. If you crave their scent in the winter months you can easily force hyacinths indoors by resting the bulbs in soil or damp pebbles.

Companion Planting and Design

Plant hyacinths near paths and doorways in order to better enjoy their powerful scent. Combining hyacinths with Dutch iris, Siberian squills, and daffodils in containers and planting beds will produce handsome color-filled displays. Black varieties look dazzling when mixed with white daffodils and other early white-blooming plants for a black-and-white themed garden. Line a bed of tall spring bulbs such as daffodils and tulips with a single row of matching color hyacinths to make the bed even more impactful.

Try These

'Midnight Mystic™' is the first truly black hyacinth. 'Multiflowering White Festival' produces several stems of flowers per bulb that are more loosely set. 'City of Haarlem' is a striking yellow. 'Sky Jacket' has a pale wisteria blue bloom, pale yellow anthers, and a slightly darker blue midrib stripe on each floret. 'Jan Bos' is an award winner with bold, dark pink florets and an intensely powerful perfume.

Lily

Lilium spp.

Botanical Pronunciation
LIL-ee-uhm

Bloom Period and Seasonal Color
Summer; all colors including white, pink, rose, yellow, peach, orange, red, and purple with striping and spots

Mature Height × Spread
2 to 8 feet × 1 to 2 feet

Lilies are the beautiful mainstay of the summer bulb garden; their bloom power defies heat and humidity, bringing color at a time when other plants fall to the hot weather. They quite often naturalize. There are dozens of colors and varieties to choose from, with many lilies having powerful scents as well as attractive hues. Not all lilies are hardy in Midwestern zones, so be sure to research before you select lilies for your garden beds. For the longest-lasting summer performance, extend the flowering with a succession of varieties that bloom throughout summer. Start at the beginning of summer with Asiatic and martagon lilies, then in midsummer follow with trumpet and Easter lilies, then in the end of summer, enjoy Oriental lily varieties.

When, Where, and How to Plant

Lilies prefer a consistently moist, rich soil with good drainage that is in mostly sun. They will survive in part shade, but the lilies might physically lean toward the sun in hopes of obtaining more exposure. Mix organic bulb fertilizer in the planting holes, planting in fall well after the last frost. Dig holes that are approximately 6 to 7 inches deep and around 6 inches apart; place the bulb in the planting hole with pointy side facing up. Cover with soil and mulch.

Growing Tips

Apply an organic fertilizer in spring when the foliage first comes out of the ground, but too much nitrogen can produce abundant leaves with weak stems. Keep soil moist.

Regional Advice and Care

Leave foliage on plants until it withers in order to put energy back into producing bulbils. Remove tops and withered material in fall. Many varieties will need support to overwinter; add extra mulch in fall to help plants survive the colder weather. Many lilies can grow up to 8 feet high, and the taller ones need staking or they will lean in the garden. Lilies can be bothered by botrytis, lily mosaic virus, or basal bulb rot from planting in shade or poorly drained soil. Treat these and other fungal issues with an organic fungicide.

Companion Planting and Design

Plant tiger lilies and Asiatic hybrids in a hummingbird garden; the other varieties rarely attract the birds, but all the varieties attract a variety of beneficial insects. Combine lilies with other plants that have similar sun, water, and growth requirements. Shorter lilies are superb in the front of garden beds.

Try These

'Casa Blanca' is a fantastic white Oriental lily with a breathtaking scent; it makes a marvelous contribution to a moon garden or night garden. 'Copper Crown' has a very fragrant trumpet with long, pink to orange blooms. 'Chameleon' is a fragrant martagon lily that has an unusual twist—it starts out pink, then turns a yellowish color. It has a lime green throat and numerous dark purple spots.

Naked Lady

Lycoris squamigera

Botanical Pronunciation
LY-kor-iss skwam-EE-ger-uh

Other Names
Surprise lily, resurrection lily

Bloom Period and Seasonal Color
Mid- to late-summer; shades of pink flowers

Mature Height × Spread
28 inches × 5 inches

While there are various types of plants called surprise lily, the only one that remains consistently hardy in most of the state is *Lycoris squamigera*, also known as the naked lady and resurrection lily. Each flower has straplike leaves in the spring that die back when the weather turns warm. Then suddenly, in the middle of summer, the lily sends up 24- to 28-inch scapes holding fragrant, pink trumpet-shaped flowers. There appears to be no leaf whatsoever at this time, so many are "surprised" to see the gorgeous plant appear as if by magic. Naked ladies are loaded with many flowers per stalk and are easy to grow. They naturalize readily, and love being crowded, making them an excellent low-care summer bulb choice.

When, Where, and How to Plant
Naked ladies prefer a richly composted soil with good drainage. Sun is preferred, but shadier conditions are fine. Mix organic bulb fertilizer in the planting holes, planting in the early spring or fall. Dig holes that are approximately 4 to 6 inches deep and about 6 inches apart, placing the bulb in the planting hole with the pointy side up. Cover with soil and mulch.

Growing Tips
Apply an organic fertilizer in the spring when the foliage first comes out of the ground. They have low water requirements.

Regional Advice and Care
Naked ladies can be propagated every three to five years by dividing the bulb clumps, but division should be done immediately after the flowers bloom or in spring after the foliage starts to die away. Plant the divided bulbs immediately or store them in a cool, dry location and replant in early fall. Naked ladies are relatively free of pests and disease. Be sure to note where you have planted them as it is easy to mistakenly dig the bulbs up when they are bereft of leaf or stem.

Companion Planting and Design
Plant naked lady bulbs in the center of container gardens surrounded by planting partners such as purple angelonia, yellow calibrachoa, and sweet potato vine. For a more harmonious blend of plants, try mixing naked lady bulbs with pale white petunia, white bacopa, and rose-colored zinnias. They are quite effective in meadows, open woodland gardens, or wild areas where the wilting late spring foliage is not a concern. Groundcovers, foliage plants, and low perennials make delightful planting partners. Ostrich fern and perennial geranium are both particularly attractive with naked ladies standing regally in their midst.

Try These
This is the only species commonly available for Zones 4 and 5. Other varieties of spider lilies, which have a similar form, do survive in Zone 6 and, if very heavily protected, in Zone 5. Try red spider lily, *Lycoris radiata*, or white spider lily, *L. albiflora*. *L. sanguinea* has shocking orange-red flowers. All spider lily varieties bloom somewhat later, flowering in October.

Siberian Squill

Scilla siberica

Botanical Pronunciation
SILL-uh sye-BEER-ih-kuh

Bloom Period and Seasonal Color
Early spring; blue, pink, white, and striped flowers

Mature Height × Spread
2 to 8 inches × 2 inches

Siberian squill is truly one of the easiest bulbs to naturalize and is quite hardy, growing all over the world, even in its namesake of Siberia. They run with abandon through garden, woodland, and grass alike, creating rivers of blue, pink, or white throughout the landscape. While some consider it invasive, I have found it easy to dig the bulbs up if necessary, and unobtrusive because the Siberian squill blooms at such time that most gardeners are not able to mow or plant yet. Without a doubt its happy springtime color is more than welcome at the end of winter. Blooming as nodding flowers with three to five star-shaped blooms lasting between two and three weeks, it has a light fragrance as well, which adds to its springtime joy.

When, Where, and How to Plant

Siberian squill love loamy, well-drained soil filled with compost and other rotted organic matter. Loosen clay soil with rotted manure and compost on first planting. While Siberian squill like all levels of sun, they do not prefer overly hot locations. Cool, slightly moist woodland locations are best. Boggy soil drowns the bulbs, so it is not advised to plant the bulbs in a heavily wet area. Plant your Siberian squill bulbs 2 to 3 inches deep and about 4 inches apart from one another in the planting holes after the first frost. Place the pointy side of the bulb facing up. Plant Siberian squill in clustered groups of twenty-four or more for strong effect in the garden.

Growing Tips

Apply an organic all-purpose granular fertilizer when new growth breaks ground and keep the bulbs well watered through the season.

Regional Advice and Care

Leave foliage on the plants until it turns brown and withers in order to help put energy back into the little bulb; foliage is quite unobtrusive because of the diminutive size of the bulb.

Companion Planting and Design

While this bulb looks excellent in all types of beds and borders, it is best suited to naturalizing. It is excellent in rock gardens and under trees and shrubs. Lawns that have been heavily planted with blue shades of Siberian squill seem to turn into a blue carpet in the spring. Siberian squill and its relatives look marvelous planted in miniature container gardens and make excellent spring fairy garden plantings.

Try These

'Alba' is a remarkable little white flower that will produce three to four thin scapes with one to three drooping, bell-like white flowers with yellow anthers. 'Prussian Blue' is a bold blue. 'Spring Beauty' is a larger-flowered, taller version of 'Prussian Blue' that has a sweeter fragrance than other Siberian squill. *Puschkinia skilloides* is a similar variety of plant that comes in pinks, various colors of blue, and stripes, often having a white, star-shaped flower with a blue stripe on the petals.

Tulip

Tulipa spp. and hybrids

Botanical Pronunciation
TOO-li-pa

Bloom Period and Seasonal Color
Spring; red, yellow, white, pink, peach, orange, purple, white, striped, blended, and variegated flowers

Mature Height × Spread
4 to 36 inches × 6 to 12 inches

Of all the bulbs, tulips are the most popular of the spring flowers. With unbelievable variety in color, form, and shape, tulips offer gardeners an interesting landscape solution that blends well with groundcovers, perennials, and annuals alike. Some tulips are excellent for naturalizing, but many need to be replanted every season as they are short-lived in our Midwestern weather. Heavy soils and hot summers make it difficult for tulips to retain their vigor; they prefer cool weather and consistent moisture to flower brilliantly every season. There are early-, middle-, and late-spring blooming varieties to choose from. Do research when planning the landscape so you can be assured the tulips will bloom when you plan for them to perform.

When, Where, and How to Plant
Drainage is *the* most important consideration for tulip planting. Plant tulips in a fertile, organically amended soil in a *very* well-drained bed. Standing water will drown the bulbs. Plant about two weeks before the ground freezes hard, usually after the first frost. Mix organic bulb fertilizer in the planting holes, but do not overfertilize as that can overproduce green stems and lessen flower development. Plant the bulbs 6 inches deep and about 8 inches apart, pointy end up.

Growing Tips
After flowers fade in the spring, fertilize with an organic fertilizer. Not too much water!

Regional Advice and Care
Deadhead the spent flower heads, but leave the foliage on the plants until it turns brown and withers to encourage the energy for future growth to go back to the bulb. Plant bulbs in cages or use chicken wire to surround the bulbs if rabbits, squirrels, or voles become an issue. Because tulips often decrease production within one to two years, particularly in the Midwest where hot summers have an effect on tulip performance, some gardeners dig up the bulbs after their initial bloom, refrigerate them for the summer to keep them cool, then replanted again in the fall.

Companion Planting and Design
When tulips leaves begin to fade and look gnarly in the garden, plant foliage-rich annuals around the spent leaves to hide them. Tulips work perfectly with other spring bulbs; try orange, red, and yellow tulips mixed with white daffodils to make a bold statement.

Try These
'Sky High Single Red' is large and stately and one of the tallest tulips available at 36 inches. 'Mr. van der Hoef' is a yellow, double, early tulip with a delicious scent. 'Little Princess' grows only 4 inches tall and is decidedly one of the shortest varieties of tulip. It has reddish orange, primrose yellow, burnt orange, and gold petal mixes and blooms heavily. Sweetly scented 'Electra' is a daring, hot pink early bloomer. 'Sunset Miami' is a surprising fringed variety that has large, iridescent, pink-magenta flowers with an ivory base.

GROUNDCOVERS
FOR INDIANA

Groundcovers are definitively a collection of low-growing plants placed together. Most groundcovers make a gorgeous contribution to a landscape and are undoubtedly the solution to the high maintenance of a traditional lawn. Where lawns need to be mowed, fertilized, edged, and watered weekly, groundcovers most typically do not need such high maintenance, making them a more sustainable choice over lawns. They are also quite fitting beneath trees and in other challenging areas where grass will not grow.

Types of Groundcovers

Groundcovers come in various forms: creeping vines, short perennials, and low-growing shrubs. One can find evergreen groundcovers that stay green all winter or deciduous groundcovers that drop their leaves in the winter but return in full force in

Lemon coral stonecrop, raspberry angelonia, and agave combine in a gorgeous, low-growing groundcover design and landscape feature. Both colorful and drought tolerant, this water-conserving design would be an excellent planting combination for a low-water-needs garden.

the spring. There are groundcovers that can withstand abuse from walking, making them suitable for path plantings, and groundcovers that will not tolerate any footsteps whatsoever. Groundcovers can be standalone rooted plants or plants that form an intricate network of underground runners that sprout shoots from the ground.

Growing & Maintaining Groundcovers

Success with groundcovers can be increased with proper preparation of the soil. Dig in several inches of compost, rotted manure, and appropriate natural soil amendments based on your soil testing results. Base spacing requirements of the plants on what you expect the mature size of the plant to be, not on the size of the seedling. If planted according to mature plant size expectations, the bed should take two years to fill in. If you plant them farther apart then suggested, then expect nearly four years of growth from planting time. Once planted, water in well and fertilize once a year in spring with an organic fertilizer.

Once you plant a groundcover, you will want to mulch to help keep moisture in the root zone and discourage weeds. However, if your particular groundcover choice needs to spread via roots from the top of the soil, mulching will slow its expansion considerably. Do not mulch these types of top-spreading groundcover plants.

All plants need some maintenance and groundcovers are no exception. Sometimes groundcovers, particularly those with underground runners, become invasive. Runner-based plants need a hard trimming back one or two times per year if they start to overflow the planting bed. Controlling rhizome-based plants can be simple if you stop them against a sidewalk or wall or with a metal or recycled plastic edging.

Low-growing deciduous perennials and shrubs collapse or lose their leaves in the fall. It is best to clean them up after the winter for a neater and more refined look when fresh growth starts the following year. For groundcovers that stay evergreen, it is best to rake the fallen leaves out of them late in the season and trim any dead or brown spots out in the spring.

Groundcovers for Wildlife

Many types of wildlife enjoy groundcovers whether the they are planted in a traditional manner in the soil or in containers as a wildlife attractant. Chipmunks, squirrels, and birds will use certain groundcovers for nesting material and as cover. Both coreopsis and geranium are low-growing perennials not listed in this chapter, yet they are excellent choices as groundcovers that attract butterflies and other pollinators. Ajuga, creeping thyme, and spotted dead nettle attract bees and butterflies. Using groundcovers as part of your plan to help the environment and encourage wildlife and pollinators is a smart idea.

Groundcovers soften and beautify a landscape, stabilize soil, hide bare areas, and attract pollinators. They are a perfect buffer between a garden and a sidewalk or grass, drawing your eye in and welcoming a visitor.

Ajuga

Ajuga reptans

Botanical Pronunciation uh-JOO-guh REP-tanz

Other Name Bugleweed

Bloom Period and Seasonal Color
Spring; white, pink, and purple flowers with dark green to bronze leaves

Mature Height × Spread
6 to 9 inches × spreading

Ajuga is a very versatile and attractive groundcover that does well in most sun situations, loves drought, withstands foot traffic, and flowers gorgeously in the springtime. This evergreen or semi-evergreen perennial spreads rapidly by stolons and can be quite aggressive in lawns, so it helps to have a border or sidewalk to stop its creeping and keep it contained. On its own, the foliage stands only 2 to 3 inches above the ground, making this a great low-grower that is a creative lawn substitute where traditional grass refuses to perform. Ajuga is an excellent plant to place on a hillside for erosion control due to its rhizomatous nature. Flowers bloom in spring and early summer and are absolutely stunning when ajuga is planted *en masse*.

When, Where, and How to Plant
Place ajuga in nearly any location, about 10 inches apart, and it will soon fill in. To help ajuga get a good start, amend soil with compost and make sure the soil is well drained. Although it likes moist conditions, it needs good drainage. Ajuga is a tough little plant and tolerates a variety of conditions, from full sun to full shade, from wet soil to dry, and from clay to sand. Do not mulch ajuga as it will spread better on its own without mulch blocking its growth.

Growing Tips
Fertilize once per month with a liquid organic fertilizer to see stronger plant performance. It likes moisture.

Regional Advice and Care
If plants get overly zealous, simply shear back their growth with clippers or dig them up and share with friends. Plants may be trimmed with a mower: set the blades high to remove spent flower blooms and tidy its appearance. If the groundcover is in a challenging garden position, simply shear back the dead flower spikes. Crown rot and other fungal conditions are a problem for ajuga. Control with an organic fungicide. While ajuga is edible, it is primarily used as an herbal tea medicinal remedy. It tastes bitter and somewhat dandelion-like in salads.

Companion Planting and Design
Ajuga is fantastic as a path plant due to its weed-suffocating tendencies and ability to handle light foot traffic. Group ajuga with small-statured plants such as heuchera, painted fern, sweet flag, and carex. It looks great at the base of bleeding hearts; when the bleeding heart collapses in the heat of late summer, remove its brown stems and the ajuga looks beautiful in its place.

Try These
'Chocolate Chip' is my favorite variety with short 2-inch chocolate brown, bronze, and maroon leaves with a purple flower in spring (see photo). 'Black Scallop' has a deeper colored leaf with blue-purple flowers. 'Burgundy Glow' has a purple flower and variegated multicolor leaves that are white, pink, green, and burgundy.

Common Periwinkle

Vinca minor

Botanical Pronunciation VING-kah MY-nor

Other Names Vinca, dwarf myrtle

Bloom Period and Seasonal Color
Spring; white, pink, purple, lilac, and blue
flowers; green and green-with-white leaves

Mature Height × Spread
3 to 9 inches × spreading

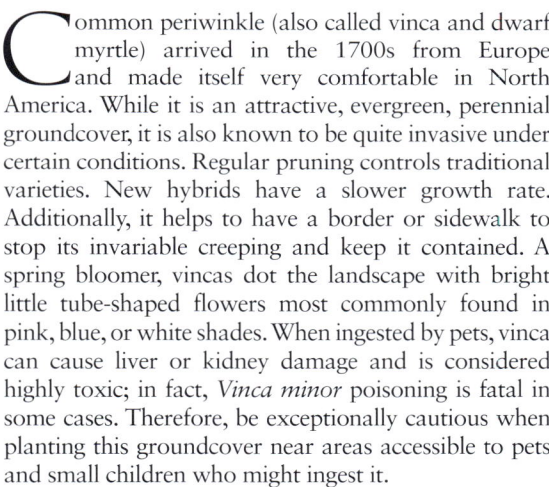

Common periwinkle (also called vinca and dwarf myrtle) arrived in the 1700s from Europe and made itself very comfortable in North America. While it is an attractive, evergreen, perennial groundcover, it is also known to be quite invasive under certain conditions. Regular pruning controls traditional varieties. New hybrids have a slower growth rate. Additionally, it helps to have a border or sidewalk to stop its invariable creeping and keep it contained. A spring bloomer, vincas dot the landscape with bright little tube-shaped flowers most commonly found in pink, blue, or white shades. When ingested by pets, vinca can cause liver or kidney damage and is considered highly toxic; in fact, *Vinca minor* poisoning is fatal in some cases. Therefore, be exceptionally cautious when planting this groundcover near areas accessible to pets and small children who might ingest it.

When, Where, and How to Plant

Easily grown in average, dry to medium, well-drained soil in full sun to shade, vinca is a very hearty groundcover. It will tolerate rocky and poor soil. Although it can be planted anytime during the growing season, it does best when planted in early spring before its first bloom in soil that has been amended with rotted manure or compost. Vinca prefers good drainage. Do not mulch vinca as it spreads with roots that develop at nodes where they touch the soil; if blocked from touching the soil, it will not spread as consistently.

Growing Tips

Fertilizer is not required; however, it will do well with a once-per-month organic fertilizer application.

Regional Advice and Care

Grass and weeds often invade vinca and can be challenging to pull out, particularly in dry shade. In spring the plants may be mowed on a higher level setting in order to remove spent flower blooms and to tidy its appearance. Root rot and other fungal conditions are a problem for vinca due to its preferred shady and moist growing conditions. Cut out diseased areas or apply an organic fungicide. If plants get too aggressive, it is easy to shear back their growth with clippers or dig them up and share with friends.

Companion Planting and Design

Large hostas, bleeding hearts, and perennial geraniums will grow through this groundcover and make fantastic features in a shaded area. Vinca can handle light foot traffic, so it does well lining woodland trails. Vinca works well in containers and wall gardens as an attractive vining feature. Forsythia has a bold yellow flower in early spring that contrasts nicely when vinca's glossy foliage is planted thickly around the base of the shrub.

Try These

'Variegata' has a bicolor leaf that brightens up shady areas with a traditional blue-purple flower. 'Atropurpurea' has a red-violet flower that fades to a bold magenta. 'Alba' has a white flower and is less invasive than traditional varieties. 'Illumination' has a bold yellow spot on the center of each leaf and bright purple blooms.

Creeping Sedum

Sedum spp.

Botanical Pronunciation
SEE-dum

Other Name
Stonecrop

Bloom Period and Seasonal Color
Summer; variously colored foliage

Mature Height × Spread
2 to 12 inches × creeping

While sedum is generally considered to be an ornamental succulent used in drought-tolerant perennial beds, the shorter creeping sedum can also be considered a groundcover because it is lower to the ground than the taller sedums and is a spreading plant. Recently, creeping sedum has become an popular substitute for some of the more highly invasive groundcovers because of its incredibly low maintenance. If you want a plant that needs to sit and be left alone, this plant is for you. Low-growing sedums have various shapes of leaf and flower, are deer resistant, attract beneficials, and can be grown in virtually any type of soil or location, from rooftop garden to container to directly in the ground, as long as they have access to regular sunshine.

When, Where, and How to Plant

Plant creeping sedum anytime there is no danger of frost. Although creeping sedum will grow in nearly any soil, it prefers a light, sandy, or gravelly area. Sites exposed to full sun are ideal but the plant will also tolerate part shade. Loosen heavy clay soils with rotted manure, compost, or gravel before planting as good drainage is the key to success with creeping sedum. Creeping sedum does not handle foot traffic well, so it's best planted along the edges of sunny paths.

Growing Tips

In summer, particularly during dry weather, water every two weeks. Moisten the soil without soaking it as the leaves of the creeping sedum (a succulent) store water, which makes heavy irrigation unnecessary.

Plants that stand in water will drown and typically suffer from root rot and fungal issues. Fertilize in early spring with an organic fertilizer; do not overfertilize as the plants will become leggy and weak.

Regional Advice and Care

In early spring, prune back any dead growth from winter. Treat botrytis leaf blotch and other fungal conditions with an organic fungicide. Creeping sedum has edible leaves that are slightly sour and can be used in salads and stir-frying.

Companion Planting and Design

Creeping sedums quickly cover large, sunny areas with poor soils. Single cultivars look gorgeous *en masse*; however, mixing colors and forms can bring a lot of color interest to a challenging landscape situation as well. They are sought after as significant rooftop and vertical wall garden plants because of their low water requirements.

Try These

'Ruby Glow' is 8 to 12 inches high and has burgundy leaves with blue tints and bold red flowers in summer. 'Cauticola' has diminutive blue-gray foliage on 2-inch stems. *Sedum spurium* 'Tricolor' has green, white, and pink leaves and stands 4 inches tall. 'Dragon's Blood' has bold purple foliage that deepens in full sun and stands 4 inches tall. *S. rupestre* 'Angelina' has chartreuse-green foliage that turns orange in winter. *S. spathulifolium* 'Cape Blanco' has the tiniest gray rosettes in tight little clusters with stems that stand 2 to 4 inches tall.

Creeping Thyme

Thymus serpyllum

Botanical Pronunciation
TY-mus ser-PIL-lum

Other Name
Wild thyme

Bloom Period and Seasonal Color
Early summer; scented foliage that blooms white, pink, and purple

Mature Height × Spread
2 to 6 inches × spreading

Creeping thyme is one of the lowest growing groundcovers, with some varieties at only 2 inches when they flower. However, it is absolutely one of the most beautiful and impactful groundcovers for full sun because when it is blooming, it is awash in a wave of color. Additionally, when it is not blooming, it is saturated in a wave of scent. Creeping thyme handles very high traffic and releases its magnificent scent when walked upon. It is perfect when placed in between steppingstones, on low stone walls, and in miniature gardens. It works very well as a creative no-mow, low-water lawn replacement, as creeping thyme loves dry conditions. Because it is an edible herb, creeping thyme can also be harvested and used in cooking.

When, Where, and How to Plant
Plant creeping thyme in spring or fall when there is no danger of frost. Although creeping thyme will grow in nearly any soil, it prefers a light, sandy, or gravelly area exposed to full sun. Loosen heavy clay soils with rotted manure, compost, or gravel before planting. Do not mulch creeping thyme as it will spread better if it has contact with the soil.

Growing Tips
Fertilize once per month with an organic fertilizer, more often in heavy traffic zones. Creeping thyme can suffer from root rot in wet situations.

Regional Advice and Care
Pulling fine grass and other weeds out of the thyme can sometimes be a challenge. Pull invading weeds out and then gently push creeping thyme back into place in the soil. Propagate by cuttings, seeds, or division of roots. Sweep fall leaves off thyme so the plant is not smothered over winter. Because creeping thyme is smaller than traditional thyme, it is not used for large culinary projects. It is best steeped for teas, used fresh off the stem in dishes, or whole stems can be used in vinegars. For fresh flavor, remove the leaves from the stems anytime.

Companion Planting and Design
It's outstanding as a path plant in ornamental landscape walkways. Creeping thyme looks stunning when flowering in pink and white flower gardens. Woolly thyme is grown for its fuzzy silver foliage and makes a great edging when tucked in to a white, black, and silver garden. Creeping thyme 'Elfin' is adorable in fairy gardens due to its diminutive size, particularly when it's planted to look like grass or groundcover.

Try These
'Coccineus' have dense mats of flowers that bloom a reddish violet. Woolly thyme has soft green-gray leaves that soften harsh edges in gardens. 'Annie Hall' has late spring, rose-red flowers that pollinators adore. 'Alba' is a darker green variety with bright white flowers. 'Goldstream' has flecks of gold in the leaves and takes a good amount of foot traffic. 'Elfin' handles only light foot traffic but has the tiniest leaves imaginable with light purple flowers.

English Ivy

Hedera helix

Botanical Pronunciation
HED-dur-uh HEL-licks

Bloom Period and Seasonal Color
Evergreen vining foliage

Mature Height × Spread
6 to 9 inches × trailing

English ivy is a tremendously versatile plant and is not to be confused with Boston ivy (*Parthenocissus tricuspidata*), which is aggressive and has been known to cover entire buildings. While it can be invasive in southern states and the Pacific Northwest, in the Midwest English ivy is used as houseplants and groundcovers, and in topiary displays, hanging baskets, and window boxes. There are many types, from huge to miniature, and almost all of them tolerate shade, atmospheric pollution, poor soil, and other extreme conditions. English ivy has woody stems and climbs by aerial rootlets that help it grab on to walls, fences, soil, and other plants. English ivy is exceptionally toxic to cats, dogs, horses, and humans. Therefore, be cautious when planting this groundcover in areas near pets and where small children might ingest it.

When, Where, and How to Plant

English ivy is easily grown in average, well-drained soil in full sun to shade; however, any organic matter added to the planting area will benefit this groundcover. Plant in a 6-inch hole, and then place plants at least 2 feet away from walls and 1 foot away from other plants. Although it can be planted anytime during the growing season, it does best when planted in early spring in soil that has been amended with rotted manure or compost. Many English ivy cultivars will not perform well in Midwestern climates; therefore, do some research and understand which planting zones the ivy will do best in.

Growing Tips

Fertilize every two months during the growing season with organic fertilizer.

Regional Advice and Care

English ivy propagates readily: simply dig up a section, being sure to get the root, and replant it in another location. Diseases that plague English ivy include bacterial leaf spot, stem canker, and fungal diseases. Prevent overly dense growth, which encourages disease, by pruning ivy in spring. Mow the groundcover with your mower blades set high and then remove all dead leaves, stems, and other plant debris early in spring. Shear it later in the season with hedge trimmers. Prevent fungal issues by letting it dry out between waterings and treat with an organic fungicide.

Companion Planting and Design

Brunnera, large hostas, and all forms of spring bulbs, particularly daffodils, will grow through this groundcover and make fantastic features in a shaded area. Aerial roots can damage brick, stone, stucco, and wood. Be aware that English ivy can be invasive under the right conditions; be cautious as to where you plant it and use climbing structures to support it rather than letting it grow up unsupported structures.

Try These

'Thorndale' survives extremely cold weather and is one of the best varieties for northern winters. 'Bulgaria' has leaves that turn purplish in winter and is tolerant through Zone 5. 'Variegata' is hardy to Zone 5 and has astounding tricolor white, pale green, and dark green foliage.

Lily-of-the-Valley

Convallaria majalis

Botanical Pronunciation
kon-vuh-LAIR-ee-uh muh-JAY-liss

Bloom Period and Seasonal Color
Spring; white and pink flowers

Mature Height × Spread
6 to 18 inches × 6 to 15 inches

Lily-of-the-valley prefers shade and moist soil and has tiny, nodding, bell-shaped flowers on short stalks in the spring. It has an absolutely mesmerizing and much loved fragrance, which makes this a sensory-rich plant that is well-placed along paths and near gates where you can enjoy its scent. There are two lance-shaped green leaves on every plant, which are quite straight, with red berries that follow after the flowers bloom. While the plants are immensely attractive, they are equally invasive and need to be placed where they are restricted and cannot escape into neighboring garden beds or lawns. Every part of the lily-of-the-valley is poisonous to mammals. Be particularly cautious when planting this toxic groundcover near pets and small children who might eat it.

When, Where, and How to Plant
Originally known as a woodland plant, lily-of-the-valley should be planted in loamy, moist, well-drained soil filled with compost and other rotted organic matter. Loosen clay soil with rotted manure and compost on initial planting. Soak lily-of-the-valley pips, its short rhizomatous roots, in warm water for a few hours before planting. Plant the pips so that their tops barely peek out of the surface of the soil about 1½ to 3 inches apart.

Growing Tips
They like some water but will do surprisingly well in drought. Total lack of water will cause the lily-of-the-valley leaves to dry and brown at the edges.

Regional Advice and Care
Divide and replant in the early fall, before the first frost has flattened the leaves. Lily-of-the-valley can have several diseases including anthracnose, leaf spot, leaf blotch, and crown rot. Wet conditions promote fungal infection and spread of the diseases, so it is best to prevent these conditions by planting in drier areas. Spider mites can be treated with a spray of soap and water. Wet conditions might encourage slugs; trap them organically. Weevils and beetles can be handpicked.

Companion Planting and Design
Because of lily-of-the-valley's astounding growth rate, they work marvelously planted on hillsides and in difficult areas to prevent erosion. Lily-of-the-valley is a superb grass replacement when planted beneath large shade trees where nothing else appears to grow. They seem to thrive in dry, shady conditions. When planted close to other perennials or groundcovers, expect traditional lily-of-the-valley to wholeheartedly invade the neighboring space and smother the other plants out. When planted in contained areas near walkways, lily-of-the-valley is a deliciously fragrant solution.

Try These
'Aureovariegata' has yellow stripes and spreads less vigorously than the common lily-of-the-valley. 'Fortin's Giant' is tall at 18 inches and has larger white bell flowers. 'Rosea' has delicate pink flowers. 'Fernwood's Golden Slippers' has striking chartreuse-yellow foliage and white flowers. 'Bordeaux' has darker green foliage, larger white flowers, and a unique burgundy plant base. 'Hardwick Hall' has a clear golden stripe on the outside of each leaf.

Pachysandra

Pachysandra terminalis

Botanical Pronunciation
pack-ih-SAN-druh tur-mih-NAY-liss

Other Name Japanese spurge

Bloom Period and Seasonal Color
Spring; white flowers with evergreen foliage

Mature Height × Spread
9 to 12 inches × spreading

Pachysandra is the quintessential no-care groundcover that, once established, spreads with rhizomes into a thick carpet. Although the plant produces small white, slightly fragrant flowers in spring, it is known more for its shiny, almost glossy green broadleaf structure. Pachysandra is a great groundcover for dense shade conditions beneath trees and shrubs, often choking out weeds or invasive plants. Employed as a tool to fight soil erosion, pachysandra provides a utilitarian service when planted on hillsides and in great drifts in deep shade where other plants will not survive. While the plant is slow to kick-start and often looks dismal the first year it's planted, it will begin to shine by year two, and by the third year will thicken substantially.

When, Where, and How to Plant

Too much sun will cause pachysandra to become abnormally yellow, or chlorotic. Therefore, plant pachysandra where it is most likely to experience shade. The leaves can burn from sun exposure in winter. Provide shade near a fence, building, or large evergreens to help prevent winter burn that will leave the plants edged in brown. Because the plants do best in rich, well-drained, woodland-like soil, be sure to amend an area with compost or rotted manure before planting in a poor soil. Space about 12 inches apart.

Growing Tips

Newly planted pachysandras require help getting established; water about 1 inch per week during this initial period of growth. When the leaves

decay, they will provide additional soil nutrients for the plants.

Regional Advice and Care

Autumn maintenance is fairly easy; when leaves fall onto pachysandra, take the back of a rake and gently rake the tops of the plants so the dry leaves fall into the bed and out of sight. The fungal disease volutella leaf blight can affect overcrowded pachysandra. Good air circulation helps prevent the blight, so periodically cutting out sections that might be overcrowded will increase its ability to resist it. When planting along driveways or throughways where salt is used to de-ice in winter, pachysandra will brown out. Protect plants from salt exposure.

Companion Planting and Design

Ornamental hakonechloa grass looks fabulous planted near pachysandra, as do certain taller ferns. Pachysandra can crowd out nearly any perennial and small shrubs planted among it, so it is best used as a wide edger, in a large rock garden, or placed in a woodland location. Under pines and other densely shaded trees, it is the perfect solution because of its evergreen nature and ability to grow where grass doesn't. Plant pachysandra against sidewalks or buildings where it can be contained.

Try These

'Variegata' or 'Silver Edge' has a frosty white rim and grayer leaves, and the plant is a bit less aggressive. 'Green Sheen' has a slower growth rate and highly shiny leaf. 'Green Carpet' is a common green type.

Snow on the Mountain

Aegopodium podagraria 'Variegata'

Botanical Pronunciation ee-guh-POH-dee-um pod-uh-GRAR-ee-uh ver-ee-uh-GAH-tah

Other Names Bishop's weed, goutweed

Bloom Period and Seasonal Color Summer; green and white leaves and small white flowers

Mature Height × Spread
6 to 10 inches × spreading

Snow on the mountain, also called bishop's weed or goutweed, is a rapidly spreading European native that has naturalized here with abandon. Variegated forms are not as fast spreading, but without containment this aggressive groundcover can become invasive. When contained within a garden, particularly within a dry area which helps limit its growth, snow on the mountain can be a glorious plant to lighten a dark, shady area. In my own garden I have a 6-foot stand of the variegated snow on the mountain, which I adore; it lines a very dry pathway filled with lime screenings. I never water or fertilize it. Weeds are completely choked out, and the only maintenance is to rake up the dried vegetation after winter.

When, Where, and How to Plant
Snow on the mountain grows easily in any average soil, but it's more likely to stay contained in dry, well-drained soil in shade. Snow on the mountain tolerates rocky and poor soil but will spread far more rapidly with enriched soil, so do not amend or fertilize. Although it can be planted anytime during the growing season, it does best when planted in early spring before its first bloom. A poor performer in heat, snow on the mountain's leaves can burn and look sparse in extremely hot weather, particularly in direct sun.

Growing Tips
There's no need to water or fertilize it.

Regional Advice and Care
If plants get too aggressive, shear back the leaves with clippers or mow the plants completely over to slow growth. Some people report skin irritation and rash when planting snow on the mountain, so be sure to wear gloves when handling the leaf and roots. Remove white flower heads to prevent additional seeding. Snow on the mountain leaves are considered an edible and are used much like spinach; harvest in early spring before it flowers. If it is picked later, it develops a pungent taste and can have a laxative effect. It has been used as a medicinal herb to treat gout and other conditions.

Companion Planting and Design
This plant is a good solution for difficult areas, covering banks, sandy bare spots, and thickly rooted tree zones. Many love this attractive, deciduous, perennial groundcover, but it should be used primarily as an edging and massing solution in very dry shade areas where nothing else will grow. It is not recommended for other landscaping purposes due to its vigorous nature. Trees and bushes will tolerate snow on the mountain at its base, but it will not partner well with perennials or annuals as it usually overtakes them.

Try These
Other species of *Aegopodium podagraria* exist, but none are appropriate for home gardening because they are even more intensely invasive. *Euphorbia marginata* is also called "snow on the mountain," but is not the same species as *A. podagraria*.

Spotted Dead Nettle

Lamium maculatum

Botanical Pronunciation
LAY-mee-um mak-yew-LAY-tum

Other Name Dead nettle

Bloom Period and Seasonal Color
Late spring; variegated leaves of green and silver; white, pink, and purple flowers

Mature Height × Spread
6 to 8 inches × spreading

L amium is well suited to dry shade and functions as a fantastic transitional groundcover plant between sunny and shady sites. Its name derives from other varieties of plants that resemble spotted dead nettle but that have hairy stinging nettles. Spotted dead nettle can be hairy, but it does not have the stinging nettles; therefore it is titled "dead." Its "spot" can be seen on the heart-shaped leaves as a bold, lightly shaded blotch that stretches across the foliage. With a long blooming season and bright variegated leaves, lamium is a showstopper. If it is placed in dry shade, lamium's spreading habit is well contained and easy to manage. However, if placed in moist, rich-soil conditions, and given no management, it can become invasive and spread outside its bounds.

When, Where, and How to Plant
Place nettle in nearly any location about 18 to 24 inches apart, and it will fill in quickly. It grows easily in any average soil but is more likely to stay contained in dry, well-drained soil in shade. Lamium can tolerate rocky and poor soil but will spread far more rapidly with enriched soil, so do not amend or fertilize. Although it can be planted at any time during the growing season, it does best when planted in early spring before its first bloom.

Growing Tips
Keep this plant, which can form dense mats, contained within raised beds, blocked in with walls or sidewalks, or tamed by spading its edges (clip its roots) in the garden beds. Divide or thin lamiums after plants finish blooming by digging rooted stems up or clipping as much as one-third of the plant back. Shear overzealous plants back to a preferred height at any time after blooms fade, and you might be rewarded with a second wave of blooms.

Regional Advice and Care
Leaves will scorch if exposed to full sun conditions. When autumn tree leaves drop, gently rake or use a leaf blower to clean the leaves out so the plant won't be smothered. Flowers and leaves are edible and can be used in herbal tea or added to stews, soups, and salads.

Companion Planting and Design
Spotted dead nettle looks marvelous when planted *en masse* beneath maple trees and other large shade trees. Lamium can be great daffodil partners; simply plant the bulbs within the groundcover. Great companion plants include brunnera, ferns, and large hostas.

Try These
'Dellam Golden Anniversary' has a scorch-resistant tricolor leaf that is chartreuse-yellow with a green interior and a silver spot. 'White Nancy' has silver leaves edged in a deep blue-green with pink flowers. 'Cosmopolitan' is a miniature variety with variegated leaves and a shell pink flower. 'Anne Greenway' has a mauve flower and astounding color with four to five colors of variegation on every leaf that run from chartreuse to deep green to silver shades.

Spring Cinquefoil

Potentilla neumanniana

Botanical Pronunciation
po-ten-TILL-a new-MAN-nee-ah-na

Other Name Spotted cinquefoil

Bloom Period and Seasonal Color
Spring to early summer; yellow blooms

Mature Height × Spread
3 to 8 inches × 6 to 12 inches

Spring cinquefoil is the low-growing groundcover potentilla, which should not be confused with the many varieties of potentilla that are shrubs. When it blooms, spring cinquefoil has an endearing 1-inch, five-petaled, buttercup-shaped yellow flower. Its dark green foliage can sometimes have a slight silvery tint, is evergreen, and is long-lasting in areas with warmer winters and protected areas. These sturdy little plants are fast growers and spread readily to form low mounds that are approximately 3 to 6 inches tall. Spreading by runners, it will happily choke out weeds. It's a good selection as a no-mow lawn substitute or as a path filler. Once established, spring cinquefoil takes abuse and can handle light foot traffic.

When, Where, and How to Plant
Plant the spring cinquefoil anytime after the last frost. This plant will tolerate any soil as long as it is well drained; however, it prefers a light, sandy, or gravelly area exposed to full sun. Heavy or wet soils should be improved with rotted manure, compost, or gravel to enhance drainage. Place plants at least 12 to 18 inches apart, and they will easily fill in. It is simple to divide: dig up a clump, then cut or pull the plant apart.

Growing Tips
Although drought tolerant, spring cinquefoil appreciates a regular watering schedule as long as it is not standing in water.

Regional Advice and Care
When planted in ideal growing conditions, spring cinquefoil sometimes reblooms in early autumn. Extreme cold in winter can cause minor damage to the tips of foliage. Sheer back any brown areas, and the plant will return quite well in the spring. It has no serious disease or insect problems, although excess water can cause root rot issues. When leaves drop in autumn, gently rake out or use a leaf blower to clean the leaves out of the groundcover so the plants aren't smothered.

Companion Planting and Design
Spring cinquefoil allows spring-flowering bulbs to grow through its foliage, so it functions as a good overplanting for daffodils, tulips, and alliums. As a groundcover, spring cinquefoil grows well in crevices, between steppingstones, and over retaining walls. It can function as a mulch when planted around shrubs and trees, helps with erosion control on slopes, and spreads readily into full sun locations that have poor soil. Spring cinquefoil shines brilliantly in the rock garden. It looks lovely at the front of borders but its spreading nature might invade the border.

Try These
'Nana', which has glossier leaves, is the common selection found in most nurseries. 'Pygmaea' has the same general habit of 'Nana' but is a pygmy version growing only 2 inches tall and 5 inches wide, which makes it an excellent selection for rock gardens and miniature gardens.

LAWNS
FOR INDIANA

O ne of my earliest memories is laying out flat on a grassy hill with my cousins. Birds flit overhead as we lay in the cool grass and count the clouds. We are stretched out with muddy knees and mosquito-bit elbows simply enjoying a sunny afternoon. It was wonderful. Midwesterners, like many Americans, have a love affair with a well-manicured lawn. Perhaps it is because of our memories of the experience of touching nature while playing in the grass as children. While our state is known agriculturally for its soybeans, corn, and other staples, the biggest agricultural enterprise here is turfgrass.

The benefits of a lawn include grass for children to run and play on, light and heat absorption in urban areas, neighborhood noise absorption, and pet walking areas. They also provide a nice place where lawn games and barbecues can be celebrated. Lawns provide a frame for your garden design picture, which often helps the landscape look finished and refined.

Unfortunately, there is an inordinately high maintenance and environmental cost to growing a lawn. Residential summer watering uses more than 40 percent of our water resources. Mowing takes hours of work weekly, and mowers can spew exhaust fumes into the air. Then there's weeding, aerating, fertilizing, watering, broadcasting, and spraying for diseases and pests. This investment of time, effort, and chemicals is costly and raises significant economic and environmental worries. But there are options.

Low-Maintenance Versus High-Maintenance Grasses

High-maintenance grass means excessive use of resources. However, there are alternatives to keep your lawn as low maintenance as possible while reducing the labor and negative environmental impact. Consider reducing the size of your lawn by increasing the size of your landscaping beds. Incorporate more trees, shrubs, and perennials in the areas that border your grassy lawn. Mowing is a major environmental and safety issue. Americans spend three billion hours annually mowing our grass or using equipment in our gardens that give off greenhouse gases. We use 600 million gallons of gas in this equipment. Beyond mowing with non-environmentally friendly tools, having a "perfect looking lawn" often involves the heavy use of chemicals such as pesticides and herbicides, which are not good for the water table or environment. Chemicals often run off into our larger water systems, causing a negative effect in your neighborhood, but also in rivers and streams, which lead to and deposit the chemicals in the ocean. Consider a more natural-looking lawn without idealized perfection. Think about pulling dandelions and other small weeds by hand or ignoring them entirely.

Mixing lawns with perennial and native plant beds within the landscape makes a more positive environmental impact than lawns alone. Surrounding structures with pollinator plants or ornamental edible garden beds can provide an attractive and utilitarian result for garden visitors and native wildlife.

Grass varieties can make all the difference. Use low-grow or no-mow grass varieties as solutions to the high-maintenance lawn: you'll increase the garden sustainability factor by reducing how often you have to mow. This type of grass saves time and money.

Types of Lower-Maintenance Grass

Imagine a lower-maintenance grass that you could allow to go natural or perhaps only have to mow about once per month. Happily, it exists. Low-maintenance grass is deep rooted, therefore, it's extremely drought tolerant and needs little water. Here are two of my favorites.

Low-Mow Fescue

Many companies sell a low-mow or a no-mow fescue seed mix. This is a fantastic solution to address the environmental concerns of a heavier-feeding traditional lawn grass. Environmentally supportive grasses usually resist lawn grubs, do not require fertilizing, and have a super slow growth rate, which reduces traditional mowing needs by 50 percent or more. Sow low-mow fescue grass at the rate of 5 pounds per 1,000 square feet.

Buffalograss (*Bouteloua dactyloides*)

Buffalograss is a native American grass that has a feathery, soft look about it that, when it has not been mowed, adds a special natural beauty to a landscape. It is seedless, thrives on little water, and is fast spreading. It has an aggressive nature, which makes it tough for weeds to invade, and it seems to thrive in hot conditions. If it is exposed to a heavy drought, it will go dormant and come back to a full green color once it's watered. It has a low pollen rate, so it is a good solution for allergy sufferers. Sow buffalograss at the rate of 4 pounds per 1,000 square feet.

Types of Higher Maintenance Grass

There are many varieties of turfgrass that will work in the Midwest. These grasses require heavy watering and fertilization to maintain a deep green, thick condition and are therefore considered higher maintenance. Here are several species.

Kentucky Bluegrass (*Poa pratensis*)

Kentucky bluegrass is the most widely used turfgrass in the region and is well adapted to this climate. High-quality Kentucky bluegrass requires regular fertilization to stay thick and at least 1 inch of water per week throughout the spring and summer. Annual core-aeration and de-thatching will also help keep the grass showy. Sow Kentucky bluegrass seed at the rate of 2 pounds per 1,000 square feet of lawn.

Perennial Rye Grass (*Lolium perenne*)

Perennial rye grass is a bunch grass that is well suited to the Midwestern climate, though it can suffer some in a late hot and dry summer. This is a cool-weather grass and is a quick germinator from seed, between four to seven days. It provides good wear resistance. Sow perennial rye grass seed at the rate of 10 pounds per 1,000 square feet of lawn.

Urban areas are filled with green lawns along city streets. These areas are particularly attractive when broken up with urban plantings of pollinator-attracting plantings such as the small streetside garden in this photo.

How To Install Grass Seed

Soil preparation is important when considering the growth of a lawn. When planning a new lawn, be sure to test the soil to find out its specific needs. Clear the planting area of debris, weed thoroughly, and roughly level the existing soil to the proper grade. On top, add 2 inches of topsoil and 1 inch of a compost mixture rich in organic matter. Be sure to add additional soil amendments if recommended by your soil test, and then combine all of this in with existing soil, digging to a depth of 6 inches. Rake and level the soil until the surface is smooth.

Seeding

Spread seed according to package directions, being sure to change the direction of your drop spreader back and forth in multiple directions. Once the seed is planted, push a roller over the soil surface, building a strong seed-to-soil contact. If seeding in early spring, it will be necessary to cover the seeds with straw to create light shade. Water the surface well several times a day until germination, but not so much that the water causes seed run-off. Do not fertilize the grass until the lawn has been well set and mowed more than once. Feed with an organic lawn fertilizer according to the label instructions.

Sodding

For best success, be sure to buy sod grown on a soil as much like yours as possible. Sod should be dark green and moist to the touch. Moisten your already-prepared soil and roll out the sod, making sure that the ends are tightly squeezed against one another. Staggering the ends between rows will help blend the sod into a natural-looking placement. Roll well to make sure there is a firm contact between soil and the bottom of the sod roll. Water well upon completion, then water daily after that until the soil has shown it is established. Feed with an organic lawn fertilizer according to the label instructions.

Thickening

Maintaining a lush, green, weed-free lawn without the use of chemicals is possible if you spread grass seed regularly over an existing lawn. By maintaining a thick lawn, you are preventing weed seeds from germinating, and the existing grass is able to reach down deep for nutrients and water, increasing root depth and the likelihood of a stronger plant. It is best to do this seeding in early fall. For thickening, spread 3 pounds of seed per 1,000 square feet.

How To Reduce Your Lawn's Water Needs

To make your lawn more sustainable and able to hold water more efficiently, apply compost as topdressing to your existing grass once per season. Manure compost is excellent for this process: it gives your lawn an organic nitrogen boost. Rake compost into grass evenly to a depth of about ¼-inch. Consider thickening your existing grass at this time as the compost helps hold grass seed in place.

If you planted a drought-tolerant grass, your watering requirements will be significantly less. However, you should practice good watering techniques as well. Lawns hold more water when watered before 10 a.m. and after 6 p.m. When watering during the main part of the day, the evaporation percentage goes up significantly; this means you are wasting water when you water at midday. Traditional grass varieties need 1 inch of water every week. It is better to heavily water your grass once or twice per week, rather than water shallowly every day. This technique forces roots to search deeper for the water and helps to build a stronger root system for your lawn. Watering more than 1 inch of water per week is wasteful as 1 inch weekly should keep your grass green throughout the season.

Mowing

Each time you mow, you should not remove more than one-third to one-half of the height of the grass. In fact, mowing grass to a height of 3 inches is effective in suppressing weeds and crabgrass, and it helps the grass look greener. Weeds are often shaded out by the taller grass. When you cut too close to the soil, thatch and roots are sometimes exposed, causing additional complications with growth. Spring's first mow is the only exception to the 3-inch rule. Cut the grass down below 2 inches the first mow of the season to help cut off the winter dead tips.

Mulching mowers are best because they leave the mulched grass trimmings on your lawn, which helps you save money on fertilizer. These clipped grass pieces decompose and contribute valuable organic matter to your soil; the technique actually adds 1 pound of nitrogen per 1,000 square feet each growth season. Keep your mower blades sharp to prevent frayed grass ends. Some say that lawn thatch is caused by grass clippings. This is not true. Excess lawn thatch is caused by overfertilization and other improper lawn care. Lawn thatch is the dead grass and root tissue that resides between the soil surface and the green part of the grass plant. When thatch gets thick, it blocks water, air, and nutrients from reaching the roots and provides a spot for insects and disease to nest.

Fertilizing

Overfeeding your lawn is bad for your lawn and the environment. Too much nitrogen and phosphorus can harm the local water systems, and excess nutrients can kill grass and plants in surrounding beds as well as cause lawn thatch. Do *not* overfertilize your lawn. Instead, better understand your soil test results, and apply only what your soil requires. Your soil ingredient composition is key to the supplements you add to make your grass grow successfully. Organic fertilizers are always the choice for a safer and healthier lawn. Once you thoroughly understand the amendments your soil needs, add organic fertilizer as label instructions direct. It is always better to apply a lower dose rather than overdo it.

Disease Control and Lawn Repair

Disease problems happen when your lawn becomes stressed. Over- and under-fertilization, heavy thatch levels, and compacted soil are several reasons your lawn can be stressed. Minor accumulations of thatch can be controlled by power-raking, but to repair an extremely heavy thatch problem, core-aerify the lawn at a rate of thirty-six holes per square foot to reduce compaction, then spray an all-natural thatch control product on the lawn, according to package directions.

Lawn diseases like brown patch, pythium blight, brown spot, necrotic ringspot, dollar spot, and rust are harmful fungi that can destroy a lawn if left untreated. These problems can be repaired in several steps. Practice smart water techniques: water in the morning so that the grass has time to dry out before evening. Mow frequently to prevent rust from maturing, and spray the diseased grass with beneficial bacteria that disrupt the fungi life cycle. Beneficial microbes like those found in an organic-certified fungicide will help prevent or control most lawn disease problems without the use of harmful chemicals.

Building a healthy lawn in early spring will help prevent disease later in the season. A mixture of natural soil amendments and compost is an effective organic solution to building a healthier lawn and landscape. A premium soil amendment like chelated iron with streptomyces lydicus bacteria will help with disease prevention and keep a lawn green and healthy. Mix a 3-pound bag of chelated iron with streptomyces lydicus bacteria into 300 square feet of compost, and distribute a ¼-inch layer of the compost mix evenly over the lawn. To repair a damaged lawn, follow the above steps, then add grass seed, spreading 1 pound of seed per 350 square feet over the top of the compost mixture. Water well.

And then sit back and enjoy your lawn! It is possible to have a healthy lawn and enjoy it too—just think about the choices you're making.

In urban areas, lawns often function as play spaces for pets and children. Maintaining a clean, grassy area can be important for parks and public walking areas as well.

NATIVE PLANTS & WILDFLOWERS
FOR INDIANA

Whether mixed in heavily or lightly in your landscape, native plants and wildflowers are an amazing addition to any garden, both for their beauty and their value to the environment. Native plants attract favorable insects, butterflies, songbirds, hummingbirds, and wildlife that live in your specific region of the state. They eliminate the need for pesticides or herbicides, require very little watering once established, and offer a gorgeous contribution to the modern landscape.

There are native plants that could fit into every garden scenario. Plants such as these trillium and prairie phlox are particularly suited for moist, part-shade conditions.

Native Plants Solve Problems

Consistently, native plants are the super-heroes in your garden as they solve many challenging problems. For example, do you have heavy clay soil in your garden? Native plants have deeper roots that break up hard clay naturally. If you have a particularly wet spot on your property where grass won't grow and other perennials drown, a native plant rain garden could solve that problem. Native plants have the ability to soak up large quantities of water, particularly if you plant water-loving natives. Alternately, the same water-loving plants will survive drought, wind, and other harsh conditions and come back swinging like a champ. There is a native plant to solve nearly any landscaping difficulty.

As convenient problem-solvers in the garden, native plants can be intermingled amongst traditional perennials, trees, and shrubs as working tools that help you with your difficult landscaping issues. They are also solutions we should all be tapping into for our environment.

Ecological Value

Encouraging biodiversity in your landscape means you are creating a more sustainable landscape that requires less maintenance and work. Native plants require minimal watering, survive difficult and variable conditions, can have four-season interest, and can live for decades. Planting natives creates a wildlife habitat, which can be a beautiful contribution to your birding or pollinator garden. More important, by bringing insects, birds, amphibians, and mammals into your landscape, you are solving a problem: the more wildlife you have, the fewer bad insects you'll have eating the plants. Native wildlife, particularly birds, eat seeds and insects.

Use native plants to help your greater community with storm water management: natives are excellent in rain gardens, bioretention areas, and wetland retention basins because they slow down and absorb masses of rainwater, enabling a reduction in the magnitude and speed of storm water run-off issues.

Native plants are often deer resistant. With well over 500,000 deer in the state, planting more native plants makes common sense if your garden is plagued by the animal. Deer do not prefer the aromatic foliage of wild bergamot or the painful barbs of prickly pear cactus, for instance. A deer-resistant garden is possible if you use a mix of the right native plants.

Beautiful Gardens

In recent years, native gardens have received praise for their low chemical needs and water retentiveness, but harsh criticism as well for their wild look in a traditional garden. Planting natives in a design just as you would a more traditional landscape tree, shrub, or perennial, and then maintaining it properly means that your garden can look attractive, not weedy or wild.

Native flowering vines, shrubs, trees, and wildflowers offer an enormous range of textures, colors, and shapes to create astounding seasonal displays. Whether you're designing a natural prairie or a contemporary urban landscape design, natives should be a part of your plan. You'll solve soil and insect problems, create a haven for pollinators and other wildlife, enjoy more success in your entire landscape plan, and help the environment as well.

Native plants such as the yellow prairie coneflower can be planted in wildflower fields, but they can also fit naturally into a modern landscape. Natives help the environment by providing food for wildlife and by utilizing less water and chemicals to maintain the plants.

Big Bluestem

Andropogon gerardii

Botanical Pronunciation
an-droh-POH-gon jer-AR-dee-eye

Other Name
Turkey foot

Bloom Period and Seasonal Color
Late summer to early fall; green or blue-green stems; russet, purple, or bronze blooms

Mature Height × Spread
4 to 8 feet × 3 feet

Big bluestem is a perennial bunchgrass with greenish blue stems that can grow between 4 to 8 feet tall. It has interesting seedheads that branch into three parts that resemble a turkey's foot, hence its nickname. Big bluestem is known as the "king of the prairie" and is one of the top four native grass species that colonized most of the prairies of central North America. Cattle have been quite destructive to this native species: because the animals are not migratory, they will decimate areas of grass to the root level. Big bluestem is an essential plant for a bird garden as it provides cover for more than twenty species of songbirds and nesting sites and seeds for sparrows, wrens, and meadowlarks.

When, Where, and How to Plant
Big bluestem prefers average, well-drained soils in full sun; plant this grass from seed or plants in spring. Once established, it readily self-seeds and has a spreading nature with good drought tolerance. Do not plant in fertile or overly moist soils as it will become taller, develop weaker stems, and topple over in windy conditions.

Growing Tips
Water well until it's established, then water infrequently if you want shorter plants, or water a bit more heavily if you prefer taller plants. No fertilizer is needed.

Regional Advice and Care
Cut or mow stems to the ground in late winter before new shoots appear in order to keep the plant clean looking in the garden; however, do not mow or cut during its active summer growth period as that could kill the plant. Big bluestem is relatively disease- and pest-free, although it's likely to have fungal spot in shadier conditions; ignore it. Once the grass is established, digging it up to split or relocate the plant will become a challenge; big bluestem's thick root base is tough to cut through and will take heavy spades or a handsaw to separate.

Companion Planting and Design
Big bluestems are a great selection for a bird garden. Birds use the grass clumps as protection, pick grass for their nests, and eat the seeds. Place the tall grass in clumps at the back of the garden area with seed-bearing flowers such as echinacea, black-eyed Susan, and coreopsis planted in front. Big bluestem is wonderful in naturalized prairies or in modern-day ornamental grass gardens. To highlight this native grass in a textural perennial bed, try planting it behind foxglove, Russian sage, and sea holly for a strong visual impact.

Try These
'Silver Sunrise' has blue-green foliage with a yellow band that turns a deeper purple in fall. 'Pawnee' is 5- to 6-feet tall with blue-green foliage that turns pale red in fall. 'Rountree' has a shorter growing season and is more tolerant of northern winters. 'Kaw' is better adapted to fields and pasture sites; it has excellent drought tolerance.

Black-Eyed Susan

Rudbeckia hirta

Botanical Pronunciation
rud-BEK-ee-ah HER-tah

Other Name
Gloriosa daisy

Bloom Period and Seasonal Color
Summer; golden yellow flowers with a deep
purple-brown eye (cone)

Mature Height × Spread
3 feet × 3 feet

Black-eyed Susans are well-loved wildflowers that are biennials or short-lived perennials native to our region. They primarily grow in dappled woodlands, along roadsides, and in moist prairie areas. This native has adapted amazingly well to the traditional garden, so much so that breeders have created many hybrids and cultivars. One can find the primary variety of black-eyed Susan in most garden centers as a plant or it is easily purchased as seed. Once established, black-eyed Susans grow hairy, 2- to 3-foot stems bearing golden yellow flowers that have a slightly orange base. While the eye of the flower is called "black," it is really a deep brown. This plant can maintain itself well in a wildflower garden due to its self-sowing nature. Other common names include coneflower and rudbeckia.

When, Where, and How to Plant
Plant in a moist, well-drained soil in full sun. If placing potted plants in a smaller bed, simply dig a hole and install the rooted plant. Black-eyed Susans are amazingly easy to grow from seed. Rake seed gently into the soil or place seed in shallow, trenched rows; cover with soil; and then lightly pat it down. Seed can be widely broadcast with other wildflower seed such as phlox or goldenrod in fields. Water regularly until well established.

Growing Tips
Keep soil moist. Rudbeckia easily adapts to natural conditions, and wildflowers such as black-eyed Susan can become leggy and weak when overfertilized or planted in soil that is overly rich.

In fact, the best soil for a native plant is the local soil. That's why you see this flower blooming without fertilizers or special soil along roadsides and highways.

Regional Advice and Care
Native black-eyed Susans can grow much taller than some varieties of the cultivated perennial. Fungal issues can arise with the plant, but typically it is best just to ignore the issue. Normally, black-eyed Susans are short-lived, but they are such reliable self-seeders that you will have blooming plants year after year once they are planted.

Companion Planting and Design
Black-eyed Susans are an admirable choice for a wildflower garden because of their long blooming period and attractive yellow flowers. Frequently used as a crucial flower in butterfly wildflower seed mixes, rudbeckia attract birds and butterflies. Because they tolerate drought and cold, and have relative insect resistance, they make an excellent feature plant in a traditional cottage garden or perennial border as well as in wildflower gardens.

Try These
There are other native wildflowers with the title "rudbeckia" such as *Rudbeckia serotina*, which does well in part shade. *R. lacinata* is taller, very hearty, with sparse petals. *R. subtomentosa* has a rounder flower, can be up to 4 feet tall, and seems to resist powdery mildew. *R. hirta gloriosa* is a hybrid that has huge flowers and multicolors ranging from gold to mahogany to red.

Blazing Star

Liatris spp.

Botanical Pronunciation
ly-AT-riss

Other Name
Gayfeather

Bloom Period and Seasonal Color
Summer; purple, lilac, and white flowers

Mature Height × Spread
2 to 6 feet × 1 to 3 feet

Blazing star is a native, clump-forming perennial that can grow quite tall. Mostly native to low grounds, marsh margins, meadows, and Midwestern ditches, most blazing star varieties can handle drought and moisture with ease. The plant is named "blazing star" because the flower heads have feathery disk-like flowers and no traditional ray blooms. Tall spiky flowers open from the top of the plant and progress downward. Liatris is versatile and wonderfully suited for native garden beds, wildflower fields, cottage gardens, and traditional perennial borders. Hummingbirds and other beneficials adore blazing star for its sweet nectar. When the flower stops blooming, the plant will attract birds that enjoy eating the seed heads. Blazing star is also edible and is primarily used in herbal teas and homeopathic cures.

When, Where, and How to Plant
Plant in a well-drained soil in full sun. Do not plant liatris in areas where water is likely to pool; the native can handle some moisture but prefers a well-drained bed. Amend soil to create proper drainage if necessary. Start either from potted plants, corms, or seed. If starting the plants from potted plants or corms, space about 10 inches apart or up to 15 inches if the potted plant is larger. Liatris seed can be started indoors or sown directly in the soil in fall or early winter. Seeds perform better when exposed to up to six weeks of cold conditions; seed-grown plants will most likely bloom in their second year.

Growing Tips
Do not fertilize blazing star as it can become gangly and weak-stemmed when overfertilized or planted in soil that is overly rich. In fact, the best soil for a native plant is the local soil.

Regional Advice and Care
Some varieties easily reach 6 feet and might need staking. Liatris is subject to many fungal diseases such as wilt, rusts, and mildew, particularly when grown in shadier conditions. Ignore if this occurs in a wildflower field or field planting area. However, to keep the natives looking good in traditional cottage gardens or perennial beds and to prevent the spread of the fungus to other ornamental plants, treat with an OMRI-certified fungicide.

Companion Planting and Design
Plant *en masse* or in drifts for a more prairie-like appearance. It looks beautiful planted with black-eyed Susans, goldenrod, and native grasses. To create a cottage garden look, consider mixing blazing star with echinacea, tall coreopsis, catmint, and lamb's ears.

Try These
Liatris spicata is often referred to as marsh blazing star because of its water-tolerant nature; it functions very well in rain gardens and drought-prone gardens alike. *L. pycnostachya* is known as prairie blazing star; it can grow quite tall but is not as drought tolerant as the other varieties. *L. aspera* is called rough blazing star; it tolerates drought well and stands 2 to 3 feet tall.

Blue Flag Iris

Iris virginica

Botanical Pronunciation
EYE-riss vur-JIN-nick-uh

Other Name
Blue flag

Bloom Period and Seasonal Color
Spring; violet flowers with yellow and white crested falls

Mature Height × Spread
1 to 3 feet × 1 to 3 feet

Blue flag is a water-loving native plant with beautiful, fragrant violet and yellow flowers that appear in spring above lance-shaped leaves. The plant needs little care once established, making it very easy to grow. Blue flag iris is planted as a solution for wet natural areas and also as an excellent rain garden plant; its natural habitats include ditches and swales along roadsides, edges of streams and ponds, swamps, soggy meadows, and black-soiled prairies. Its ability to attract hummingbirds and beneficial insects is just the beginning of its environmental benefits. It functions as a home for lizards, snakes, and frogs. Birds and other animals eat its flower seeds. And roots of the blue flag work to stabilize river edges and marsh areas; clumps spread by creeping rhizomes to form colonies.

When, Where, and How to Plant

Plant the rhizomatous roots of blue flag iris near the surface of the soil. Blue flag prefers rich, organic, boggy soil that rarely dries out. Seeds should be planted in the autumn and prefer a cold overwintering period in order to properly establish. While blue flag iris can be grown from seed, it is much easier to propagate through division. Cut rhizomes so that each section contains a portion of the stringy feeding roots, the rhizome, and a leaf fan. Divide roots every 4 to 5 years for best performance.

Growing Tips

Like other natives, no additional fertilizer is needed. Keep soil moist.

Regional Advice and Care

Common pests include aphids, iris borers, snails, and slugs. Spray aphids off with a strong squirt of water or treat with soapy water. Trap slugs and snails. Iris borers can be a serious issue; clean beds of dead foliage regularly to prevent iris borers. If you see the tips of the foliage turn yellow, or other signs of their presence, dig the rhizome after blooming is finished, inspect it carefully, cut out rotted or mushy areas, and then replant. Some people report skin irritation and rashes when planting blue flag iris; wear gloves when handling the leaf and fleshy roots. Be sure to keep small children and animals away from these slightly toxic plants.

Companion Planting and Design

Blue flag irises are particularly valuable in Midwestern landscapes as rain garden and water-absorbing plants. Naturalizing flood areas and effectively treating challenging water conditions within a traditional landscape is easy for this water-loving workhorse. It's beautiful when planted as a meandering colony through wet pastures and meadows. Mixed along the edges of a garden pond, blue flag irises make a tall contrast to floating water lilies.

Try These

'Contraband Girl' is a larger flowered cultivar that typically grows 2 to 4 feet tall. 'Alba' has a large white flower with yellow falls. With a strong magenta-pink form, 'Rosea' is quite attractive with its yellow signals and pink-veined falls. 'Pond Lilac Dream' is slightly shorter with a lilac-pink flower.

Butterfly Weed

Asclepias tuberosa

Botanical Pronunciation
ass-KLEE-pee-us too-bur-O-suh

Other Names Indian paintbrush, pleurisy root

Bloom Period and Seasonal Color
Summer; orange to orange-red flowers

Mature Height × Spread
1 to 3 feet × 1 to 2 feet

Smothered with butterflies throughout summer, butterfly weed is a good-looking, sweet-scented plant that attracts beneficial insects of all sorts. It is a relative of the common milkweed but does not have the sticky sap associated with that taller plant. It is exceptionally drought tolerant and stunning both in native plant and traditional gardens. Butterfly weed is native to Midwest prairies, and its bold orange-red flowers can bloom continuously until the first frost if it's placed in full sun. Hummingbirds *love* the flowers, but deer will not typically eat it. Butterfly weed's long taproot was chewed by Native Americans as a cure for pleurisy and other pulmonary ailments, giving it the name pleurisy root. However, this practice is no longer recommended as butterfly weed can be quite toxic.

When, Where, and How to Plant

Butterfly weed will grow in nearly any soil, but it actually prefers poor soil to rich. Do not plant in areas where water is likely to pool; this native can handle some moisture but prefers a well-drained bed. Amend soil to create proper drainage if necessary. Start either from potted plants or seed. Butterfly weed seed can be started indoors or sown directly in the soil in fall or early winter. It performs significantly better when exposed to up to six weeks of cold conditions before it produces growth and can take up to 3 years to develop flowers. Be sure you place the butterfly weed in its permanent location because its long taproot is not easily dug up, and if it is broken during transplanting, the plant often dies.

Growing Tips

New butterfly weed plants may benefit from a weekly watering until the taproot is well established. After that, only water if there is an ongoing drought. Feeding is not needed.

Regional Advice and Care

For more abundant flower production, deadhead regularly. Aphids can be sprayed with soapy water or blasted off with a stream of water. This plant is considered poisonous; insects eat the toxins within the nectar and become toxic and distasteful to their natural predators. Discourage small children and animals from touching or eating the plants as these toxins can harm mammals.

Companion Planting and Design

Because butterfly weed tolerates drought and cold, with relative insect resistance, they make an excellent feature plant in a traditional cottage garden or perennial border as well as in wildflower gardens. Butterfly weed makes a fantastic addition to one-color garden that could also feature marigolds, zinnia, coneflower, lilies, and other orange-colored flowering plants. It makes an excellent contribution to a butterfly garden with other plants such as butterfly bush, blazing star, coreopsis, lantana, salvia, and yarrow.

Try These

'Gay Butterflies' produces large 6-inch clusters of bold flowers that are good cutting flowers that combine red, yellow, orange, and deep rust. 'Orange' is the common variety of butterfly weed found most commonly in native planting sites throughout the Midwest.

Eastern Prickly Pear Cactus

Opuntia humifusa

Botanical Pronunciation
oh-PUN-tee-uh hew-mih-FEW-zuh

Other Name Devil's tongue

Bloom Period and Seasonal Color Summer; yellow flowers with striking red centers

Mature Height × Spread
1 to 1½ feet × 2 feet

Eastern Prickly pear cactus is a beautiful, ground-hugging, native, multistemmed cactus that survives northern winter snow and harsh weather with ease. Growing this cactus is easy, and it can be quite a novelty in the garden. Prickly pear cactus has the most astonishing, crowdstopping 3- to 4-inch yellow flowers, but its beauty is tempered by its spiny cactus nature. Handle the pads carefully; while there are fewer spines on this variety than other cacti, it can be a painful experience to come into contact with its needlelike bristles. After the flowers complete their bloom, a deep red fruit called a *tuna* may appear that has a slightly sour taste and can be made into jellies and jams. All parts of the prickly pear cactus are edible except the spines and prickles.

When, Where, and How to Plant
Prickly pear cactus will grow in nearly any site with full sun, but it prefers sites with poor, sandy, well-drained soil. Start either from potted plants or seed. Prickly pear cactus seed needs to be exposed to up to six weeks of cold conditions before it will produce growth. If branches break off of the cactus, do not remove them from the site. Simply replant the pad or branch about 2 inches into the soil, water sparingly, and it will take root and thrive.

Growing Tips
No fertilizer is needed, and there's no need to water.

Regional Advice and Care
It has no insect or disease pests that will seriously affect it. In winter the prickly pear cactus looks deflated, but it will perk up again in spring. Use thick rose gloves and kitchen tongs to weed nearby, to help harvest the cactus pads, or move the plant, being particularly cautious of the tiny, fuzzy prickles, which look unassuming but hurt and itch relentlessly if embedded under the skin. Peeled prickly pear cactus is edible and was used by Native Americans for medicinal purposes. Nopalitos is a Mexican dish prepared from prickly pear cactus pads, which have a slightly tart taste and crisp texture. Prickly pear cactus is made into soups, salads, and main dishes. Its fruit juice is used in candies, jellies, and desserts.

Companion Planting and Design
Prickly pear cactus looks delightful planted in rock and alpine gardens. Xeriscape gardens mulched with rocks and planted with flowering sedum in the foreground, prickly pear cactus in the middle, and Russian sage in the background look stunning and have practically no maintenance requirements beyond weeding. Used as a front edger, its sharp spines will deter rodents and wild pests from entering your perennial beds.

Try These
Opuntia macrorhiza is known as the big-rooted prickly pear; it has a thicker tuberous root and extra spines. *O. fragilis* is called brittle or fragile prickly pear and is smaller than the eastern prickly pear; its stems easily break off.

Foxglove Beardtongue

Penstemon digitalis

Botanical Pronunciation
PEN-stih-mun didge-ih-TAY-liss

Other Name   Beardtongue

Bloom Period and Seasonal Color
Mid-spring to early summer; white flowers

Mature Height × Spread   3 to 5 feet × 3 feet

This native delivers impressive 1-inch-long, tubular white flowers on top of strong, green, panicled stems and bloom profusely through early summer. This native plant is extremely easy to grow and attracts abundant quantities of beneficial insects such as bees, sphinx moths, and hummingbirds. Foxglove beardtongue survives wet conditions well if the water drains off quickly and the roots are not left standing in water for long periods; this makes the plant a smart candidate for rain garden plantings. Beardtongue has a short rhizomatous root system and is relatively drought tolerant. When extreme drought occurs, expect the plant to turn slightly yellow and wilt. Beardtongue's clumping nature makes it a good choice for both traditional perennial gardens and all-native wildflower beds.

When, Where, and How to Plant
Plant this native in moist, well-drained, loamy soil in full sun. It will adapt to all types of soil including sand. If placing potted plants in a garden bed, simply dig a hole and install the plant so that the rootball is level with the soil's surface.

Growing Tips
Beardtongue requires very little attention and no fertilizer whatsoever. Apply a thin layer of compost as a mulch seasonally for a light soil conditioning. Water regularly throughout the first season until well established, then ignore the plant unless there are signs of wilting.

Regional Advice and Care
When the flowering stalk has finished blooming, it will turn brown and you will see oval brown seed capsules where the flowers were. Seeds can be carried in the wind but are more likely to land next to the native plant, overwinter, then self-sow in spring. Trim seedheads off of the leafy basal portion of the plant to prevent self-sowing. Foxglove beardtongue is called "beardtongue" because the sterile stamen inside the white flowers has a tiny tuft of small hairs. Beardtongue can be susceptible to wilt or fungal issues on their leaves in shady, wet conditions. Prevent these problems by planting in full sun, and do not overwater.

Companion Planting and Design
While the flowers have no scent, they make a fine addition to a cut flower display. Use foxglove beardtongue as a transitional plant between tall native grasses and shorter plants such as black-eyed Susan or butterfly weed. Beardtongue is a stupendous naturalizer for prairies and wildflower areas. It's spectacular when clumps are planted at the edge of a part sun rain garden mixed in with cinnamon ferns. Its white flowers work very well when planted in a more traditional all-white garden bed.

Try These
'Husker Red' has bronzy red leaves when grown in full sun, plus burgundy stems and white flowers (the leaves sometimes can fade). 'Mystica' blooms the first year with lavender-pink flowers and burgundy shaded leaves. 'Dark Towers' is slightly taller and has more reliable deep purple-red leaf color in shade and sun, with pink flowers.

Indigo

Baptisia australis

Botanical Pronunciation
bap-TIZZ-ee-uh aw-STRAY-liss

Other Names Baptisia, wild blue indigo, false indigo

Bloom Period and Seasonal Color
Late spring to early summer; purple, blue, yellow, and white flowers

Mature Height × Spread 3 to 5 feet × 3 to 5 feet

Native plants are often quite versatile as well as beautiful; baptisia is definitely one of those. This herbaceous, branching plant, sometimes called wild blue indigo or false indigo, with its tall, late-spring, flowering racemes, can be a significant contribution both to native landscapes and traditional garden designs. American colonists and Native Americans used the flowers of the plant to make indigo-colored dyes and boiled the roots of the plant to create an antiseptic. Modern-day medicinal uses of the plant include antiseptic and laxative purposes. Baptisia is considered edible, but use caution as consuming too much of the plant can be toxic. Baptisia is long-lived and remarkably tough and reliable. Faded blooms mature into interesting black seedpods, which sound like a rattlesnake's tail when they're shaken.

When, Where, and How to Plant

Indigo tends to sprawl in part shade, so it is best to find a spot for it in full sun. The plant requires good drainage and a medium-fertile soil. Amend soil to create proper drainage if necessary. Start from plants or seed, keeping placement in mind as baptisia has a large taproot that does not like to be disturbed. Seeds perform better when exposed to up to six weeks of cold conditions, most likely blooming in the second year. A surprising benefit is that indigo will help add nitrogen to the garden soil it is planted in. This occurs because all *Baptisia* plants belong to the Fabaceae or pea family, and pea plants naturally return nitrogen to the soil.

Growing Tips

Without a doubt, this is one of the easiest plants to grow. Water well the first season but ignore the plant thereafter as it typically requires no watering and no fertilization.

Regional Advice and Care

Indigo will self-seed, but the plants are very slow growing so will take many years to flower. Should baptisia become too floppy or take over an area in the garden, feel free to cut back the plant by one-quarter to one-third. Leave the black seedpods on for winter interest, but if you want to prevent self-sowing, simply cut the seedpods out as soon they form.

Companion Planting and Design

Plant *en masse* or in drifts for a more prairie-like appearance. Because it only blooms in early spring, most of the summer baptisia can be an astounding green backdrop for native plants such as blazing star, butterfly weed, beardtongue, and tickseed. To create a cottage garden look, consider mixing baptisia with peony, foxglove, lilies, catmint, and lamb's ears.

Try These

'Solar Flare' is vigorous, with up to 100 flower stems and lemon yellow flowers that take on an orange to violet blush with age. 'Midnight' has deep midnight blue flowers and a double bloom cycle, extending its bloom time. 'Twilite' has violet-purple and yellow flowers; three-year-old plants can produce upward of 100 flowering stems.

Joe-Pye Weed

Eupatorium purpureum

Botanical Pronunciation
you-puh-TORE-ee-um pur-PUR-ee-um

Other Name
Purple boneset

Bloom Period and Seasonal Color
Summer; rose-purple flowers

Mature Height × Spread
3 to 10 feet × 3 feet

Joe-pye weed is rumored to be named after a Native American herbalist who used the plant as a medicinal herb to help cure fever-centered illnesses in early American history. This herbaceous perennial is often called "queen of the prairie" because of its 10-foot stature and regal crowning flowers that are a rose-purple shade and attract butterflies and bees by the hundreds. Plants have a lovely vanilla scent, and the flowers make extraordinary cut flowers. If you have a bird garden, do not deadhead the flowers as the seedheads attract all types of feathered friends. While Joe-pye weed has been considered medicinal, it is rarely used in modern times because it is considered highly toxic to pets and humans when it's not consumed as directed.

When, Where, and How to Plant
Although Joe-pye weed prefers full sun, it will do well in part sun but might sprawl if its spot is too shady. Joe-pye weed prefers rich, humusy, moist soils. Improve soil where needed with rotted manure and compost. Plant either from seed or potted plants. If it's planted early enough, Joe-pye weed should flower by the end of its first season of growth.

Growing Tips
Encourage shorter plants by pinching back early in the spring growing season. Consider planting in wet soils near rivers, streams, ponds, and as a plant for wetland mitigation.

Regional Advice and Care
Maintenance includes cutting down the plant completely in early winter. Typically Joe-pye weed has very little insect or disease problems, although overcrowded, shady, and consistently wet conditions can lead to fungal problems. Give the plants lots of space in the planting beds in order to help prevent these issues. Treat fungal spot and powdery mildew with an organic fungicide.

Companion Planting and Design
Joe-pye weed naturalizes very well both in prairies and along the borders of woodlands. It makes an outstanding rain garden plant and looks good combined with grasses and water-loving iris. Because it is such an exceptionally tall prairie plant, it is best used at the very back of borders, as a natural fencelike border plant, and mixed in with other natives in prairies and meadows. Joe-pye weed is a must-have choice for a butterfly garden and works well planted in the center of an island of mixed butterfly shrubs and perennial plants. In a more drought-tolerant border, consider placing Joe-pye weed at the back with ornamental grasses, Russian sage, goldenrod, and butterfly weed, mulching the garden well to help hold moisture.

Try These
The species Joe-pye weed can be found most commonly at garden centers throughout the region. For a more compact plant that only grows to 4 feet, try *Eupatorium dubium* 'Little Joe'. *E. purpureum* subsp. *maculatum* 'Gateway' has wine-red stems and brighter pink flowers.

Milkweed

Asclepias syriaca

Botanical Pronunciation
ass-KLEE-pee-us seer-ee-AK-uh

Other Name
Common milkweed

Bloom Period and Seasonal Color
Summer; pale pink flowers

Mature Height × Spread
5 feet × 2 feet

When I was a young girl growing up on a Midwestern farm, milkweed grew prolifically in ditches and along fence rows. The plant looks rather uninteresting on a day-to-day basis, but it is truly an essential monarch butterfly garden plant. When they bloom, the air is filled with the most magnificent fragrance from the milkweed flower. Seductively sweet milkweed blooms attract butterflies to their nectar, particularly monarch butterflies that use the plant as a host to lay their eggs, harbor the monarch caterpillar, and feed the newly emerged butterflies. Native Americans used milkweed for making twine, rope, and medicines. Milkweed plants can be toxic to pets and humans, so place the plants in gardens away from areas where children and pets might be tempted.

When, Where, and How to Plant
Milkweed is fairly drought tolerant and performs well in dry, poor soils. Do not plant in areas with standing water. It's most commonly and easily propagated via seed; milkweed will self-seed in the landscape if seedpods are not removed prior to splitting open. Milkweed should be planted in fall when the seeds will be exposed to up to six weeks of cold conditions. Milkweed can spread somewhat rapidly by rhizomes and often form extensive colonies.

Growing Tips
There's absolutely no need to fertilize; don't overwater.

Regional Advice and Care
While aphids and a variety of milkweed beetles can commonly be found on milkweed, do not spray or treat the plants in any way as the butterfly larvae on the plant will be killed with chemical treatments. Cut stems at the base of the plant in late winter in order to clean up the garden and prepare them for the spring growth season. No other heavy maintenance or care is required. Broken stems produce a white, sappy latex liquid that can cause skin irritation. Wear gloves when transplanting or digging the milkweed. To collect milkweed seeds directly from the plant, collect the seedpods after they have split. Hold the end and gently strip the seeds. These seeds can be stored in a paper bag in a cool, dark location until ready to use. It typically takes two to three seasons for the seedlings to develop into flower-producing plants.

Companion Planting and Design
While this plant is considered to be too vigorous and weedy for borders, it does marvelously in butterfly gardens or naturalized in prairies, meadows, and native plant areas. Plant milkweed with sunflowers, Russian sage, black-eyed Susans, butterfly weed, and other drought-tolerant plants for a colorful and ongoing variety of bloom throughout summer.

Try These
While there are many varieties of milkweed as a family, there is only one variety of *Asclepias syriaca*. Swamp milkweed, *A. incarnata*, is a variety of *Asclepias* that is better grown in wet regions and rain gardens.

Prairie Dropseed Grass

Sporobolus heterolepis

Botanical Pronunciation
spore-OB-uh-lus het-ur-oh-LEEP-iss

Other Name Northern dropseed

Bloom Period and Seasonal Color
Late summer to early fall; green stems; pink and brown blooms

Mature Height × Spread 2 to 3 feet × 2 to 3 feet

Prairie dropseed is a perennial clumping bunchgrass with green stems and pinkish brown blooms that can grow between 2 to 3 feet tall. Its lovely light and airy late-summer blooms smell like an interesting mix of buttered popcorn and coriander, which makes it an admirable candidate to line sidewalks, place near gates, and use in low-growing borders so visitors can appreciate the fragrance. While other ornamental grasses can spread aggressively, this native grass stays relatively contained. Seedheads are feathery and when they are mature the husks drop their seeds onto the ground; hence, the common name of the plant. The small seeds are highly sought after by ground-feeding birds such as turkeys, buntings, juncos, larks, longspurs, and sparrows.

When, Where, and How to Plant
While some grasses prefer full sun only, this particular grass grows rather well both in full sun and part shade situations. Prairie dropseed enjoys average, well-drained, even rocky or sandy soils. It does not like wet feet and can tolerate considerable drought (and heat), but it does appreciate water. Seeds prefer exposure to winter, so plant them in fall. Plant bare-root or container plants in spring or fall.

Growing Tips
Prairie dropseed takes at least three to five years to mature, but once established it's tremendously low maintenance. Water well until established; after that water infrequently as prairie dropseed prefers dry conditions. Don't fertilize.

Regional Advice and Care
Leave the plant alone for a totally natural look or cut stems to the ground in early spring before new shoots appear in order to keep the plant looking clean in the garden. Dividing older clumps of prairie dropseed can be quite challenging because of the thickness of the grassy root system. Use heavy spades or a hand saw to separate.

Companion Planting and Design
Prairie dropseed will not be flattened by winter snow; therefore, it makes an appealing show in a winter interest garden. Dried grass clumps that have been cut and tied can be formed into interesting natural wreaths for fall decoration. Perfect in a wildflower birding garden, prairie dropseed looks delightful along front garden borders. This plant is a fantastic contributor to an ornamental grass garden, naturalized prairie or meadow, or planted *en masse* as a focal center point in a modern contemporary garden. It is absolutely magnificent planted in drifting waves with purple liatris and Russian sage. Create a xeriscape garden with prairie dropseed, prickly pear cactus, and indigo. It's beautiful mixed with annuals such as celosia, calibrachoa, and zinnias in a container garden.

Try These
'Tara' is a dwarf prairie dropseed that grows 24 to 36 inches high but only 18 inches wide. 'Morning Mist' has more upright foliage with a larger quantity of blooms, which are held on red stems. Most common is the species, which is easily found in garden centers.

Prairie Phlox

Phlox pilosa

Botanical Pronunciation FLOCKS pih-LOE-zuh

Other Names Downy phlox, fragrant phlox

Bloom Period and Seasonal Color
Late summer to early fall; green stems; pink and purple blooms

Mature Height × Spread
18 to 24 inches × 12 to 24 inches

Habitats of the native prairie phlox tend to be dry to moist black soil prairies, oak savannas, and open woodlands. It seems to love hugging the edges of woodlands and can be found blooming throughout the region near wooded glens. This plant provides benefits for all types of wildlife and has the perfect flared flower with a long tube that butterflies adore (it's also called the fragrant phlox). It is the only known food source for the rare phlox moth. Groundhogs, deer, and rabbits also find the prairie phlox irresistible, particularly in its early shoot stages. Hummingbirds enjoy supping the fragrant phlox blossoms, which come in shades of pink and violet. Prairie phlox's lower leaves will turn yellow and drop off if the plant is stressed.

When, Where, and How to Plant

Prairie phlox is best grown in fertile, well-drained soil. It prefers full sun but will do well in part shade and likes dry to moist soil. Although it does not like wet feet, it does appreciates water, and can tolerate considerable heat and drought. Seeds prefer exposure to winter, so plant them in the fall. Plant bare root or container plants in the spring or fall. Mulch the soil once plants are well established to help hold water.

Growing Tips

Water prairie phlox well until established; after that, it is only necessary to water the plant if it looks wilted from excessive drought. No fertilizer is needed.

Regional Advice and Care

While not invasive, prairie phlox does spread by rhizomes to form clumps that can eventually become colonies. The rhizomes are less likely to spread in drier soil. While some perennial phlox is prone to powdery mildew, prairie phlox rarely gets it. If it does seem affected by fungus or powdery mildew, treat with an organic fungicide. Clean up phlox in fall as the phlox plant bug, which sucks the juices from perennial phlox, has eggs that overwinter on the dead phlox plant matter; nymphs of the bug emerge in early summer. This little orange-and-black bug can be quite destructive, so preventing its spread is encouraged.

Companion Planting and Design

Prairie phlox is a delightful plant for a butterfly garden. Native butterfly gardens might include Joe-pye weed, milkweed, liatris, black-eyed Susans, and asters. Prairie phlox looks beautiful planted in drifts along woodland areas. Prairies and meadows are quite attractive when dotted with native prairie phlox. Phlox will work in a rain garden if the garden drains immediately after a heavy rain.

Try These

'Ozarkana' is a slightly shorter pink to magenta-pink variety. 'Forest Frost' is an 18-inch-tall variety with white flowers. 'Slim Jim' is a summer dormant variety that grows only 12 inches high. 'Sun Kissed' is a pink, groundhugging prairie phlox that gets no taller than 15 inches.

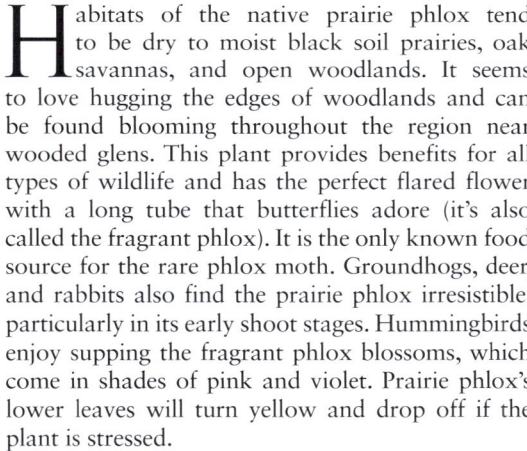

Shooting Star

Dodecatheon meadia

Botanical Pronunciation
doe-duh-KAY-thee-un MEE-dee-uh

Other Names
Prairie shooting star, Midland shooting star

Bloom Period and Seasonal Color
Late spring; white, pink, and purple blooms

Mature Height × Spread
8 to 24 inches × 12 to 24 inches

Shooting star is an adorable, charming native woodland and prairie plant that has a basal rosette of lanced foliage. From each rosette comes one to four stems, and each 20-inch stem supports a flowerscape with eight to twenty nodding flowers. Each flower is about 1 inch long and has five reflexed petals and a collection of yellow stamens that form a peak, giving the flower the fascinating appearance of a shooting rocket or falling star. Shooting star is considered poisonous in its raw state, so it should not be grown near an area where pets or children might investigate its edible properties. These herbaceous perennials become dormant in the summer. It's also called prairie shooting star and Midland shooting star.

When, Where, and How to Plant

Preferring part shade to full shade, shooting star is best grown in a soil with medium moisture and the strong humus and rich, organic content mix that is found in woodlands. Amend soil with rotted manure and compost to encourage growth. Wet soils, particularly over winter, will drown its root system and lead to rot. Shooting star seeds need to be overwintered in order to propagate. With the proper conditions, shooting stars will self-seed to form large colonies, but it takes the seeded plants five to six years to develop flowers.

Growing Tips

Water regularly upon initial installation, but the plant should survive dry conditions as long as the soil is rich. Shooting star will be more prolific in moister, shadier conditions.

Regional Advice and Care

Only divide clumps that are quite large because smaller clumps will not tolerate division as well. Snails and slugs enjoy the basal foliage and must be trapped to prevent large populations from decimating the plants.

Companion Planting and Design

Shooting stars are waning in the wild due to overzealous collectors, and they are easily crowded out by more aggressive native plants in the wild as well. Planting these in their own spot in the garden away from potential aggressors will help ensure more prolific success. A particularly beautiful spring meadow plant, shooting star is eye-catching when it is planted in a naturalized area. It works very well when grown *en masse* along a woodland border or as an understory planting in a forested area. It performs well as a spring feature in rock gardens. Mix shooting star with white daffodils and other late-spring bloomers for a lovely spring garden display.

Try These

'Queen Victoria' is a bright pink flower with a white and yellow rim at the base of the bloom. 'Alba' is a lovely white variety. There are other varieties of *Dodecatheon*, but only a few in the specific *Dodecatheon meadia* family are considered native to the Midwest region of the United States.

Tickseed

Coreopsis Spp.

Botanical Pronunciation
kor-ee-OP-sis

Other Names
Prairie coreopsis, stiff coreopsis

Bloom Period and Seasonal Color
Early summer; yellow flowers with a golden eye

Mature Height × Spread
12 to 30 inches × 18 to 24 inches

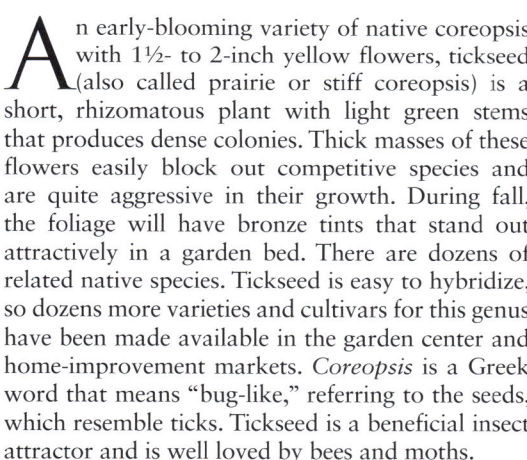

An early-blooming variety of native coreopsis with 1½- to 2-inch yellow flowers, tickseed (also called prairie or stiff coreopsis) is a short, rhizomatous plant with light green stems that produces dense colonies. Thick masses of these flowers easily block out competitive species and are quite aggressive in their growth. During fall, the foliage will have bronze tints that stand out attractively in a garden bed. There are dozens of related native species. Tickseed is easy to hybridize, so dozens more varieties and cultivars for this genus have been made available in the garden center and home-improvement markets. *Coreopsis* is a Greek word that means "bug-like," referring to the seeds, which resemble ticks. Tickseed is a beneficial insect attractor and is well loved by bees and moths.

When, Where, and How to Plant
Tickseed is not fussy and will grow in nearly any type of soil: clay, loam, sand, or gravel. Most important to its growth is good drainage and full sun exposure. Place potted plants directly into the soil with no special preparations. Rake seed gently into the soil; do not cover as the seed needs light to germinate. Seed can also be widely broadcast in fields with other wildflower seed such as black-eyed Susan or goldenrod.

Growing Tips
Water regularly until well established, but be careful not to overwater as drowned roots in boggy situations will kill the plant. Surprisingly heat and drought tolerant, tickseed easily adapts to natural conditions and requires very little care. Do not fertilize in native growing situations as the plant will spread even more insistently.

Regional Advice and Care
Shady sites encourage sprawling plants and fungal disease, so it's best planted in full sun. Give plants as much room as possible and feel free to cut it back at any time during the summer and fall should the plants grow out of bounds and look sloppy. Consistent deadheading or shearing of spent blooms will ensure more prolific blooming and stop aggressive self-sowing.

Companion Planting and Design
Tickseed is a tough plant, sometimes used in the Midwest as a roadside planting because of its ability to outcompete weeds. This is a top choice for a native pollinator garden. Tickseed works brilliantly on hillsides to prevent erosion and looks marvelous when planted in waves against native grasses such as prairie dropseed. For a seasonal bloom of yellow flowers, try planting tickseed with black-eyed Susans and prickly pear cactus. Wildflower gardens look marvelous edged in tickseed, and it will bring a touch of seasonal yellow color to the fields if planted throughout prairies and meadows.

Try These
Other native tickseeds in the genus include large-flowered coreopsis, *Coreopsis grandiflora*, which has a larger, threadier flower. Lance-leaved coreopsis, *C. lanceolata*, has more pronounced pointy-shaped leaves. Tall coreopsis, *C. tripteris*, can grow between 4 to 8 feet high and attracts butterflies.

Wild Geranium

Geranium maculatum

Botanical Pronunciation
jur-AY-nee-um mack-you-LAY-tum

Other Names
Spotted geranium, wood geranium

Bloom Period and Seasonal Color
Late spring; lilac, pink, and white blooms

Mature Height × Spread
18 to 30 inches × 12 to 24 inches

Wild geranium is a native woodland plant that is sturdier than the traditional perennial geranium. Stiff upright limbs grow in mounded clumps with attractive five-lobed leaves that resemble an outstretched hand with the fingers held wide. Flowers are lilac, pink, and white, and bloom prolifically in spring but do not typically rebloom; however, the attractive foliage will remain throughout the growing season. Wild geranium (also known as spotted or wood geranium) was used by Native Americans as a medicinal plant for its astringent and diuretic properties. The roots have strong tannin content, and can be used as a brown dye. This plant thrives in low light and shady conditions, particularly in moist areas where other understory plants are likely to grow, such as a woodland edge.

When, Where, and How to Plant
Preferring part to full shade, wild geranium's flowers can offer flowering variety to dark areas. Although it does not like standing in water, it does like a consistently medium moisture and rich, humusy soil with lots of natural materials mixed in; rotted manure, compost, and worm castings make perfect soil amendments. Wild geraniums seem to be more prolific in areas that are wet in the spring, but dry out later in the season. Plant from seed in fall or potted containers in spring.

Growing Tips
Water regularly upon initial transplanting, but the plant should survive dry conditions well as long as the soil is rich. No fertilizer is needed.

Regional Advice and Care
Like wild petunia, wild geranium has a unique exploding seedpod that throws seeds quite a distance from the plant after flowering ends in early summer. Divide wild geranium by digging up the rhizomes and cutting them between stems. A new cluster of basal leaves and flowering stems will crop up from the thick, branched, horizontal rhizomes. Deadheading is not recommended because the plant only blooms once. Even under the best growing conditions, wild geranium is not considered overly aggressive or invasive, which makes it optimal for planting in traditional gardens as well as native gardens and woodlands.

Companion Planting and Design
Wild geranium is loved by beneficial insects and wildlife so is quite appropriate when planted in a shady pollinator garden. Woodlands and forest borders look beautiful with wild geranium planted *en masse*. Wild geranium is a great accompaniment to wild columbines, trilliums, and Virginia bluebells in the native landscape. In traditional garden beds, consider mixing wild geranium with hostas, carex, and ferns.

Try These
'Espresso' has an unusual chocolate-brown leaf that makes the pink flowers pop out like beacons of light in a shaded area. 'Elizabeth Ann' has a similar chocolate leaf to 'Espresso' but with bronzy hints and a lilac-pink flower. 'Alba' is shorter than the species, growing only to 12 inches but with clear white blooms. 'Beth Chatto' has a delicate flower that is a pale shade of lilac.

Wild Petunia

Ruellia humilis

Botanical Pronunciation
roo-ELL-ee-uh HEW-mih-liss

Other Names
Hairy wild petunia, fringeleaf wild petunia

Bloom Period and Seasonal Color
Summer; lavender blooms

Mature Height × Spread
12 to 24 inches × 8 to 12 inches

Wild petunia is a happy little plant with a compact form and prolific pale lavender flowers that are 1½ to 2½ inches wide. While the wild petunia resembles hybrid petunias, they come from different families and perform differently. Wild petunia flowers open in the morning, available and ready for pollinators, and by evening the flower is done blooming and will fall off the plant. It is low to the ground, growing sporadically, and does not form dense colonies like other native plants, enabling it to be planted in height-restricted prairies. Wild petunia has a flower that is built for easy access by regional native butterflies and long-tongued bees, making this a good selection for pollinator gardens. Other common names include hairy wild petunia and fringeleaf wild petunia.

When, Where, and How to Plant
Plant seeds or potted plants in a well-drained soil in full sun; it prefers sandy, rocky, and native soils. Wild petunia does *not* like overly moist soil; if it must be planted in a moister area, it is best if wild petunia does not have to compete with other plants since it does not have enough root strength to compete with aggressive neighbors in wet soils.

Growing Tips
Do not overwater and do not fertilize.

Regional Advice and Care
Under the right conditions, after the flowers of the wild petunia have receded, listen for the popping sound of exploding seedpods. Wild petunias are known to shoot their seeds up to 10 feet away from the original plant in order to self-seed. Wintering over seems to encourage the seeds to germinate, and gardeners can find new plants in sidewalk cracks, flagstone edging, and between steppingstones the following spring. Vulnerable to fungal diseases and root rot when planted in deeper shade with wetter conditions, wild petunia needs air circulation and sun to stay healthy. Very few insects or pests harm this petunia, although its distinct lack of scent and softer leaves can sometimes attract deer.

Companion Planting and Design
With its compact perennial habit and interesting flora, this makes a fine plant for container gardens and more traditional flower beds as well as the native prairie. Wild petunia performs well in rock gardens. For an ongoing summer display of purple flowers, mix wild petunia, blazing star, and monarda. Wild petunia is a lovely border or edging plant for traditional and native garden beds. While it is a shorter-lived petunia than traditional varieties, it looks exquisite in a small container garden.

Try These
Other wild petunias in the genus might be suitable in similar regional planting situations but are not all native to this specific region. Varieties include *Ruellia nudiflora*, which has more trumpet-shaped flowers. *R. caroliniensis* has long, pointed leaves beneath the flowers. *R. brittoniana* 'Purple Showers' is a 3-foot-tall shrub with similar flowers to the other *Ruellia* species.

ORNAMENTAL GRASSES

FOR INDIANA

Ornamental grasses offer a fantastic, low-maintenance, sustainable solution for landscaping design. Many have four-season interest, are mostly drought tolerant, need no staking or pruning, and have no regular insect or disease problems. This means less watering and virtually no pesticides or herbicides are needed.

Grasses, or *Poaceae*, is a large genus of plants with over 10,000 varieties of species that represents the fifth-largest plant family in the world. Grasses feed most of the world: wheat, millet, rice, and corn are all from the grass family. Bamboo is considered a grass and is harvested widely in Asia for its thatch, and both ethanol alcohol and ethanol fuel are produced from grain. Ultimately, these plants feed, clothe, and house much of the earth, and their sustainable nature makes them an excellent choice for home gardening as well.

Ornamental grasses are particularly low maintenance and look well in a prairie setting, as standalone feature plants, in containers, or as seen here, mixed in the landscape with other perennials and shrubs.

How to Grow

Ornamental grasses have two distinct growth habits—clumping or rhizomatous. Clumping plants are more like a traditional perennial in that the grass will grow in neat mounds. While you can expect some seeding, the plant will generally not become invasive and will get larger in circumference over time. Grasses with rhizomes spread by underground stems and can become intensely invasive. Placing a rhizomatous grass in your perennial border might result in an invasive growing disaster. Examples of severely invasive grasses in the Midwest include blue lymegrass, running bamboo, and cordgrass. Understanding the variety of ornamental grass and its growing nature can prevent a landscape disaster.

Plant ornamental grasses in the spring or fall when conditions are somewhat rainy to assist in their establishment. Most ornamental grasses prefer full sun, but this is not always true, so be sure you understand conditions for the individual grass selected. Prepare soil for planting by mixing in 2 to 3 inches of organic matter in the planting bed and adding any soil amendments your soil tests have shown you need.

Maintenance

Grass maintenance is fairly easy. In order to have four seasons of interest, it is best to leave your grass standing all winter. In spring, cut the grass back by shearing it off near the base. Cut back to 2 to 3 inches for shorter grasses, 4 to 5 inches for taller grasses. Every three to four years or so, you can divide the plant or spade it back in size if it should start to grow out of its planting area. Sometimes the center of a grass clump dies out as a plant gets older. If this happens, divide the plant, saving some of the plant for the original planting area and give away or replant the remainder.

Ornamental grasses often respond to and get a growth kickstart based upon temperature. Some grasses grow more readily in early spring's cool weather while others wait until the soil is warm and temperatures are more consistently hot to begin new growth. Cool-season grasses such as fescues and tufted hair grass prefer cool weather, need more frequent dividing, and will go dormant during drought. Warm-season grasses love warm weather and are generally more drought tolerant. Warm-season grasses include pampas and fountain grass.

Diverse Uses For Ornamental Grasses

With a wide range of sizes, ornamental grasses can be substituted for nearly any role in the perennial bed that a perennial or shrub might normally fill. For example, some varieties like plume grass or dwarf pampas grass grow taller than a person and make an excellent hedge or screen. Feather reed grass makes a wonderful substitute for a fence line, while small carex can be a groundcover solution.

Blue Fescue

Festuca ovina var. glauca

Botanical Pronunciation
fes-TEW-ka oh-VYE-na GLAW-ka

Other Names
Gray fescue, sheep fescue

Bloom Period and Seasonal Color
Early summer; blooms green with a purple highlight in early summer; blue-gray foliage

Mature Height × Spread
6 to 14 inches × 6 to 14 inches

Blue fescue has become intensely popular because of its impressive, ornamental, steely blue foliage. While the grassy flowers can be quite attractive, the plant is far more desirable in modern gardens because of its foliage. With radiating foliage, this small-sized grass seems to grow in a rounded clump, usually reaching 6 to 12 inches tall. Under the right conditions blue fescue can live for eight to ten years, providing a reliable, long-lasting perennial feature in the landscape. Planting blue fescue in wet conditions can result in parts of the plant becoming browned out and dead looking. Floppy, yellowed, and unattractive growth can be the result of too little sun exposure; fescue thrives in hot, full sun locations. Blue fescue may also be called gray fescue or sheep fescue.

When, Where, and How to Plant
Blue fescue enjoys good drainage and full sun exposure. Plant this ornamental grass in nearly any type of soil: clay, loam, sand, or gravel. If soil is heavy and wet, be sure to loosen existing soil by adding compost or other organic amendments to improve drainage. Plant grass seed or potted plants into the ground in spring.

Growing Tips
Water regularly until established. Mulching blue fescue means it will become even more drought tolerant as the mulch helps hold moisture at the root level.

Regional Advice and Care
Cut seedheads off before flowering to keep the plant tidy and prevent self-sowing; seeds do not consistently grow into a plant that is the original color from seed drop. Therefore, it is better to propagate by division. Divide plants every three to four years to keep the plant fresh. Use a sharp spade or saw to cut through the thick, mounded foliage. Do not cut this grass back in winter as it provides lovely winter interest, with semi-evergreen foliage and interesting color when it peeks through snow. Full sun is critical to its growth, but during excessively hot summers, blue fescue has been known to die back. Simply trim off dead growth. There are no diseases or insect pests that seem to affect these plants.

Companion Planting and Design
Blue fescue can be rather stunning when planted *en masse* in xeriscape gardens. Planted more tightly together in straight lines, blue fescue functions as an admirable border or edging plant for the traditional or ornamental grass garden. Grouping the grass in odd numbers and planting in drifts adds visual interest and creates the effect of a blue wave. They make wonderful feature plants in rock gardens. Blue fescue is an amazing design contrast when planted near burgundy-leaved plantings.

Try These
'Elijah Blue' actually has several variants that have intensely blue foliage in sunnier locations. 'Sea Urchin' has tight foliage, is silvery blue, and is slightly wider, averaging 8 inches tall and 12 inches wide. 'Boulder Blue' is more silver-gray in tone.

Carex

Carex spp.

Botanical Pronunciation
KAIR-ex

Other Name
Sedge

Bloom Period and Seasonal Color
Year-round; chartreuse, green, tan, orange, burgundy, brown, and striped foliage

Mature Height × Spread
12 to 30 inches × 12 to 24 inches

Carex is an incredibly versatile foliage plant in the garden. While it looks like an ornamental grass, it is really a perennial plant with grassy-looking plant leaves. These leaves can be striped or range in color from soft pink and burgundy all the way to olive or chartreuse green. There are over a thousand varieties of native sedges growing in almost every place on earth. In the past, the plants were overlooked as ornamental landscaping plants because they looked too much like grass. With perennial gardens incorporating grasses of every sort in more recent times, the plant has grown in popularity; there is a carex plant for every garden situation imaginable. Gardeners love carex because the plant adds interesting textures and forms into the shade garden.

When, Where, and How to Plant
Generally speaking, carex prefer rich, consistently moist soil. Consider amending native soils with rotted manure, compost, and worm castings to enhance water retention and improve soil content. Place container plant in spring. Carex does not like to be located in dry or windy sites. There are so many different varieties of carex that it's easy to find one for your specific needs. Do some research to make sure you have the right carex for your location. For example, some carex spread by rhizomes, while others have more traditional roots. While some prefer full shade and bog, others might need a drier spot. There are many variables to consider.

Growing Tips
Most carex love moisture, and its leaves can turn brown and crispy in hot, dry summers. Mulching is critical for carex in helping its root systems retain moisture.

Regional Advice and Care
Leave the foliage up for winter interest and cut it to the ground in late winter. There are no serious diseases or insect pests that seem to affect these plants.

Companion Planting and Design
Carex can become a lawn substitute planted *en masse*, particularly for a small feature area in a shady spot where grass will not normally grow. Gorgeous as a path edger or border plant, carex can enliven a dull pathway. Place carex in containers, window boxes, and vertical wall gardens for vertical interest.

Try These
Many carex varieties are not hardy in Zone 5; read the labels to understand which variety will perform best in your planting zone. 'Bowles Golden' has astoundingly bright yellow-green leaves in early spring. 'Evergold' is a Japanese sedge that has evergreen leathery leaves with a creamy, off-white stripe down the center of the leaves. 'Shima-nishiki' or 'Island Brocade' sedge is a wide-leafed, striped plant that forms a thick groundcover and has 9-inch-long leaves. 'Fox Red' has red stems that arch up to 30 inches high.

Dwarf Pampas Grass

Cortaderia selloana 'Pumila'

Botanical Pronunciation
kor-ta-DEER-ia sel-o-AH-na PU-mi-la

Other Name Pampas grass

Bloom Period and Seasonal Color
Late summer; green arching grass with creamy white plumes

Mature Height × Spread 4 to 6 feet × 3 to 4 feet

Dwarf pampas grass, specifically *Cortaderia selloana* 'Pumila', is a great substitute for the giant pampas varieties, which are extremely invasive and not consistently hardy in many Midwestern zones. Dwarf pampas grass is a clumping herbaceous perennial that can be hardy to Zone 6 and Zone 5 with heavy protection. Worth the extra effort in northern gardens, dwarf pampas grass is boldly showy and can produce more than 100 swaying flowering plumes per plant. Most pampas grasses are prolific reseeders, but this particular variety is nearly sterile and does not reseed readily. Dwarf pampas grass flower plumes are outstanding both in freshly cut and dried arrangements. They feel silky soft and dance attractively in a light breeze in the landscape.

When, Where, and How to Plant

Plant dwarf pampas grass in full sun to part sun exposures. This ornamental grass will be happy in almost any type of soil, including clay, loam, sand, or gravel. However, the soil needs to be very well drained. If conditions are heavy or wet, loosen existing soil by adding compost or other organic amendments to improve drainage. Place potted plants into the ground in spring.

Growing Tips

Water occasionally until well established. Dry conditions are best; water infrequently in normal conditions. If suffering from extreme drought, water more in its first season. No regular watering is required once the plant is well established. Healthy plants don't need fertilizer.

Regional Advice and Care

Tie the grass together with twine in late fall to help keep moisture off the plant's leaves and plumes. Mulch heavily, particularly if in a Zone 5 garden, as extreme temperatures can kill this grass. Prune in late winter or early spring with pruners or electric trimmers. Be sure to wear gloves when managing the plant, as its blades are fairly sharp.

Companion Planting and Design

While dwarf pampas grass is shorter than traditional varieties, it is still tall and bushy and can interfere with lines of sight for vehicles. Do not place near driveways, sidewalks, and roadways. Do not place close to central air conditioning units or outdoor machinery where the leaves can become trapped. Dwarf pampas grass is an architectural feature and works as an accent plant in the center of the garden. Its height lends itself to the back of large borders where you can place the plant in rows or long drifting waves. This grass looks magnificent when planted in a tall mixed border with Joe-pye weed, milkweed, and sunflowers.

Try These

There are no other recommended varieties of pampas grass that are hardy in most Midwestern zones. However, a newer variety called 'Ivory Feathers®' has flower plumes that stretch to 8 to 10 feet; however, it will have to be replanted each year as it is only hardy to Zone 7.

Feather Reed Grass

Calamagrostis x acutiflora

Botanical Pronunciation
kal-uh-muh-GRAHSS-tiss uh-kew-tih-FLORE-uh

Bloom Period and Seasonal Color
Early spring; bronzy purple foliage; golden tan seed heads in fall

Mature Height × Spread
4 to 6 feet × 2 feet

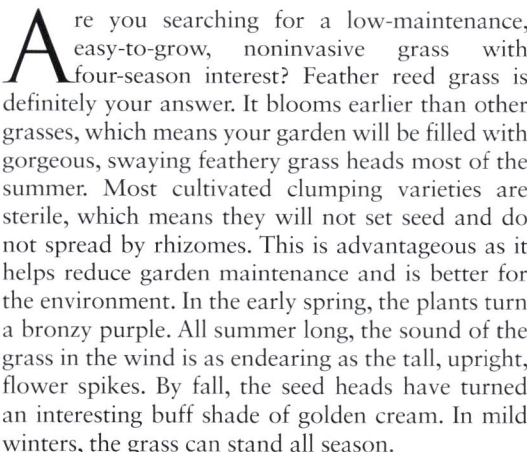

Are you searching for a low-maintenance, easy-to-grow, noninvasive grass with four-season interest? Feather reed grass is definitely your answer. It blooms earlier than other grasses, which means your garden will be filled with gorgeous, swaying feathery grass heads most of the summer. Most cultivated clumping varieties are sterile, which means they will not set seed and do not spread by rhizomes. This is advantageous as it helps reduce garden maintenance and is better for the environment. In the early spring, the plants turn a bronzy purple. All summer long, the sound of the grass in the wind is as endearing as the tall, upright, flower spikes. By fall, the seed heads have turned an interesting buff shade of golden cream. In mild winters, the grass can stand all season.

When, Where, and How to Plant

Plant this grass in full sun to part shade, in soil that has excellent drainage. Place potted plants into the ground in spring. If roots are potbound or matted, be sure to cut through the rootball in several places before planting.

Growing Tips

While feather reed grass is drought tolerant, it also enjoys regular water and will grow taller flower heads if watered regularly throughout the season. There's no need to fertilize.

Regional Advice and Care

While it is fine to cut back grasses in fall, most gardeners prefer to wait until late winter or early spring to preserve the plant's attention-grabbing winter interest throughout the season. Cut back to 6 to 9 inches above the soil. An easy way to cut the grass is to wrap the entire plant with twine or tape to hold the grass together, then use pruning shears or a hedge trimmer to cut the plant at the base. Propagating feather reed grass is fairly simple if you enjoy grappling with a bear; the extremely thick, mounded foliage is very challenging to cut through. Divide every three to five years in early spring or late fall by using a sharp spade or saw to cut through the roots. If you cut the plant into very small pieces it may take several years to reflower, so dividing in half is a good rule of thumb.

Companion Planting and Design

Excellent companion plants for feather reed grass include tall sedum, particularly the burgundy-stemmed 'Matrona', Russian sage, bee balm, and yarrow. Native plant partners such as blazing star, black-eyed Susan, and tickseed work brilliantly. Feather reed grass makes an impressive natural dividing wall or fence when planted in a straight row due to its tall flower spikes. Feather reed grass is a gardening solution for growing beneath or near black walnut trees.

Try These

'Karl Foerster' is the most popular and widely available variety. 'Overdam' is more compact and has variegated foliage. 'Avalanche' has a strong variegated leaf with a white stripe and green margins.

Fountain Grass

Pennisetum alopecuroides

Botanical Pronunciation
pen-i-SEE-tum al-o-pe-kur-OH-deez

Bloom Period and Seasonal Color
Late summer; cream, bronze, and black blooms; leaves have interesting fall color

Mature Height × Spread
1 to 3 feet × 1 to 3 feet

Fountain grass is aptly named because its plant form is shaped much like a fountain, lending an interesting, arching habit to perennial garden beds. Many varieties of fountain grass are only hardy to Zone 6, and in Zone 5 they need heavy protection. Be particularly cautious when reading plant tags and doing research to make sure you are getting an ornamental grass that will survive your garden conditions. There are several varieties listed here that do marvelously well in northern zones. But fountain grasses not hardy in Midwestern zones can still be planted in container gardens as a tall feature to give height to the container's design. Fountain grass is a versatile plant for urban plantings because it survives air pollution and can help control erosion.

When, Where, and How to Plant
It's best in full sun, but this grass will tolerate shadier conditions with less flower production. Although it will survive drought, fountain grass adores moist, well-drained soils. Consider amending native soils with rotted manure, compost, and worm castings to enhance water retention and improve soil content. Plant the grass in spring or fall. If roots are potbound or matted, cut the rootball with a sharp knife in several areas before planting. Wear gloves during transplanting to protect your skin from grass cuts.

Growing Tips
To keep this grass looking its best, occasionally give it a deep watering during drought conditions as the leaves will curl and brown with heavy drought. Skip the fertilizer.

Regional Advice and Care
Leave the foliage for winter interest, and then cut fountain grass back to 3 inches in late winter. An easy way to cut the grass is to wrap the entire plant with twine or tape to hold the grass blades together, and then use pruning shears or a hedge trimmer to cut the plant at the base. Fountain grass has virtually no pest or disease issues; however, it will sometime self-seed. Pull up seeds as plants will rarely bloom true to the cultivar's original form.

Companion Planting and Design
Planting fountain grass *en masse* produces a remarkable visual result because it appears to be a wide swath of undulating waves when gently pushed by a breeze. Fountain grass, particularly miniature or dwarf varieties, look elegant as a path edger or border plant. Design dwarf fountain grass containers, window boxes, and vertical wall gardens for vertical garden interest.

Try These
'Moudry' is a black-flowering fountain grass that has glossy foliage and large dark flowers. Shorter than most varieties, it is hardy to Zone 5 and adds interest and texture to the garden. 'Hameln' has cream-colored flowers that float above bright green grassy blades; its leaves turn russet in fall and it is hardy to Zone 4. 'Little Bunny' is a dwarf that only grows to 12 inches high and wide and is splendid in children's gardens.

Hakonechloa

Hakonechloa macra

Botanical Pronunciation
ha-koe-neh-KLOE-uh MA-kruh

Other Names
Japanese forest grass, golden variegated hakonechloa

Bloom Period and Seasonal Color
Season long; chartreuse, green, burgundy, and variegated foliage; tan or copper orange in fall

Mature Height × Spread
8 to 36 inches × 24 inches

Hakonechloa is native to Mount Hakone, Japan, and is a long-lived herbaceous ornamental perennial that is a graceful, low-spreading foliage plant. Originally a woodland plant, hakonechloa can truly light up the dark understory of a wooded area with its waterfall-like foliage. Its graceful leaves are magic in the perennial garden as well, seeming to lean toward pathways and garden visitors. It is considered a lovely plant for urban gardens because it is slow growing and noninvasive. It is ideal in tight spaces, can tolerate air pollution, and adores shade. While hakonechloa prefers moist sites, it is drought tolerant and can handle most conditions in the garden except full sun, which burns its leaves. Hakonechloa adds unique form and texture to the shade garden. It's also called Japanese forest grass or golden variegated hakonechloa.

When, Where, and How to Plant
These plants prefer very rich soil that has good drainage but remains consistently moist. To help it survive drought, consider amending native soils with rotted manure, compost, and worm castings to enhance water retention and nutrient content. Plant in spring, well out of full sun as the leaves can suffer scorch; shady conditions are preferable.

Growing Tips
Keep soil moist. Although many varieties are hardy to Zone 5, safeguarding the plant is helpful: keep it well mulched for weed prevention, moisture retention, and cold protection. No fertilizer is required.

Regional Advice and Care
Prune anytime, however the foliage is quite striking with snow resting on it and many gardeners prefer to leave it up for winter interest. Cut to 3 or 4 inches above the ground in late winter using pruners or hand clippers. There are no serious diseases or insect pests that seem to affect these plants. Hakonechloa only need dividing once every five years or so if it becomes crowded. In spring, use a sharp spade to cut roots and then replant divisions.

Companion Planting and Design
Hakonechloa is a very adaptable plant for design because of its finely textured leaves; it works particularly well as an edger or border plant. Use it in woodland settings planted in naturalized drifts. Plant this grass to surround Japanese maples with deep burgundy leaves for a bold contrast. Combine hakonechloa with large, deep blue hostas for a spectacular shade statement. Use as a groundcover in shady urban areas such as along a sidewalk or side entry. Place in front of tall ferns and cimicifuga. It also works as a shade planting under black walnut trees. Use as a spectacular feature plant in large containers or drooping over ponds and waterways.

Try These
'All Gold' is a compact golden variety that stays only 12 inches high. 'Naomi' has burgundy leaves. 'Fubuki' is a newer variety that is only 8 inches high with white-and-green striped margins; it's tinted pink in fall. 'Aureola' has tried-and-true variegated green-and-yellow foliage. 'Nicolas' is an amazing fall color feature with leaves that turn intense red-gold shades.

Plume Grass

Saccharum ravennae

Botanical Pronunciation
suh-KAIR-um rav-EN-nay

Other Names
Ravenna grass, northern pampas grass

Bloom Period and Seasonal Color
Summer; silvery blue-gray blooms

Mature Height × Spread   8 to 12 feet × 6 feet

Plume grass is an extraordinary vertical interest plant for northern landscape and is often called northern pampas grass because it looks very similar to the invasive, full-sized pampas grass. In northern zones, pampas grass reaches 10 feet, but, in southern zones, it can easily reach 12 feet, and sometimes taller in a good year. Plume grass is only around 4 feet tall, but the fuzzy plumes reach up later in the season to add outrageous heights. Strong winds can knock the plants over, so staking might be necessary in challenging weather seasons. Most of the summer plume grass has green foliage, but in fall the leaves develop gradually into a delightful bronze-red. Plumes can be used for striking cut flower arrangements.

When, Where, and How to Plant

While plume grass can be drought tolerant, it also enjoys regular water and will grow taller flower heads if given consistent water throughout the season. Plant the grass in full sun where it has excellent drainage in spring. Too much shade can also create a weaker limb. Plume grass does not appreciate overly fertile soils; plant in the native soil. If roots are potbound or matted, cut the roots with a sharp knife in several areas of the rootball before planting.

Growing Tips

Do not fertilize as overfertilization can result in a floppy plant with bent and falling stems. Healthy plants don't need fertilizer. Mulch the plants well both for moisture retention and root protection

Regional Advice and Care

Plume grass's unique flowers and foliage can be attractive in winter, but the plant sometimes needs heavier cold protection, particularly in northern Midwestern zones. Plume grass can self-seed and escape into other garden beds. Propagate by division every several years by sawing the plant down to 6 inches in fall, then use a sharp spade or saw to divide the plants into multiple divisions for replanting. To cut it down, wrap the entire plant with twine or tape to hold the blades together, and then use pruning shears or a hedge trimmer to cut the plant at its base. Be cautious in placing near machinery or air conditioning units as the grass can become trapped in the equipment.

Companion Planting and Design

Most notably, plume grass's strength is that it adds vertical interest in the landscape. Plume grass is frequently used as a tall screen in landscape design as it is a lovely substitute to full-sized pampas grass in northern climates. Because of its incredible height, plume grass can be used as a standalone bush or tree substitute. Plume grass makes a spectacular backdrop against fences or at the rear of a border.

Try These

There is only the species. Plume grass is listed as both *Saccharum ravennae* and *Erianthus ravennae*; however, they are the same grass.

Tufted Hair Grass

Deschampsia cespitosa

Botanical Pronunciation
deh-SHAMP-see-uh sess-pih-TOE-suh

Bloom Period and Seasonal Color
Fall; gold, russet, and purple shades; spring blooms of pale green

Mature Height × Spread
1 to 4 feet × 1 to 2 feet

Birds love the grassy mounds of the tufted hair grass for nest materials and for seed that drops from ripened flowers. It is a cool-season, semi-evergreen grass in mild winters, and a champion performer in damp shade. Abundant, silvery buff-colored flowers top airy stalks in early summer. Popular for its rather dainty flower heads, its flower stalk floats nearly 2 feet above its short grass and resembles fluffy clouds when the plant is in bloom. While primarily found in its native state in woodlands, bogs, and along rivers, it also makes a superb urban grass as it has a high tolerance for soils contaminated by metals and can survive in nearly any soil condition. Thick groupings of the flower heads can be cut and made into wreaths.

When, Where, and How to Plant
Tufted hair grass prefers good drainage and light humusy soil that remains consistently moist. To help it survive drought, consider amending native soils with rotted manure, compost, and worm castings to enhance water retention and improve soil content. Plant in spring well out of full sun as leaves can suffer scorch; shady conditions are preferable. But while tufted hair grass likes shady and dappled conditions, it will not flower excessively in deep shade.

Growing Tips
Because tufted hair grass needs consistent moisture throughout all four seasons, it is best to mulch well. Tufted hair grass is well suited as a plant that can border rain gardens and bioswales; while the roots do not like to be constantly under water, it can help mitigate certain water concerns. Fertilizing isn't needed.

Regional Advice and Care
Divide in spring or fall using a sharp spade to cut through the grassy tussock. Prune the plant anytime; however, the foliage is attractive and gardeners often prefer to leave it up for winter interest. Cut to one-third of its height in late winter or early spring by using pruners or hand clippers. Tufted hair grass is sometimes affected by rust, a fungal condition. Treat with an organic fungicide.

Companion Planting and Design
Tufted hair grass in an especially good grass to use in areas of soil that need help with erosion control. Because it can survive and process difficult soil situations, it is also an extremely useful plant in urban gardens and roadways. Building the plant into a shade garden with large hosta, tall ostrich fern, wild geranium, and spring-blooming bulbs makes a lovely statement. The grass is delightful as a naturalized plant along the edges of ponds and streams.

Try These
'Northern Lights' is a beautiful green-and-white variegated form that turns an interesting pink shade in fall (see the photo). 'Gold Tau' has golden yellow flowers that stand out over a deeper green foliage. 'Bronzeschleier' has a compact habit and slightly bronze flowers. 'Schottland' is Scottish tufted hair grass and grows to 4 feet with a silky flower head.

PERENNIALS
FOR INDIANA

Perennials are a long-term investment for your garden as they come back every spring with beauty and grace. Consider planting flowering perennials that both look attractive and promote local pollinators within your neighborhood. A perennial plant lives for two years or more, though many perennials can live for ten or even twenty years if cared for appropriately. Typically, most perennials in the Midwest die back during winter and return every spring with an explosion of gorgeous greenery to start the process anew. Perennials are the primary plants in cottage gardens and English perennial beds, but they have made the jump to be a standard in all types of Midwestern garden landscaping. With careful landscape planning and a good understanding of the perennial plants' flowering cycle, you can plan gorgeous flowering and foliage displays that will help support your local wildlife.

Landscaping with perennials and annuals can produce amazing results. Here is a beautiful woodland path planted with a combination of ferns and hostas mixed with magenta-colored coleus.

How to Grow Perennials

You can plant perennials anytime, but they establish best in the spring or fall. Understanding a plant's growth habits, watering needs, and sun requirements are particularly important in the planting process for a plant that will be in the ground multiple seasons. Therefore, determine a plan by drawing out a rough design. Be sure to consider the expected mature size of a plant so you do not overcrowd the beds.

Although many recommend double-digging a perennial bed, I have found it is better to preserve the deep soil structure by raising the bed above the ground whenever possible. Raise your bed by placing 6 to 12 inches of good compost and planting soil mix on top of the ground after all grass has been removed. Then, plant perennials directly into the new soil. Eventually the worms and microbes will do their work and the soil you have placed on top of the ground will begin to loosen and blend with the decomposing soil beneath. However, if you can't build a raised bed, then remove all grass and weeds and prepare the existing bed by mixing 3 inches of organic matter in with the topsoil. Consider using worm castings, rotted manure, and leaf mold as well as adding any soil amendments your soil tests have shown you need. Plant perennials, add 2 inches of mulch, and water the garden well. Maintain the garden by adding more compost and organic soil amendments to your perennial beds in future years as you are able. By improving the soil regularly over the seasons, your perennial plants will live longer.

Design Ideas

There are several design techniques I use with perennial gardens. One concept is to put all the tall perennials in the back, the medium-height plants in the middle, and the short plants in the front of a planting border. This works well up against a fence or wall. If planting an island perennial garden, plant all the tall perennials in the middle of the bed, circled by medium-height plants, with an outer ring of short plants. Much like hanging pictures in your home, I focus on planting in odd numbers: one, three, five, seven, and so on. Odd numbers of plants look better grouped together. In the end, there are no hard and fast rules in design. I have planted monochromatic beds, perfectly even beds, foliage-only beds, herbal perennial beds, and so much more.

Your imagination is the only limit on the design ideas you might use to build your little piece of garden heaven.

Planting perennials in the landscape *en masse* can lend interesting seasonal color changes. Nepeta is a delicious pollinator attractant and flowers magnificently on the sunny edge of this woodland border and path.

Aster

Aster spp.

Botanical Pronunciation
AS-ter

Bloom Period and Seasonal Color
Fall to late fall; white, blue, lavender, and pink flowers

Mature Height × Spread
1 to 3 feet × 1 to 5 feet (variable)

Asters are daisylike flowers named after the Greek word for "star." When blooming, its stems seem almost invisible, making each flower seem to float starlike above the rest of the bed. There are spring- and summer-blooming aster varieties; however, the most popular varieties in garden centers are typically fall-blooming. During the bloom season, an aster can bring a remarkable amount of color and personality to a perennial border which might be ebbing in its growth and browning up for the year. Growth habits vary from compact mounds to larger perennials nearly 5 feet wide. Asters look surprisingly unattractive until they bloom, something like green sticks with tiny buds. But when cool weather hits, the flowers explode like colorful fireworks show.

When, Where, and How to Plant

Asters do well in normal to clay soil, are drought tolerant, and look marvelous naturalized, particularly along a woodland border. Plant in full sun whenever possible, though the plant does well in part sun conditions. When planting, mix into the soil organic matter such as rotted leaf compost or composted manure to keep this long-lived plant happy. Richer soils will produce taller plants that occasionally grow beyond the predicted height and spread.

Growing Tips

Fertilize rarely as overfertilization results in a large floppy plant. If you get less than 1 inch of rain per week, you should supplement with additional water. Some asters are quite sensitive to water issues; too little or too much water can result in lower leaf drop and less flowering. Consistent watering provides a better environment for your aster plants.

Regional Advice and Care

Asters are susceptible to powdery mildew, so they should be watered at the base of the plant in the morning whenever possible and allowed to dry out before evening. Divide the plants in the spring every three years or so. Tall asters can benefit from staking. Pinching the plants back until the first of July will keep the plant more compact.

Companion Planting and Design

Understand the growing nature of your aster before you plant it so that you know where it might fit best within your garden beds. For example, if it is a dwarf cultivar, it will do well planted as an edger along the front of the border. If it is a taller aster, plant at the back of the border. Asters look fantastic as a companion plant in front of artemisia and goldenrod. Try mixing asters in with ornamental grasses for a shot of amazing color during bloom time.

Try These

Aster oblongifolius 'October Skies' is a powerhouse in the late fall and my absolute favorite, blooming through October when the other plants have gone to sleep. *A. amellus* 'King George' has extra-large violet-blue flowers that make a big impact in the fall garden. *A. novi-belgii* 'Bonningdale White' is a remarkably hardy white variety.

Astilbe

Astilbe spp.

Botanical Pronunciation
uh-STILL-bee

Other Names
False spiraea, false goat's beard, meadowsweet

Bloom Period and Seasonal Color
Summer; lavender, purple, rose, magenta, red, burgundy, cream, and white blooms

Mature Height × Spread
6 to 40 inches × 2 to 30 inches

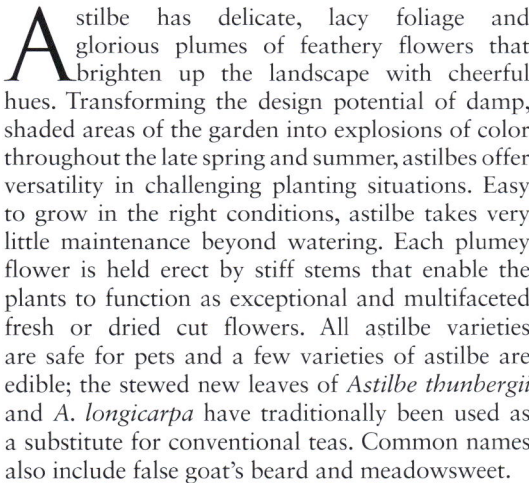

Astilbe has delicate, lacy foliage and glorious plumes of feathery flowers that brighten up the landscape with cheerful hues. Transforming the design potential of damp, shaded areas of the garden into explosions of color throughout the late spring and summer, astilbes offer versatility in challenging planting situations. Easy to grow in the right conditions, astilbe takes very little maintenance beyond watering. Each plumey flower is held erect by stiff stems that enable the plants to function as exceptional and multifaceted fresh or dried cut flowers. All astilbe varieties are safe for pets and a few varieties of astilbe are edible; the stewed new leaves of *Astilbe thunbergii* and *A. longicarpa* have traditionally been used as a substitute for conventional teas. Common names also include false goat's beard and meadowsweet.

When, Where, and How to Plant
While astilbes love shade, they will have more flowers if exposed to some sun, so they do their best in part sun or part shade. They prefer rich, organic soil. Consider amending native soils, whether they are heavy clay or sandy, with rotted manure, compost, and worm castings to enhance water retention and soil content. This hardy herbaceous perennial performs better in areas with cool summers and needs more water during dry or hot summers, so be sure to plant with water access in mind.

Growing Tips
Mulch astilbes well to help retain water through dry summers, but do not smother the crown of the plant. Astilbes are heavy feeders and while mixing a heavy level of organic matter in the soil is good, supplementing with an organic fertilizer will help the plant along. Astilbes like acid, so consider using an organic fertilizer with elemental sulfur added. Mixing in mulched oak leaves annually will also help increase the acid level of the soil.

Regional Advice and Care
Water at the root level of the plant instead of on the leaves to prevent fungal conditions such as wilt or powdery mildew. These fungi issues can be controlled with an organic fungicide sprayed as a preventative or to treat specific issues. Divide astilbe every two to three years, or when they become crowded.

Companion Planting and Design
Astilbes look gorgeous planted *en masse* in curving swaths through the landscape. Iris of all types look wonderful planted amidst astilbe groupings. Ferns, hostas, cimicifuga, and ligularia offer interesting foliage combinations within shady borders. Plant in containers and raised beds with annuals like alyssum and coleus, and with ornamental edibles such as lettuce and Swiss chard.

Try These
'Look At Me' has bright red stems and pale pink flowers on a more compact form. 'Maggie Daley' is a bold magenta flower with bronzy green leaves; it's rumored to be more drought tolerant than other varieties. 'Diamonds and Pearls' has an astounding quantity of whitish cream flower buds. 'Ostrich Plume', also known as 'Straussenfeder', has tall, arching, pendulous pink plumes.

Bee Balm

Monarda spp.

Botanical Pronunciation
muh-NAR-duh

Other Names
Bergamot, horsemint, monarda

Bloom Period and Seasonal Color
Summer; red, magenta, lilac, pink, and white blooms

Mature Height × Spread
10 inches to 4 feet × 2 to 3½ feet

Essential to hummingbird gardens, bee balm is a powerful beneficial insect and hummingbird attractor due to its delicious nectar and bold flower coloring. Bee balm is part of the mint family and has a wonderful scent. Native Americans used the plant for various medicinal applications, and modern-day herbalists use all parts of the foliage and flowers for aromatic teas. Blooms of bee balm can be eaten as well; they look beautiful when sprinkled on salads. Bee balm has uniquely shaped flowers: daisylike in shape but with tubular flower petals that jut out from the flower head. If conditions are right, bee balm can multiply invasively with underground stems or stolons, so be sure to give it plenty of room to spread. Look for it listed as bergamot, monarda, or horsemint too.

When, Where, and How to Plant
Plant in a moist, well-drained soil, preferably in full sun. Bee balm likes rich soil amended with compost or rotted manure. If planting in shadier conditions, expect floppy plants and more center clump die-off.

Growing Tips
Water regularly until well established. Mulch well for water retention and weed control. No extra fertilizer is needed.

Regional Advice and Care
Bee balm is particularly susceptible to powdery mildew, especially if planted in shade. When watering the plants, be sure to water at the base of the plant instead of on the leaves to prevent fungal

problems. These fungus issues can be controlled with an organic fungicide sprayed as a preventative or used to treat specific problematic issues. Divide bee balm every two to three years or when they become crowded. Pinch back in the spring to increase the plant's bushiness. Cut down entirely in late fall or early winter to clean beds. To make a bee balm tea, harvest leaves and flower petals, and dry them in a paper bag. Sprinkle one teaspoon of the dried herb in one cup of boiling water and sweeten to taste.

Companion Planting and Design
Be cautious of planting bee balm too close to other plants because of its spreading nature. Plant bee balm near walls and sidewalks or plant in raised beds and use underground barriers to help contain aggressive runners. It is better in cottage and informal gardens because of its likelihood to be aggressive. Bee balm can come in a variety of sizes from dwarf to tall. Placement in the landscape is dependent upon the size of plant you select. Red varieties are used as hummingbird attractors.

Try These
'Petite Delight' grows 10 to 12 inches high and has resistance to mildew. 'Coral Reef' has a beautiful coral-pink flower with strong resistance to mildew. 'Fireball' is a bright red variety that grows to 24 inches and is very tolerant of urban pollution. 'Snow White' has bright white flowers on 2- to 3-foot stems. 'Jacob Cline' has red flowers that grow to be 4 feet tall.

Blackberry Lily

Iris domestica

Botanical Pronunciation
EYE-riss doe-MESS-tih-kuh

Other Name
Leopard lily

Bloom Period and Seasonal Color
Summer; orange flowers specked with red

Mature Height × Spread
24 to 30 inches × 12 to 18 inches

Blackberry lily is a rhizomatous flowering perennial that has flat, sword-shaped foliage that resembles an iris plant. Blackberry lily is sometimes called leopard lily because each plant bears several six-petaled orange flowers with red, leopard-like spots. Flowers are unscented and bloom for a day. When plants are done blooming, the petals offer a fascinating twisting feature; the flowers dry into a tight spiral, and then fall off once pods begin to develop. Green pods grow in place of the flower and eventually split open to show shiny black seeds. Although these black seeds are attractive, they are also poisonous and plants should not be grown where pets or children might eat them. To prevent self-seeding from the blackberry-like seeds, snip off pods before seeds develop.

When, Where, and How to Plant
Preferring well-drained sites, blackberry lilies can be drought tolerant and do not like excessive moisture. They do well in sandy soil. Blackberry lilies like full sun best and prefer rich soil with considerable organic amendments. If planting by seed, cover the seed since they prefer darkness to germinate. Potted plants can be found at garden centers quite easily.

Growing Tips
Do not overwater the blackberry lily, particularly during winter. Root rot can occur if the plant sits in water. Use an organic fertilizer and fertilize regularly to see more prolific blooms.

Regional Advice and Care
Clumps expand by a slowly creeping rhizome that is easily divided. Dig up the plant and examine its root system; cut through rhizomes leaving branches or eyes on each piece. Replant each cut section. In the right conditions, seed drop can cause the plant to invade. Because of its iris-like rhizomatous root system, blackberry lily can be attacked by the iris borer and various fungal and bacterial diseases similar to iris. Keep the planting beds clear of debris, and water at the base of the plants to help prevent some of these issues. Watch the leaves for spots, stripes, or dead areas. Treat fungal issues with an organic fungicide.

Companion Planting and Design
Blackberry lilies have blue-gray lanced leaves that look good all season. It looks wonderful in informal cottage gardens mixed with Siberian iris and summer lilies. Plant blackberry lily in dry beds with lavender, yarrow, and Russian sage. It is an excellent plant for rock gardens and xeriscape plantings.

Try These
'Freckle Face' produces lighter orange flowers that bloom the first season if planted early. 'Hello Yellow' is a dwarf variety that only stands 20 inches tall and has butter yellow flowers. Due to limited variety selection, × *Pardancanda norrisii* 'Park's Candy Lily' is a species that resembles the blackberry lily flower and can be substituted. Candy lilies have more color varieties to choose from. Blackberry lily was once known botanically as *Belamcanda chinensis* and is still sometimes listed with its former Latin name.

Blanket Flower

Gaillardia hybrids

Botanical Pronunciation
gay-LAR-dee-uh

Other Name
Firewheel

Bloom Period and Seasonal Color
Summer; red, orange, yellow flowers

Mature Height × Spread
12 to 48 inches × 12 to 36 inches

Blanket flower is a native perennial that absolutely adores hot and sunny locations. Branched stems have showy, radiating daisylike flowers with petals that have red at their base and yellow on the toothed edges, with a bronze-shaded eye. Traditional colors on the flower are said to resemble a Native American blanket weaving. Most varieties are hardy to Zone 3; however, a few varieties are only hardy to Zone 7, so read plant tags carefully. Blanket flower's bold colors look wonderful in borders. Butterflies and bees love the long-blooming blanket flower's nectar and will spend hours dancing among a mass planting of the bright flowers. Blanket flower is a short-lived perennial but can readily self-seed, which will extend its life in the garden.

When, Where, and How to Plant
Plant blanket flower in well-drained soil in full sun. While they seem to adapt to nearly any location, they perform better in a soil that is nutrient rich. Amend soil with compost or rotted manure if soil is heavy and water retentive. Grow from potted containers or from seed. Wear gloves when transplanting as a skin rash can develop from exposure to the sap of some gaillardia species.

Growing Tips
Water regularly until established, but do not overwater. Apply a couple inches of organic matter in the spring and no fertilizer after that; it is simply not needed.

Regional Advice and Care
Pests for blanket flower are rare, but it can be susceptible to aster yellows. Aster yellows is a disease that is spread by aster leafhoppers. Symptoms include chlorosis and curling of leaves, no seed development, and distortion of flower petals, sometimes with peculiar growths of leaves developing in the center of the flower. If flowers decline and brown during midsummer, deadhead or prune back flower heads to encourage new growth and a second, late-season bloom. Fungal conditions can bother blanket flower, particularly when it is planted in wet or shady conditions.

Companion Planting and Design
This plant is a fantastic xeriscaping garden companion to the prickly pear cactus, ornamental grasses, and Russian sage. Nepeta, lamb's ears, yarrow, and bee balm also make wonderful drought-tolerant combinations. While some consider the colors too brash, I have found they make an excellent contrast to blue and purple flowers in cottage gardens, traditional borders, and native prairies. Cut flowers are long lasting.

Try These
'Burgundy' has wine-red petals with yellow tips and blooms nearly all summer. 'Fanfare' has interesting tubular flower petals with frilly ends and grows 18 inches tall. 'Goblin' is a short 12-inch variety with extra bold burnt-orange and yellow flowers. 'Fanfare Blaze' is a bold red with the same unique tubular flower petals of 'Fanfare'. 'Amber Wheels' is a taller gaillardia at 32 inches with wide yellow flowers that have frilled petals around a bronze eye.

Bleeding Heart

Lamprocapnos spectabilis

Botanical Pronunciation
lam-pro-CAP-nus spek-TAH-bi-lis

Other Name
Dutchman's breeches

Bloom Period and Seasonal Color
Late spring; pink, red, and white flowers

Mature Height × Spread
2 to 4 feet × 2 to 3 feet

Bleeding heart is a late spring or early summer blooming flower that makes an astounding show with what appears to be "bleeding hearts"—upside-down, heart-shaped, pendulous flowers that hang on long, arching stems above deeply cut leaves. Bleeding hearts were once called "lady-in-the-bath" by gardeners from the Victorian era because when you turn a bleeding heart flower upside down and spread it gently apart, it looks like a lady sitting in a bathtub. Bleeding heart goes completely dormant in late summer, turning yellow and collapsing entirely to the ground. This could happen earlier in the season when stressed by drought or heat. Do not worry about the plants' tragic death; simply clean up the dried foliage and the plant will return with a passion the following spring.

When, Where, and How to Plant
Shade-loving bleeding hearts adore woodland conditions and prefer to be planted in rich, organic soil. Consider amending heavy clay or sandy native soils with rotted manure, compost, and worm castings to enhance water retention and soil content. This hardy perennial performs better in cool, moist summers and is considered easy to get started from potted plants within the garden. Seed must be planted in fall and overwintered in order to perform.

Growing Tips
Mulch bleeding heart to help retain water through the dry season and prevent its dormancy; do not smother the crown of the plant. Bleeding hearts do not typically need to be fertilized as you can easily create more leaves and fewer flowers by stimulating green growth.

Regional Advice and Care
Avoid standing water at the roots as this can rot the plant, particularly in winter. Bleeding hearts can reliably endure stronger sun conditions if kept watered and cool at the root level. Water at the base of the plant instead of on the leaves to prevent fungal conditions such as powdery mildew. Overcrowding can cause fungal issues as well, so divide the plant every three to four years in response to growth. Slugs and snails can eat new growth; trap if necessary.

Companion Planting and Design
Bleeding hearts look fantastic in the middle of the shade border. Mix with perennial geranium, astilbe, hosta, and ferns. Try planting shade-loving annuals beneath the plants such as New Guinea impatiens, coleus, or begonia to fill in and grow tall when the bleeding heart dies back for the season. It's fantastic when naturalized in a wooded lot or near a forest path.

Try These
'Valentine®' is a breakthrough cultivar with deep red bleeding hearts, bronzy green foliage, and red-toned stems. 'Gold Heart' has bright chartreuse leaves with pink flowers. 'Alba' has grass green foliage and bright white flowers. *Lamprocapnos spectabilis* formerly was known botanically as *Dicentra spectablis* and is still sometimes listed with the former Latin name as a synonym.

Brunnera

Brunnera macrophylla

Botanical Pronunciation
bruh-NER-uh mack-roe-FILL-uh

Other Names
Siberian bugloss, false forget-me-not

Bloom Period and Seasonal Color
Midsummer; blue, white, and white with blue margin blooms; foliage is variegated white, yellow, and green

Mature Height × Spread
12 to 24 inches × 12 to 24 inches

When I first met 'Jack Frost', an amazing brunnera with silvery, stained-glass foliage and tiny blue flowers, I immediately fell deeply and passionately in love. Brunnera is a rhizomatous perennial that has stunning, large, heart-shaped leaves, and tiny forget-me-not blue flowers on racemes that dance above the foliage. Multicolored foliage is offered in many varieties of brunnera. Many people who visit my garden stop at the brunnera and ask, "What is this?" Of course, the flowers are adorable, but it's the leaf that captures your eyes and creates an interesting resting stop in dark shade. Brunnera is a fantastic design solution for a dark, shady niche in the landscape, both for its foliage and its lovely blue spring flowers. You may also see it listed as false forget-me-not.

When, Where, and How to Plant
Brunnera loves part-shade to shade and prefers rich, organic soil. Consider amending native soils, whether they are heavy clay or sandy, with rotted manure, compost, and worm castings to enhance water retention and soil content. Plant a bare-root brunnera by digging a hole, then placing the top of the crown about 1 inch below the soil level. This hardy herbaceous perennial performs better in cool weather and needs more water during dry or hot summers.

Growing Tips
Mulch brunnera well to help retain water through dry summers. These are light feeders; do not fertilize heavily. Too much sun without moisture will scorch the plant's leaves.

Regional Advice and Care
To prevent self-sowing, deadhead blooms. Cut the plant back in late winter or early spring. Divide brunnera every two to three years or when they become crowded. Slugs and snails can be a problem and can be trapped if necessary. When watering brunnera, water at the root level of the plant instead of on the leaves to prevent fungal conditions such as wilt or powdery mildew. These fungal issues can be controlled with an organic fungicide.

Companion Planting and Design
Brunnera functions as a delightful groundcover or edging plant as much as a feature plant within a path garden. It looks gorgeous planted *en masse* in curving swaths through a woodland garden. Group several together in odd numbers for a shade garden accent. It is interesting and beautiful when planted in rows next to heucheras and similarly sized hostas.

Try These
'Betty Bowring' flowers in white. 'Starry Eyes' has white flowers with royal blue edging on each flower petal. 'Hadspen Cream' produces light blue flowers over light apple green leaves with irregular creamy white-and-yellow margins. 'Jack Frost' is my favorite; it has silver-white leaves with strong dark green veins and clearly defined margins that resemble frosted glass. 'Diane's Gold' has golden yellow leaves. 'Looking Glass' has green veining similar to 'Jack Frost', but the leaf fades to a brighter silver by midsummer.

Coneflower

Echinacea spp.

Botanical Pronunciation
eck-ih-NAY-see-uh

Other Name
Gloriosa daisy

Bloom Period and Seasonal Color
Summer; pink, purple, red, orange, yellow, and white flowers

Mature Height × Spread
12 to 48 inches × 12 to 36 inches

Coneflowers are perfect plants for birding gardens. Goldfinches spend hours tussling over coneflower heads. Bees and butterflies also love this flower. Coneflower species are native and are one of the toughest perennials you can find for hot, dry locations. In recent years, the flower has experienced a revolution; a resurgence of hybridization interest which has caused a significant change in color and form for the plant. Cultivated coneflower species such as *Echinacia purpurea* and *E. angustifolia* can be found as single or double forms and in a rainbow of color selections. Coneflowers are traditional prairie plants and have been used for medicinal reasons for centuries. Varieties such as *E. pallida*, *E. tennesseensis*, and *E. paradoxa* can be found in native nurseries across the region.

When, Where, and How to Plant

Plant coneflowers in well-drained soil in full sun. While coneflowers seem to adapt to nearly any location, they perform better in a soil that is nutrient rich. Amend soil with compost or rotted manure. Flowers that drop seed will not always return true-to-form, so obtain plants and seed from a reliable source. Propagate by division when plants become crowded; divide every three to five years.

Growing Tips

Water regularly until established, but do not overwater as coneflowers like it dry. Apply a couple inches of organic matter in spring and no fertilizer after that; it is simply not needed.

Regional Advice and Care

Pests on a coneflower are rare. Handpick any Japanese beetles that attack the flower heads. Leave stems and cones standing for winter interest, then cut down in late winter or early spring. A disease that is of concern for the coneflower is aster yellows. While it sounds like the name of a plant, aster yellows is actually a name of a disease that is spread by aster leafhoppers. Symptoms include chlorosis, curling of leaves, no seed development, and distortion of flower petals, sometimes with peculiar growths of leaves developing in the center of the flower. There is no cure. Remove and destroy the plant.

Companion Planting and Design

Some coneflowers have unattractive branches. They resemble sticks when not in bloom. Position other foliage plants such as daylilies, nepeta, and ornamental grasses to aesthetically cover the bare coneflower's limbs. Cottage gardens, traditional borders, and native prairies are all enhanced with clumps of coneflowers growing throughout.

Try These

'Ruby Giant' has giant 7-inch flower heads. 'Supreme Cantaloupe' is a long-blooming, 26-inch-tall double that is the same shade as a slice of cantaloupe. 'Raspberry Tart' is a dwarf at only 18 inches high and has pink flowers. 'Julia' is a bright orange dwarf that grows to 18 inches high. 'Supreme Elegance' is a pink double with superior branching and prolific blooms. 'Cheyenne Spirit' is a mix of intense colors: bright orange, red, golden yellow, purple, and white with a large brown eye.

Coreopsis

Coreopsis verticillata

Botanical Pronunciation
ko-re-OP-sis ver-ti-si-LA-ta

Other Name
Threadleaf coreopsis

Bloom Period and Seasonal Color
Summer; yellow, orange, white, and bicolor flowers with a golden eye

Mature Height × Spread
1 to 2½ feet × 1 to 2½ feet

Threadleaf coreopsis is a delicate-looking herbaceous perennial with airy cut-leaf foliage, small abundant flowers, and an exceptionally long bloom period. It performs well in urban areas because of its smaller form and tolerance for drought and a variety of soil conditions. Coreopsis is a prolific bloomer that continues through most of the summer garden season. New cultivars for the plant have expanded its color offering to include various shades of yellow, white, orange, and yellow mixed with burgundy. Its ferny leaves melt into the background once the plant starts blooming, creating the effect of floating stars in the garden. Waves of color can be achieved by massing these low-maintenance plants in large groupings. Nearly all threadleaf coreopsis varieties have strong heat and drought tolerance.

When, Where, and How to Plant

Threadleaf coreopsis is not finicky and will grow in nearly any type of soil from clay, loam, sand, or gravel. Most important to its growth is good drainage, consistent moisture, and full sun exposure. Loosen soil to increase drainage by adding compost, gravel, and rotted manure. If planting by seed, do not cover since the seed needs light to germinate.

Growing Tips

Water regularly until well established. While coreopsis likes moisture, its rhizomatous roots do not like to be drowned by boggy conditions. There's no need to fertilize.

Regional Advice and Care

In the right conditions, rhizomes can spread rapidly, so divide or cut back approximately every three years. Threadleaf coreopsis is relatively free of pests and attracts butterflies and other pollinators. Shady situations encourage sprawling plants and fungal disease, so the plant is best planted in full sun. Give plants as much room as possible, and feel free to cut them back anytime throughout summer and fall should the plants grow out of bounds and look sloppy. Consistent deadheading or shearing spent blooms will ensure more prolific blooming and stop aggressive self-sowing.

Companion Planting and Design

Coreopsis is a long seasonal bloomer and quite remarkable in rock gardens, dry hillsides, and in drought-tolerant beds. Planted *en masse*, the little coreopsis looks like a wave of astounding color. It is an adaptable plant to use as a border or edging perennial either in traditional gardens or along paths. It's excellent as a filler planting between larger perennials or potted up in containers and window boxes.

Try These

'Sienna Sunset' is a beautiful burnt orange flower with yellow tips. 'Route 66' has what appears to be an irregular bright splash of burgundy-red on the center of each flower. 'Zagreb' is yellow and has an exceptionally long bloom time. 'Alba' has a pristine white flower and is shorter at only 12 inches. 'Golden Gain' has larger golden flowers and a more vigorous habit. 'Moonbeam' has pale yellow flowers and tolerates salt, making it a good selection along sidewalks that are treated with salt in winter.

Daylily

Hemerocallis spp.

Botanical Pronunciation
hem-ur-oh-KAL-iss

Bloom Period and Seasonal Color
Summer; all colors, variegations

Mature Height × Spread
12 to 42 inches × 12 to 24 inches

Daylilies are named for their bloom, which flowers for only one day, then closes up and dies. It is an attractive, yet virtually indestructible perennial with the ability to be bred quite quickly. Cold hardy and drought tolerant, daylilies are also continual bloomers with up to 30 flowers residing on a single stem above grasslike foliage. They are suited to an inordinately large range of soils and climates. Perhaps this is part of the reason that this delightful perennial has captured the hearts of millions of gardeners. There are more than 60,000 registered daylily cultivars with thousands of color combinations. While daylily has the word "lily" in its name, it is not a lily species although the flowers do look similar to true lilies.

When, Where, and How to Plant
Be sure to locate this perennial in full sun or part sun with at least six hours of direct sun exposure every day. Daylilies typically come bareroot or in potted containers. Plant daylilies in well-drained soil during spring. Daylilies do not like overly fertile soil, but they do need a loose, well-drained area.

Growing Tips
While daylilies are quite drought tolerant, they do appreciate water. Regular watering increases the size and number of daylily blooms. Daylilies also benefit from deeper watering rather than more frequent watering. Mulch well to help the soil hold moisture. Should the daylilies be planted in particularly poor soil, consider fertilization. However, most daylilies need light fertilization or none at all.

Regional Advice and Care
Flowers and leaves can get sunburnt water spots on them, so it is better to water the plant at its base whenever possible. Clean debris and old leaves in the planting bed to prevent disease or pests. Do not compost diseased materials; throw them away. Overcrowding, shady, and wet conditions can lead to fungal diseases. Propagate by division when plants become crowded; divide every three to five years.

Companion Planting and Design
Daylilies look best planted in clumps and groupings in the landscape. When I was a little girl, I grew up on a farm where my grandmother created a "rain garden" before the term was commonly used by planting large clumps of daylilies within several giant wet areas in her 2-acre lawn. These areas would hold 2 inches of water in early spring and prevent her from mowing them. Filling these areas full of orange ditch daylilies solved the water problem.

Try These
'Purple de Oro' is a purple dwarf variety that grows between 12 to 20 inches tall. 'Ferengi Gold' is a pale yellow, ruffled, early-bloomer with 5-inch flowers and a 19-inch height. 'Red Ribbons' is a red and gold spider-type daylily with a 42-inch height. 'Black Fury' has 5-inch blooms that are black with a red edge. 'Lady Elizabeth™' is a white daylily that reblooms at 18 inches tall.

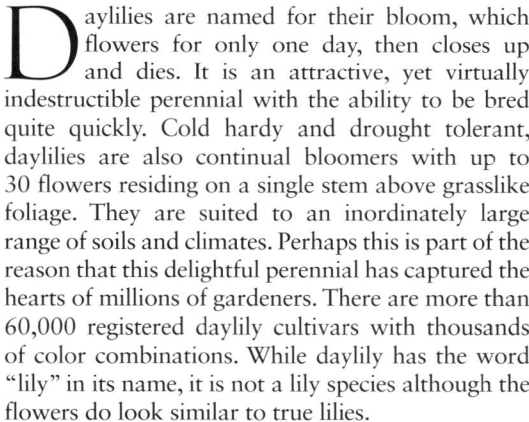

Delphinium

Delphinium elatum

Botanical Pronunciation
del-FIN-ee-um uh-LATE-um

Other Name
Larkspur

Bloom Period and Seasonal Color
Summer; blue, indigo, violet, magenta, red, and white flowers

Mature Height × Spread
2 to 8 feet × 1 foot

My first experience with the tall flower spikes of the delphinium was growing them from seed. I had never seen their blooms in person but had passionately admired them in garden catalogs for years. With determination, I planted 'Pacific Giant' seed and was surprised that such tiny bits of life could grow into incredibly tall, majestic, true-blue flowers only a few months later. Delphinium can grow up to 8 feet tall, but usually get no taller than 5 to 6 feet in the Midwest. They are a non-aggressive plant that demands maintenance: fertilizing, staking, and deadheading. Best kept at the back or center of the border, delphinium plants can be toxic and should be kept away from animals and small children.

When, Where, and How to Plant
Delphinium is a heavy feeder and likes a rich, humusy soil with lots of natural amendments mixed in: rotted manure, compost, and worm castings make perfect soil additions. Plant from seed or transplants; a protected area is wise as strong winds will knock the plants down. Stake each bloom for better wind protection.

Growing Tips
Fertilize with an organic fertilizer upon planting and once every few weeks thereafter. Although delphinium does not like standing in water, it does like consistent moisture.

Regional Advice and Care
Deadhead flowers by cutting back to the nearest new lateral flower spike. Once the plant finishes spring blooming, cut the stalks back to the basal foliage at the bottom of the plant to encourage a rebloom in fall. Propagate by division or seed. This is a short-lived perennial and will begin to die back in the third year. Delphinium is a high-maintenance plant susceptible to cyclamen mites that cause a condition called "blacks" as well as various fungal and bacterial diseases. Keep the planting beds clear of debris and water at the base of the plants to help prevent some of these issues. Treat fungal issues with an organic fungicide. Watch the leaves for spots, stripes, or dead areas.

Companion Planting and Design
Traditionally, tall delphiniums have been planted in country gardens and landscape designs that incorporate a cottage garden look. Delphinium hybrids come in an amazing selection of heights and colors that are wonderful to mix in clumps throughout perennial borders. The shorter modern hybrid delphiniums work well in the middle of the garden, and their common true-blue color makes it possible to build red, white, and blue color combinations.

Try These
'Black-eyed Angel' grows to 5 feet and has clear white flower spikes with a black eye in the middle of each bloom. 'Blushing Brides' is a rose pink and stands between 3 to 4 feet. 'Guardian Lavender' is a stunning lilac blue that stands 3 feet. 'King Arthur' is 4 to 6 feet tall and has a deep purple bloom with a white eye.

Ferns

Many genera, species, and varieties

Botanical Pronunciation
Various

Bloom Period and Seasonal Color
Various and seasonal foliage

Mature Height × Spread
6 inches to 6 feet × 1 to 3 feet

Spring marks the moment when ferns' curling fiddleheads gradually twist open to become delicately arching fronds to celebrate the joy of a new season. Ferns grow in nearly every part of the world, and more than 12,000 species of plants belong to the fern families. They have neither seeds nor flowers, yet they are an important component to our native woodland systems, garden beds, and natural environment. Ferns reproduce via spores, but most ferns also have a complex rhizomatous root system that helps spread the plant by way of runners. Ferns live in a wide variety of habitats and conditions, which might or might not be woodland, but most varieties of ferns that are available to the contemporary gardener have requirements for moist shade.

When, Where, and How to Plant
Find a planting site that is well drained, moist, and rich; ferns prefer organic matter. Amend soils, whether they are heavy clay or sandy, with rotted manure, compost, worm castings, and other organic ingredients to enhance water retention and soil content. Lay bare-root ferns in a shallow trench with buds facing up, and then cover with an inch or so of soil. Crown-type ferns should be planted similarly with the crowns just peeking through the soil surface. It can take one to three years to see new growth on some types of ferns, but most will take off by the next season.

Growing Tips
Ferns can be damaged if a fertilizer that's too strong is used, and with the proper soil amendments, fertilizer should not be required. Only add a light organic fertilizer in the early spring at the first signs of new growth if you feel you must. Mulch ferns well and keep them evenly moist. Ferns love water, and their fronds will collapse to the ground in late summer if suffering from drought.

Regional Advice and Care
Ferns are rarely bothered by diseases or pests. Slugs and snails can be a problem and can be trapped if necessary. Remove debris and dead plant material in the fall. Fiddleheads are edible in some species of ferns but not in others. Do not prepare the fiddleheads unless you know they are safe and nontoxic.

Companion Planting and Design
Ferns can have incredible fall color. Choose Japanese fern, autumn shield fern, sensitive fern, and royal fern as selections that display remarkable fall shading in the garden. Ferns look lovely when planted with hostas, heuchera, bleeding hearts, and brunnera. Smaller ferns are delightful as path border plants. Ferns look majestic when planted in large groupings.

Try These
Ghost fern has silvery gray-green foliage and is a bright standout in deep shade. Japanese painted ferns have silver and burgundy markings and are quite colorful. Lady fern is relatively drought tolerant and will do better in dry shade conditions. Ostrich and cinnamon ferns are excellent in wetter conditions.

Hardy Geranium

Geranium spp.

Botanical Pronunciation
jur-AY-nee-um

Other Name
Cranesbill

Bloom Period and Seasonal Color
Late spring; purple, lilac, pink, magenta, white, and striped blooms

Mature Height × Spread
6 inches to 4 feet × 1 to 4 feet

Hardy geraniums have a similar name to the traditional annual plant we know as a geranium, and yet they are significantly different. *Pelargonium*, or annual geranium, is a tender perennial with thick, succulent-like stems and rounded, boldly colored flower heads. Hardy geranium is a charming, mounded, rhizomatous, herbaceous perennial that blooms and reblooms nearly all spring. Its delicate-looking 1-inch flowers come in a variety of colors and have five petals. Geraniums can form dense colonies if given room to flourish. There are varieties that are low growing which make perfect groundcovers for tight spaces and larger varieties that can easily stretch 4 feet tall and wide. While most geraniums prefer sun to part sun, many will easily perform in the shade.

When, Where, and How to Plant
Choose the planting site depending upon the variety of geranium you have chosen and its sun preferences. Although geraniums do not like standing in water, they do like a consistent medium moisture and a rich, humusy soil with lots of natural items mixed in; rotted manure, compost, and worm castings make perfect soil amendments. Plant potted containers in spring after the last frost or from seed in fall or in spring if the geranium seed has been cold treated.

Growing Tips
Water regularly upon initial transplanting, but it should survive dry conditions well as long as the soil is rich.

Regional Advice and Care
Geranium has an exploding seedpod, which throws seeds quite a distance from the plant after the flowering has ended in early summer. It can be divided by digging up the rhizomes and cutting them between stems. A new cluster of basal leaves and flowering stems will crop up from the thick, branched, horizontal rhizomes. Shear back flower stems after the first bloom to help tidy the plant. Prune if the plant grows out of bounds at any time. Hardy geranium has relatively few pests or diseases; however, if watered heavily from the top of the plant in shadier conditions, it can develop powdery mildew and fungal problems. Cut off infected leaves and throw them away.

Companion Planting and Design
For larger, rambling varieties of geranium, consider cottage-garden placement; plant in front of hollyhocks, iris, Shasta daisies, and poppies. Lower-growing geraniums look magnificent as border and pathway edging; mix with lamb's ears and groundcover sedum. In part shade, try naturalizing geraniums or planting near hostas.

Try These
For a versatile, short, magenta-flowered groundcover that tolerates hot sun, dry, and wet conditions well, try 'Biokovo Karmina'. 'Rozanne' is a 20-inch geranium with very prolific lilac-blue flowers. 'Orkney Cherry' is a striated, rosy pink flower that grows to 12 inches and has bronzy green foliage. 'Dark Reiter' has burgundy foliage, a lilac flower, and is only 10 inches high. *Geranium psilostemon* can grow over 4 feet high and has a magenta flower with black eye.

Hellebore

Helleborus × hybridus

Botanical Pronunciation
hel-LEB-or-us HY-brid-us

Other Names
Christmas rose, Lenten rose, Easter rose

Bloom Period and Seasonal Color
Late spring; black, purple, red, burgundy, pink, green, white, yellow, peach, striped, and variegated blooms

Mature Height × Spread
1 to 4 feet × 1 to 3 feet

The legend of the Christmas rose is that a girl began to cry when she had nothing to offer Jesus for a gift upon His birth, and flowers sprouted where her tears dropped. While the flowers do not typically bloom at Christmas in the Midwest, hellebores are one of the earliest blooming perennials, sometimes blooming in February with some varieties showing their delightful downward-facing blooms until April. Hellebore flowers are actually made from their sepals and are intensely beautiful. Modern hybrids come in shades that range from black all the way to white and any variation in between. Hellebores are poisonous, and pets and humans have been known to get painful, burning rashes from touching this evergreen plant. Sometimes they are called Lenten rose or Easter rose.

When, Where, and How to Plant
Hellebores will do well in nearly any shade or part-shade garden bed, but they prefer consistent moisture and a rich, humusy soil. Good drainage is important, so if the soil is heavy, amend it with rotted manure, compost, and worm castings to increase drainage. Plant from seed or from potted containers in spring. Hellebore is likely to become rootbound, so loosen roots before planting to encourage growth.

Growing Tips
Most hellebores appreciate consistently moist soil, and while it is possible for hellebores to thrive in dry shade, they do better with regular waterings.

Hellebores are sometimes slow to establish; be patient and fertilize upon planting and during times of plant growth.

Regional Advice and Care
While hellebores will sometimes bloom when there's snow on the ground, their foliage can become burnt and ripped in harsh winter weather. Mulch to help protect the plant from winter's cold and summer's heat. Pests and diseases rarely bother it, although fungal problems are more likely in shady, damp areas.

Companion Planting and Design
Plant hellebores under deciduous trees and shrubs that normally offer deep shade, but in the winter months might offer dappled light. Hellebores are magnificent when planted in large groupings. They are great perennials to feature along paths and by doorways as early harbingers of spring. Try planting black hellebore varieties as features in black-and-white themed garden beds.

Try These
'Night Coaster' is a deep black hellebore with 2½-inch flowers. 'Gold Collection® Pink Frost' blooms very early and has flowers that range from pale pink to light red and leaves that have a silvery sheen. 'Ivory Prince' has warm ivory blooms tinged with pink. 'Winter Thriller™ Grape Galaxy' is a spotted purple flower with an ivory eye. 'Winter Jewels™ Golden Lotus' has astounding double blooms that have pointed petals.

Heuchera

Heuchera spp.

Botanical Pronunciation
HEW-kur-uh

Other Names
Coral bells, alumroot

Bloom Period and Seasonal Color
Late spring and summer; foliage in a wide range of shades with white, pink, and red blooms

Mature Height × Spread
12 to 18 inches × 12 to 18 inches

Heuchera (also known as coral bells and alumroot) have delicate, almost bell-like flowers that attract pollinators and hummingbirds, but the real reward is that they have the most superbly magical foliage colors: chartreuse, green, golden, peach, bronze, burgundy, purple, black, and variegated. Originally a native plant to North America, heuchera has been pounced on by brilliant hybridizers who have brought forth a dazzling rainbow of new color offerings for the public. Heuchera are short-lived, mounded, herbaceous perennials with leaves that grow from solid woody stems above fibrous roots. Leaves differ in shape and size; most are lobed and rounded while some are hairy or ruffled. Leaf color can vary throughout the year depending upon how much sun, heat, and moisture it receives. Darker varieties do better in full sun than lighter-leaved plants.

When, Where, and How to Plant

Plant heucheras in fertile, rich, well-drained soil. It is particularly important to have a well-drained site over winter. Heuchera do much better in part-sun or part-shade locations; too much sun can burn the leaves of the plant and not enough sun can produce lowered flowering. To plant, bury the crowns up to the depth of the plant's lower leaves, placing plants approximately 15 inches apart.

Growing Tips

While heuchera enjoy moisture, once the plant is established, it will not require heavy watering and can easily survive drought. Direct sun with low moisture can bring on leaf scorch; keep well watered if it's planted in a hot zone. Fertilize lightly in spring.

Regional Advice and Care

Heuchera can suffer from frost heave, which is a condition where the crown is shoved above the shallow-rooted plants during winter. This can result in serious injury to the plant. To guard against frost heave, be sure to mulch the area. Also divide and replant heuchera every three years in the spring, making sure to add additional soil or placing the plants crown and roots back below the soil. Wet shade can be damaging to the crown, which will rot without proper drainage; it can also bring on fungal issues, particularly heuchera rust and powdery mildew. Move plants to a drier, sunnier location or treat fungal issues with an organic fungicide. Flowers are surprisingly long-lasting as cut flowers.

Companion Planting and Design

Heuchera look fabulous planted *en masse* as waves of color leading through a shaded garden area. Chartreuse bleeding heart 'Gold Heart' looks magnificent with berry-colored heuchera planted in groupings along a path. Black-leaved varieties can contribute to a black-and-white themed garden. Ferns, hostas, and hakonechloa are terrific behind heucheras. Use heuchera as a groundcover along border edges and paths.

Try These

'Berry Smoothie' has berry-colored, silver-metallic leaves. 'Black Taffeta' has ruffled black leaves. 'Lime Rickey' has yellow-green foliage and white flowers. 'Peach Flambe' is slightly taller at 20 inches and has warm peach-colored leaves.

Hosta

Hosta spp.

Botanical Pronunciation
HAH-stuh

Other Name
Plantain lily

Bloom Period and Seasonal Color
All season; grown for foliage; lavender or white summer blooms

Mature Height × Spread
3 inches to 4 feet × 6 inches to 6 feet

Hostas are a reliable and easy-to-grow shade garden perennial with dozens of varieties that offer an equal number of color variations. A hosta's primary beauty is its leaf, which ranges from tiny to enormous with colors that celebrate white, yellow, green, and blue shades. Hostas can be quite exciting and present a glorious color pop in deep shade when planted with multiple varieties. Hostas offer a great variety of design and planting ideas for the shade. Some varieties are quite huge and are excellent as specimen plantings, while other hosta cultivars are especially small and function brilliantly in miniature gardens. Flowers tend to be attractive white or lavender, often having a sweet scent, and they attract pollinators and hummingbirds on tall scapes.

When, Where, and How to Plant

Hostas prefer rich, organic soil and do best in shade, part-shade, and part-sun conditions. Understanding the mature size of a hosta is important when planning your garden so you don't crowd neighboring plants in the bed. Hostas can be planted anytime, but perform best when installed in the cooler temperatures of spring or fall. Well-drained and moist soil encourages growth. Loosen soil by digging a hole 6 inches wider than the diameter of the planting container and mixing in soil amendments to enhance the soil's water retention. Mulch carefully; do not smother the crown of the plant.

Growing Tips

Hostas do not need fertilizer; however, adding organic soil amendments with strong nitrogen content, such as blood meal, will increase the leaf size. Feed organic fertilizer monthly through summer. Hostas love water but survive drought as well. Soak the plants well during dry, hot weather.

Regional Advice and Care

Hostas get attacked by a variety of pests. Select plants with leaves that are corrugated and thick to resist snails and earwigs. Chemical-free solutions include beer traps or diatomaceous earth for snails. (Diatomaceous earth is a crushed rock consisting of sharp fossilized diatoms.) Spread it over the soil to kill pests. Wet a rolled-up newspaper and lay it out at night to collect earwigs. In the morning, remove the newspaper (and earwigs) and throw it away. While hostas do not need to be divided, dividing regularly can keep your garden from looking overcrowded.

Companion Planting and Design

Hostas are used in landscape design as a mass or as a cluster-planted perennial. With the amazing selection of unique leaf colors and designs available to the Midwest gardener, hostas are also recognized as a feature specimen that makes a striking statement in a shady bed. Wonderful companion plants include hakonechloa and heuchera.

Try These

Bright green cultivars like 'August Moon' shine in a shade garden. My favorites include 'Guacamole', a large-leafed variety with white flowers and 'Halcyon', a low-growing blue. 'Empress Wu' is an enormous deep blue variety growing 4 feet tall and 6 feet wide. 'Blue Mouse Ears' is a small hosta at just 6 inches tall.

Iris

Iris spp. and hybrids

Botanical Pronunciation
EYE-riss

Bloom Period and Seasonal Color
Spring and summer; unlimited and diverse flower colors in solids, stripes, and variegations

Mature Height × Spread
6 to 50 inches × 2 to 30 inches

Irises are hardy, easy-to-grow perennials that have stunning flowers. There are dozens of cultivars and diverse species from short to extremely tall with differing growing needs. You will find a flower that can fit in nearly any growing condition. Irises are typically statuesque stars of the early summer garden, which helps give the landscape architectural strength. From small to large gardens, irises offer great versatility for design. Their flowers are enjoyed by hummingbirds, moths, and other pollinators, and when planted correctly, they are virtually trouble-free. Once the flowers are done blooming, clip the stems at the base of the plant and enjoys its interesting foliage throughout the rest of the season. Many irises make excellent cutting flowers; tall bearded iris are particularly stunning in a tall vase.

When, Where, and How to Plant
Research the variety of iris you are planting to determine the best soil conditions. Louisiana and Siberian iris do well in damp situations, for instance. Bearded iris prefers well-drained sites without excessive moisture; it's immensely drought tolerant. Most irises do better in full sun or part sun and tolerate most soils, although they prefer soil with considerable organic amendments. Plant iris rhizomes *on the top* of the soil; do not bury roots deeply.

Growing Tips
Use an organic fertilizer regularly; this is particularly important for new hybrids that have larger, more prolific blooms, and therefore need more energy for growth.

Regional Advice and Care
If flowers seem smaller and perform inadequately, perhaps the roots have become crowded; try dividing the plants. Most iris can be divided every three years or so by cutting through roots or rhizomes and replanting the divisions. Some iris can be attacked by the iris borer and various fungal and bacterial diseases. Keep the planting beds clear of debris and water at the base of the plants to help prevent some of these issues. Watch the leaves for spots, stripes, or dead areas. Treat fungal issues with an organic fungicide.

Companion Planting and Design
Iris's unique lanced leaves look brilliant all season and make the plant a great selection to clump throughout cottage and formal gardens alike. Plant black and white irises in with other black and white flowering plants like hollyhock, tulips, and petunia for an interesting color-themed garden. Siberian iris is often less finicky about planting conditions, and its swordlike leaves are very appealing.

Try These
'Mystifier' is a bright yellow spuria iris that is a heavy feeder and can grow up to 5 feet tall in the garden. 'Superstition' is a bearded iris so deeply purple that it looks like black velvet. 'Ten Carat Diamond' is an exceptionally strong, white bearded iris with gold-gilded ruffles; it has outstanding vigor and show-quality blooms. 'Caesar's Brother' is a remarkably hardy purple Siberian iris that handles drought and wet with equal aplomb.

Japanese Anemone

Anemone × hybrida

Botanical Pronunciation
an-eh-MOE-nee HIB-rih-duh

Other Name
Windflower

Bloom Period and Seasonal Color
Late summer to early fall; pink, lavender, and white flowers

Mature Height × Spread
3 to 4 feet × 3 to 4 feet

Japanese anemone, or windflower, is a diverse group of remarkably easy-to-grow perennials that have stunning flowers that dance above its deep green foliage, captivating passersby. Truly the queen of the fall-flowering garden, Japanese anemone blooms prolifically in late August and early September. During bloom time, you can watch masses of bees smother the blossoms, burying their entire bodies in the golden yellow pollen, pressing their heads deep into the flowers' centers. Once the flowers are done blooming, seedheads form on the delicate stems, and little cottonlike seed puffs are released to ride the wind to their next destination. Foliage is slow to start in spring but is full and interesting throughout the summer season.

When, Where, and How to Plant
Location is very important; when given the right conditions it can become invasive and aggressively colonize a large area. Find an area where the roots can be contained in sun, part-sun, or part-shade conditions. Spring is the best time to plant windflower; place it in a rich, loamy soil amended with compost and organic ingredients, which encourage good drainage. Patience is important as the trick with a windflower is getting it established. Because this plant does not like to have its root system disturbed, it takes a painfully long time to take hold. I spent two years babying my little anemone children until they finally decided to bloom their heads off. It was a worthy endeavor as the plant has been virtually no effort since.

Growing Tips
Windflowers spread by runner and rhizomes and become quite aggressive. As long as the plant looks healthy, there is no need for fertilizer. Adding organic amendments and mulching in subsequent years should be satisfactory. Establish plants by watering frequently. Established windflowers are fairly drought tolerant and do not need frequent watering.

Regional Advice and Care
Leaves can turn black in winter and can be left standing for winter interest, or cut down in fall. Contain windflowers' aggressive growth by creatively blocking off root expansion areas, planting against a wall or fence, in a garden next to a sidewalk, or in raised beds and containers.

Companion Planting and Design
Windflowers look stunning when planted in a bed all to themselves. In a border garden, plant next to blue-flowered perennials such as 'Rozanne' hardy geraniums, delphinium, nepeta, and baptisia for an interesting effect. While windflowers look wonderful massed near woodlands, be cautious that this perennial does not overtake the native plant life with its rampant wanderings.

Try These
Anemone tomentosa 'Robustissima' grows 36 inches, has a fantastic pale pink flower, and handles extreme drought well. 'Andrea Atkinson' is a 30-inch-tall prolific bloomer with interesting maple leaf-shaped foliage. 'Whirlwind' is a tall-statured double white.

Lamb's Ear

Stachys byzantina

Botanical Pronunciation
STAY-kiss biz-un-TYE-nuh

Other Name
Woolly betony

Bloom Period and Seasonal Color
Summer; white fuzzy foliage with lilac-pink
or white flowers

Mature Height × Spread
6 inches to 1½ feet × 1 to 1½ feet

When visitors come to my garden and see the low-growing herbaceous perennial with white fuzzy flowers, they all say the same thing, "I love these leaves!" Indeed, it is easy to fall in love with the soft, furry, grayish white leaves of lamb's ear. It performs well in urban areas because of its groundcover-like form and tolerance for drought, heat, and a variety of soil conditions. While it is primarily grown for its lightly scented foliage, the flowers are also beneficial insect attractors. Bees and butterflies constantly smother the plant's tall spiky blooms, making it an excellent selection for butterfly and pollinator gardens. Fun facts: lamb's ears have been used as toilet paper and bandages, and the leaves are edible and are used for teas.

When, Where, and How to Plant

Growing in nearly any type of soil, lamb's ears are an excellent solution for a difficult full-sun location. Plant where there is good drainage and loosen the soil to increase drainage by adding compost, gravel, and rotted manure where needed. If you're planting by seed, bury the seed about ¼ inch under the soil.

Growing Tips

Water regularly until well established. Lamb's ear is remarkably drought tolerant, requiring minimal watering after initial establishment.

Regional Advice and Care

Lamb's ear is both a self-seeder and a creeper, which means a small planting can easily grow to a large colony within a few years. Cut flowers off before seeding to prevent self-sowing. To refresh a planting in late winter or early spring, take a vigorous rake to lamb's ears plantings, raking up any dead or browned-out foliage. Shady sites encourage sprawling plants with less flowering and some fungal disease, so the plant is best planted in full sun. Lamb's ears sometimes have problems with the center of the plant dying out; divide every three to four years to prevent this and encourage new growth. Share divisions with your neighbors. Standing water drops on foliage can scorch holes in the leaves.

Companion Planting and Design

Lamb's ears are the quintessential children's garden plant; kids love to play with the fuzzy foliage. Lamb's ears can be a fantastic groundcover for sunny and dry areas where very little seems to grow. Plant with other drought-tolerant plants in borders such as short sunflowers, zinnias, marigolds, black-eyed Susans, prickly pear cactus, and sedum. Use as an edger in white-themed garden beds.

Try These

'Big Ears' has large leaves up to 8 inches long and rarely bears flowers. 'Cotton Boll' has very unusual white flowers that resemble cotton balls. 'Primrose Heron' has yellow-green leaves in the spring and the fall, but traditional silver leaves the rest of the season. 'Silky Fleece' is a dwarf lamb's ear, growing only to 6 inches tall, and has the tiniest flowers ever. It prefers cooler summers with less heat.

Lavender

Lavendula spp.

Botanical Pronunciation
Luh-VAN-dew-luh

Bloom Period and Seasonal Color
Summer; purple, sometimes white flowers

Mature Height × Spread
6 to 36 inches × 12 to 48 inches

Used as a culinary herb for centuries, lavender is also a surprisingly attractive border perennial that attracts bees and butterflies with abandon. Lavender has silvery green foliage and astounding flowers that bloom in various shades of blue-purple that also have a beautiful fragrant scent. Lavender does best in hot and sunny locations with a meager soil, much like the Mediterranean climate where the plant originates. Lavender is used fresh in everything from ice cream to main courses. It is also made into sugars, teas, and liquor distillments. Oil from the lavender flower has been used for perfumes and pomanders for more than 2,500 years. In the modern-day garden, it is used in herbal gardens, to frame garden beds, and as a defining walkway edger.

When, Where, and How to Plant
Plants prefer warm weather and average to poor soils that are loose, gravelly, sandy, or loamy. Be sure the soil drains extremely well. Sow seeds indoors four weeks before last frost or sow seeds early in the season, covering *lightly* with ⅛ inch of organic seed-starting soil. When planting potted lavender, simply dig a hole, loosen the roots, place the plant in the hole, and gently cover roots. Water regularly until established, but do not overwater.

Growing Tips
Do not fertilize. Lavender that is regularly fertilized can have flowers that are less fragrant, and the plant is more likely to suffer from legginess and fungal diseases. Wetness is the enemy of a lavender plant and will cause the leaves to yellow. Excessively wet seasons, watering too much, or planting in shaded and damp areas can lead to plant disaster from fungal conditions and root rot.

Regional Advice and Care
Mulch lavender plants well for winter protection. Help establish lavender by cutting off any flower buds that develop in the first season so the plant can focus on root growth. Later, once flowers have bloomed, cut back to about one-third of the new growth. Plant in open, airy, sun-filled locations in the proper soil. Plants sometimes become ragged-looking; remove and replace these.

Companion Planting and Design
For a quirky and fun xeriscaped garden, try planting with moss rose, prickly pear cactus, and Russian sage. Shorter varieties of lavender look delightful at the front of borders. It's perfect in an herb garden or planted *en masse* along sidewalks and paths and as a frame or border for garden beds.

Try These
'Provence' is a 36-inch tall plant that tolerates heavy soil and one of the best culinary lavenders as its leaves are double the length of traditional lavenders. 'Ellagance Ice' is a diminutive silver plant with white flowers that grows to 14 inches high. 'Hidcote Superior' makes an excellent low hedge with bright purple scented flowers and a strong upright habit. 'Dwarf Silver' is only 6 inches high and has silver leaves; it's perfect for a rock garden.

Ligularia

Ligularia spp.

Botanical Pronunciation
lig-you-LAIR-ee-uh

Other Name
Leopard plant

Bloom Period and Seasonal Color
Summer; yellow flowers

Mature Height × Spread
20 to 72 inches × 18 to 36 inches

Ligularia is a large, clump-forming perennial that can grow up to 6 feet tall and will wow visitors to your garden with amazing golden flowers. There are more than 140 ligularia species in the genus, with most of them sporting golden yellow flowers of various shapes and designs. *Ligularia przewalskii*, or Shavalski's ligularia, has radiating palmate-lobed, almost handlike leaves with deep purple stems. *L. dentata* has large, heart-shaped, purplish green leaves and golden flowers similar to daisies. *L. stenocephala* also has interesting foliage but with a tall, golden, spikey flower head. All ligularias prefer consistently wet soil conditions or their large leaves will wilt and flower production will be harmed. Parts of this herbaceous perennial are toxic if consumed by pets and humans.

When, Where, and How to Plant

Ligularias enjoy rich, loamy, wet soil that never dries out and do best in part-sun, part-shade, and shade conditions. While some plants of the genus will do well in full sun, gardeners typically find it challenging to provide consistent moisture in hot summer sun conditions. Plant the perennials either in spring or fall when conditions are cooler. Loosen soil by digging a hole 6 inches wider than the diameter of the planting container and mixing in organic soil amendments such as rotted manure, compost, or worm castings to enhance the soil's water retention.

Growing Tips

Mulch the ground around the ligularia plants to help ensure moisture retention. Overfertilization can lead to weaker limbs, which attract aphids.

Therefore, consider light fertilization or none at all. Without consistent water, particularly in a hot summer or drought, ligularias go limp and the leaves will brown and die. Be sure to soak the plants well during challenging weather.

Regional Advice and Care

Snails and slugs can attack ligularia. Chemical-free solutions include beer traps or diatomaceous earth. (Diatomaceous earth is a crushed rock consisting of sharp fossilized diatoms.) Spread it over the soil to kill pests. Wet a rolled up newspaper and lay it outside at night to collect earwigs. In the morning, remove the newspaper and throw it away. Clean debris and browned leaves up after the weather turns cold in fall.

Companion Planting and Design

Ligularias are perfect plants for rain gardens because of their intense need for wet soil. They work well massed along woodlands or as a large feature plant in a border. Plant ligularias in a mixed part-shade bed with other plants that enjoy wet feet such as cannas, elephant ear, obedient plants, cardinal flowers, and ostrich ferns.

Try These

'Gigantea' is sometimes referred to as "tractor seat ligularia" because it has unbelievably huge leaves, up to 18 inches across. 'The Rocket' is a hummingbird favorite and produces masses of tall, spiky, yellow flowers that can reach 6 feet tall and wide. 'Brit Marie Crawford' has bronzy, dark chocolate leaves and grows 4 feet tall.

Nepeta

Nepeta spp.

Botanical Pronunciation
NEP-ih-tuh

Other Name
Catmint

Bloom Period and Seasonal Color
Summer; scented foliage with purple, lilac, and white flowers

Mature Height × Spread
1½ to 3 feet × 1½ to 3 feet

Nepeta is a lovely, free-blooming, herbaceous perennial with scented gray-green foliage and an affinity for hot, dry locations. Some members of the *Nepeta* genus are known as catnip, so the entire genus is commonly referred to as catmint. The plants contain nepetalactone, which binds to a cat's olfactory receptors and causes the animal to react with excitement. That same ingredient is also supposed to be more effective than DEET at repelling insects, which makes nepeta a marvelous plant to place around patios and public walkways. Catmint is remarkably hardy and drought tolerant, requiring little maintenance in the garden. Typically a sprawling perennial with effusive blooms, catmint looks pretty planted along the edge of sidewalks as it breaks up the harsh line of cement.

When, Where, and How to Plant
Best planted in full sun, catmint will tolerate light shade conditions with less flower production. It prefers dry, well-drained conditions. Consider amending clay soils with rotted manure, compost, and gravel to loosen the soil and enhance drainage. If roots are potbound or matted, cut them with a sharp knife in several areas of the rootball before planting in spring or fall. Planting from seed can sometimes be challenging, but it is possible. Purchase fresh seeds as many catmint hybrids are sterile and do not produce viable seed from the parent plant.

Growing Tips
While surprisingly heat and drought tolerant, nepeta benefits from being well mulched. Because the majority of catmints prefer a lean soil with dry conditions, plants rarely or never need to be fertilized. Be careful not to overwater as wet situations will kill the plant. The one exception is *Nepeta subsessilis*, which prefers moist situations and partial shade.

Regional Advice and Care
Catmint is an adaptable plant that rarely suffers from disease or pests; however, planting in wet, overly crowded, or shady conditions can sometimes lead to fungal leaf spot. Remove infected leaves and throw them away; there is no need for additional control. Prune back catmint by two-thirds in July to encourage blooms in late summer. Clean up beds by cutting the wiry stems down in late winter to encourage new growth in spring.

Companion Planting and Design
Catmint is remarkably versatile and can be used as an accent perennial or planted in large masses. It looks particularly beautiful when planted in beds of contrasting color filled with yellow and purple flowers such as yarrow, iris, hardy geraniums, black-eyed Susans, and coreopsis. It is a tremendous plant as a path edger. Shorter varieties of catmint are lovely underplantings to roses.

Try These
'Six Hills Giant' grows tall flower spikes over 3 feet high that hummingbirds love. 'Little Titch' is a short groundcover-like plant at 8 inches high. 'Snowflake' is 14 inches high and has white flowers. 'Kit Cat' grows 18 inches high, has a purple flower, and is quite wonderful in containers.

Oriental Poppy

Papaver orientale

Botanical Pronunciation
puh-PAY-vur ore-ee-un-TAY-lee

Other Name
Poppy

Bloom Period and Seasonal Color
Early summer; white, plum, pink, salmon, orange, and crimson flowers

Mature Height × Spread
8 inches to 3 feet × 1 to 3 feet

Poppies have some of the most brilliantly eye-catching flowers in the plant world; they are large, some over 6 inches wide, and appear to be made from delicate crêpe paper. I have always loved the bright spot of color in the early summer garden that poppies offer. When I purchased and planted my first orange-flowering poppy, nothing could have prepared me for the shockingly beautiful bloom that emerged in June. Although the cut flowers are lovely, they only last a short time in flower arrangements, and the tips of the cut stems must be sealed by searing with a match. But save the dried seedheads for dried flower arrangements and wreaths. Most plant parts are considered toxic to humans and pets.

When, Where, and How to Plant
Preferring rich, loamy, soil that has excellent drainage, poppies do better in full sun. Consider amending soil with rotted manure, compost, and worm castings to enrich soil and enhance drainage. Plant the perennials either in spring or fall when conditions are cooler. Oriental poppy has a rather long taproot; to transplant, dig a hole 10 to 12 inches deep, and cover at least 3 inches of the crown with soil. Avoid high wind locations, or provide protection, as the petals can get blown off quite easily in a storm.

Growing Tips
Mulch the ground well to ensure moisture retention and provide winter protection. Poppies go dormant after flowering, meaning their leaves and stems turn brown and fall to the ground. Without consistent water, particularly in a hot spring or drought conditions, poppies go dormant sooner. Therefore, keep the plant well watered throughout spring and early summer growing seasons. Fertilization is not necessary.

Regional Advice and Care
Papaver somniferum is not the same as *P. orientale*; however, it can still be used in the garden. It is the only poppy variety that culinary poppy seeds come from. The word *somniferum* means "sleep-bringing," and the seeds from the same poppy variety are used to produce opium and heroin. It is legal to grow *P. somniferum* for garden and culinary spice purposes, but it is, of course, illegal to manufacture opium from the poppies.

Companion Planting and Design
Oriental poppies are beautiful in cottage gardens; their flowers seem to float above other perennials. Daylilies and ornamental grasses are great companion plants as they hide the poppy foliage after its bloom time is finished. Shasta daisy, delphinium, and lamb's ears make great blooming planting partners.

Try These
'Watermelon' has rosy red petals the same shade as the interior of a watermelon. 'Royal Wedding' is a bright white with a black eye. 'Helen Elizabeth' is a delicate salmon pink color. 'Patty's Plum' is a bold, purplish berry color with single blossoms. 'Salmon Glow' has bright salmon coloring and is heavy with blossoms; it's almost a double-flowering variety.

Peony

Paeonia hybrids

Botanical Pronunciation
pee-OH-nee-uh

Bloom Period and Seasonal Color
Late spring and early summer; white, pink, magenta, coral, yellow, and bicolor flowers

Mature Height × Spread
2 to 3 feet × 2 to 3 feet

My grandmother had the most gorgeous bright pink peonies growing in her front garden, and as a little girl, I would help her cut them every Memorial Day. We would make homemade flower vases by lining old coffee cans with aluminum foil, and then fill the cans with water and dozens of gorgeously scented peonies to place on Great-Grandpa's grave. It is a memory filled with the beauty and fragrance of cut peony flowers. Peonies are long lived—up to 50 years—and they flower in early summer. They are particularly good growers in Midwestern gardens because they require an extended cold period of dormancy to perform. Peonies are edible and bring color to salads, party punches, and are easy to boil into a tea.

When, Where, and How to Plant
Peonies prefer rich, loamy, soil that has excellent drainage. Consider amending soil with rotted manure, compost, and worm castings to enrich soil and enhance drainage. They perform better in full sun. Fall planting is best as these perennials seem to take better when conditions are cooler.

Growing Tips
Mulch the ground around a peony to ensure moisture retention and provide winter protection; prolonged drought and heat stress can cause a plant to go into early dormancy. Fertilize peonies at time of planting and during active spring growth. Keep the plants well watered throughout the spring and early summer growing seasons.

Regional Advice and Care
While most herbaceous peony hybrids look very shrubby, they are strong-stemmed perennials. When flowers are finished blooming, trim off the flower head from the top of the stem unless you would like it to set seed. Foliage continues to look attractive until the first frost. Remove dried debris and trim stems down to the ground after they collapse in the fall. Plants grown in shadier conditions might be prone to powdery mildew, which can be controlled with an organic fungicide. Ants on the heads of the peony buds are totally harmless; they are attracted by a sugary substance put out by the plant.

Companion Planting and Design
Peonies are tried-and-true flowers for the perennial border; however, they sometimes need staking because the flower heads can become extremely heavy in bloom. Partner perennial plants around peonies that could hide the peony stakes such as daylilies, Russian sage, taller hardy geraniums, and nepeta. Groundcovers such as Ajuga 'Chocolate Chip' make excellent underplantings.

Try These
'Bartzella' is a yellow variety of peony with a red center. 'Gay Paree' has a frilly, off-white center with raspberry outer petals. 'Coral Charm' has semi-double coral blooms. 'Pillow Talk' has an incredibly full double, pale pink flower. "Tree peonies" are different from these herbaceous perennials and are considered woody shrubs.

Phlox

Phlox paniculata

Botanical Pronunciation
FLOCKS puh-nick-you-LAY-tuh

Other Name
Garden phlox, summer phlox

Bloom Period and Seasonal Color
White, pink, coral, red, purple, and bicolor flowers blooming in summer

Mature Height × Spread
2 to 4 feet × 2 to 3 feet

Tall garden phlox is the joy of the midsummer garden with its tall panicles filled with fragrant, colorful, tubular blooms. Gorgeous in the cottage garden, garden phlox seems to thrive in the heat of summer, often reblooming if deadheaded. In its native form, prairie phlox is known more as a woodland flower, but garden phlox has been hybridized and grown for increased disease resistance and placement in sun locations. Garden phlox makes a good contributor to hummingbird and butterfly gardens because of its tall tubular flowers. Many varieties have an attractive, delicate scent and are delightful as a cut flower. Other common names include summer phlox and garden phlox.

When, Where, and How to Plant

Plant garden phlox in rich, organically amended soil in full sun. Consider amending native soils, whether they are heavy clay or sand-like, with rotted manure, compost, and worm castings to enhance water retention and improve soil content. This hardy perennial is considered easy to get started from potted plants within the garden.

Growing Tips

Mulch garden phlox well to help retain water through the dry season but do not smother the crown of the plant. Fertilize with an organic fertilizer at planting and once a month through the summer. Extreme heat and drought can attract pests and cause leaf drop, so water garden phlox regularly.

Regional Advice and Care

When watering phlox, avoid standing water at the roots as this can rot the plant, particularly in winter. Water at the base of the plant instead of on the leaves to prevent fungal conditions such as wilt or powdery mildew, to which garden phlox is susceptible. Overcrowding can cause fungal issues as well, so be sure to divide the plant every three to four years in response to growth. Treat with an organic fungicide. Help keep plantings disease free by clearing debris and cutting back plants in fall.

Companion Planting and Design

Garden phlox look beautiful in front of dwarf pampas grass and other tall grasses. Sun lovers such as tall sedum, Russian sage, black-eyed Susans, coneflowers, and coreopsis complement the garden phlox's blooms. Tall garden phlox is the perfect butterfly garden plant; it acts as a beacon to butterflies, and I have seen several varieties on the plants at one time.

Try These

'Shockwave' has lilac-shaded flowers and astounding deep green-and-yellow bicolor foliage that stands out significantly in a garden border. 'Orange Perfection' is a deep orange variety standing 36 inches tall. 'Red Riding Hood' is a medium-tall red at 20 inches tall that attracts hummingbirds. 'David' is a bright white that can grow up to 48 inches tall and has mildew resistance. 'Peppermint Twist' has a pink-and-white striped flower.

Pincushion Flower

Scabiosa spp.

Botanical Pronunciation
skab-ee-OH-suh

Other Name
Scabiosa

Bloom Period and Seasonal Color
Summer; purple, rose, and white flowers

Mature Height × Spread
12 to 18 inches × 12 to 18 inches

Pincushion Flower is a delightfully long-blooming herbaceous perennial that is compact and has lacy, silvery green foliage. Blooms seem to dance above the basal foliage on breezy days, and they relish sunny spots. It is a remarkably hardy and drought-tolerant plant that requires little maintenance in the garden. Pincushion flowers get their name because they resemble a seamstress's pincushion. I have a fond place in my heart for 'Butterfly Blue' scabiosa and its tough nature as it was the very first perennial I was able to overwinter successfully outdoors in a container without additional protection. They self-seed, but not aggressively, so they can often be found in the spring in interesting locations all over the garden. Scabiosa attracts butterflies and makes marvelous long-lasting fresh-cut flowers.

When, Where, and How to Plant
Best planted in full sun, pincushion flower will tolerate light shade conditions with less flower production and shorter stems. It prefers fertile, well-drained circumstances, particularly over winter when it is most likely to suffer root rot. Consider amending clay soils with rotted manure, compost, and gravel to loosen the soil and enhance drainage. Plant these perennials from containers in spring or fall. If planted by seed, the plant can take several years to flower.

Growing Tips
While pincushion flower can benefit from regular organic fertilizer, I have never fertilized mine and find them quite prolific. They do enjoy being mulched. While they prefer soil with dry conditions, it is important to water regularly in order to see stronger flower production. Be careful not to overwater as wet situations will kill the plant via root rot.

Regional Advice and Care
Pincushion flower is an adaptable plant that rarely suffers from disease or pests; however, wet, overly crowded, or shady conditions can sometimes lead to fungal leaf spot. Remove infected leaves and throw away; there is no need for more control. Deadhead plants to continue blooming. These plants will self-seed into cracks and edging, but not belligerently.

Companion Planting and Design
Scabiosa looks very attractive planted in a rock garden as it brings a pop of continual color through most of summer. Plant a row of pincushion flowers in the very front of a butterfly garden or utilize as a colorful low-growing edging plant. It's pleasing when planted below roses or peonies, and scabiosia works very well in cottage gardens as its basal foliage is often hidden and the flowers appear to float above the plant. Pink pincushion varieties are lovely contributors to all-pink flower beds.

Try These
'Beaujolais Bonnets' has mauve pink flowers with deep burgundy centers. 'Butterfly Blue' has a purple-blue bloom with a long bloom time. 'Fama' has exceptionally large 3- to 4-inch, bright purple flowers with white centers. 'Pink Mist' has a pale pink flower. 'Alba' is a long-lasting white variety. 'Yellow Chaenactis' is a yellow variety with prolific blooms that resemble dandelion heads.

Russian Sage

Perovskia atriplicifolia

Botanical Pronunciation
pur-OV-skee-uh at-rih-pliss-ih-FOE-lee-uh

Bloom Period and Seasonal Color
Summer; scented foliage, purple flowers

Mature Height × Spread
1½ to 4 feet × 1½ to 4 feet

When I first placed Russian sage in my garden, I learned the true meaning of drought tolerant, and it has been a favorite purple-flowering perennial ever since. Russian sage is a silvery green, semi-woody perennial with an astoundingly prolific and long bloom time. Its spiky purple flowers revel in heat and laugh at drought. It attracts bees, butterflies, and hummingbirds *en masse* while blooming its proverbial head off all summer long. Russian sage is entirely wonderful for urban locations as it absorbs air pollution well and can be seen growing in surprising locations, usually in dried, cracked soils with no special attention whatsoever. Because of its leggy, spiky, architectural nature, Russian sage can be grown in very creative and advantageous design locations.

When, Where, and How to Plant

Russian sage should only be grown in a full sun site. While it will survive in part shade, the plant will be floppy and less vibrant. It prefers dry, well-drained conditions. Fertility will improve its growth; however, overly fertile soils are not required. Consider amending clay soils with rotted manure, compost, and gravel to loosen soil and enhance drainage. If the roots of potted plants are potbound or matted, cut the roots with a sharp knife in several areas of the rootball before planting in spring or fall. Planting from seed is possible; be sure to barely tap into the soil as the plant needs light to germinate.

Growing Tips

While surprisingly heat and drought tolerant, Russian sage benefits from being well mulched. Do not fertilize unless you see the plant look as if it is declining. Be careful not to overwater as wet situations will kill the plant.

Regional Advice and Care

Should this woody perennial become too overgrown, simply prune it back within bounds at any time. Trimming branches back in early spring will help control height. Pests and diseases rarely bother Russian sage; however, planting in wet, overly crowded, or shady conditions can sometimes cause the plant to die back. Clean up beds by cutting the wiry stems down to the ground in late winter to encourage new growth in spring. Russian sage is toxic if eaten. Wear gloves when handling the plant as it can sometimes cause a rash.

Companion Planting and Design

Russian sage is an essential in a pollinator garden. Most varieties of this perennial are tall, so placement at the back of garden beds is best; however, there are shorter varieties that work well in the middle of the border. It's superb when planted in large masses. In urban plantings, Russian sage looks magnificent in tall containers, raised beds, and roadway medians.

Try These

'Little Spire' grows 2 feet tall and has the same form as larger Russian sage. 'Filigran' grows 3 to 4 feet high and 3 feet wide. 'Longin' is taller at 4 feet high and wide.

Shasta Daisy

Leucanthemum × *superbum*

Botanical Pronunciation
loo-KAN-thuh-mum soo-PUR-bum

Other Name
Oxeye daisy

Bloom Period and Seasonal Color
Summer and early fall; white flowers

Mature Height × Spread
8 inches to 3 feet × 8 to 18 inches

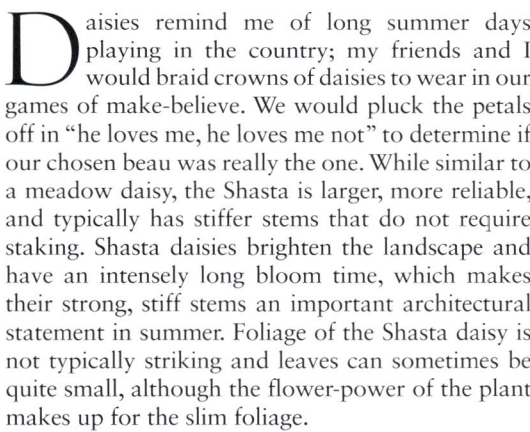

Daisies remind me of long summer days playing in the country; my friends and I would braid crowns of daisies to wear in our games of make-believe. We would pluck the petals off in "he loves me, he loves me not" to determine if our chosen beau was really the one. While similar to a meadow daisy, the Shasta is larger, more reliable, and typically has stiffer stems that do not require staking. Shasta daisies brighten the landscape and have an intensely long bloom time, which makes their strong, stiff stems an important architectural statement in summer. Foliage of the Shasta daisy is not typically striking and leaves can sometimes be quite small, although the flower-power of the plant makes up for the slim foliage.

When, Where, and How to Plant
Best in full sun, Shasta daisy will tolerate light shade conditions, but sometimes with less flower production. It prefers moist, fertile, well-drained conditions, particularly over the winter when the perennial is most likely to suffer root rot. Plant the perennials from containers in spring or fall. If planted by seed, the plant can take one year to flower.

Growing Tips
Shasta daisy can benefit from organic fertilizer at planting time. Do not overfertilize as it can lead to less flower production; it's helpful to condition the soil by applying a thin layer of compost during the growth season in spring. Water Shasta daisy clumps about 1 inch per week at the base of the plant. They also enjoy being mulched to keep their roots well protected.

Regional Advice and Care
Deadhead plants to help keep them continually blooming. Overcrowding and shady conditions can cause fungal issues, so be sure to divide the plant every three to four years in response to growth. Handpick pests or spray bugs with a soap and water mixture if infested.

Companion Planting and Design
Shasta daisies work equally well in garden borders and meadow plantings. They are absolutely superb in an all-white flower garden and with their many different growing heights, can represent a solution in various locations in the front, middle, and back of the garden. Shasta daisies make some of the best flowers for vase arrangements; consider planting a cutting garden with Shasta daisies, zinnias, cockscomb, and sunflowers for very interesting container designs. As container-grown plants, their flowers function marvelously as a tall center feature but require more water than traditionally planted Shasta daisies.

Try These
'Becky' is one of the tallest Shasta daisies at 4 feet with very sturdy stems that do not require staking. 'Tinkerbell' is a dwarf variety that grows only 8 to 12 inches high. 'Marconi' has giant semi-double flowers up to 5 inches across. 'Amelia' is over 3 feet tall with 5-inch flowers. 'Crazy Daisy' stands 2 feet, has a double flower frilly, twisted petals.

Stonecrop

Sedum spp.

Botanical Pronunciation
SEE-dum

Other Name
Tall sedum

Bloom Period and Seasonal Color
End of summer or fall; various colored foliage
that bloom white, pink, burgundy, and purple

Mature Height × Spread
15 inches to 3 feet × 15 inches to 2 feet

Stonecrop is a species related to the groundcover creeping sedum, yet its height makes it significantly more versatile in the landscape. It is a terrific ornamental succulent that can be used in xeric and drought-tolerant perennial beds. Stonecrop has various shapes of leaf and flower, is deer resistant, attracts beneficial insects, and can be grown in virtually any type of soil or location, from roof to container to ground, as long as they have access to regular sunshine. Stonecrop is the perfect butterfly garden plant; it attracts both bees and butterflies in large quantities when it blooms in the late summer or early fall. Some varieties of stonecrop are edible and are particularly good in stir-frying, but eating stonecrop raw can upset your stomach, so make sure you cook it first.

When, Where, and How to Plant
Stonecrop will do well in most any soil but prefers a light, sandy, or gravel area exposed to full sun. Loosen heavy clay soils with rotted manure, compost, or gravel before planting as good drainage is the key to success with the plant. While full sun is its preference, it will tolerate part shade but can become floppy and have weak stems in shady, moist conditions.

Growing Tips
In summer, particularly during dry summer weather, water every two weeks. Moisten the soil without soaking it as the leaves of this succulent store water, so heavy irrigation is not necessary. Plants that stand in water will drown and typically suffer from root rot and fungal issues. Fertilize in early spring with an organic fertilizer and prune back any dead growth from winter. Do not overfertilize as the plants will become leggy and weak. I once planted 'Matrona' in a pile of rotted manure and the leaves achieved a giant size, larger than my hand, but the stems became gangly and floppy.

Regional Advice and Care
Shade and overcrowding can cause fungal issues. Treat botrytis leaf blotch and other fungal conditions with an organic fungicide. While resistant to deer, some regions see deer eating this plant to the ground; it depends on the area and level of wildlife exposure.

Companion Planting and Design
Stonecrop looks amazing in border gardens, large landscape installations, and containers. It's a fantastic solution for difficult locations like busy urban areas because it looks great even after being exposed to high levels of air pollution, poor soil, and low water conditions.

Try These
'Matrona' is an amazing 2- to 3-foot-tall plant with reddish burgundy stems and pale pink flowers. 'Black Jack' is a variation of 'Matrona' and has leaves that are such a deep purple-burgundy they are almost black. 'Neon' has very bright pink flowers and stands 18 inches tall. 'Frosty Morn' has blue-green leaves edged in white and stands 15 to 18 inches high.

Yarrow

Achillea spp.

Botanical Pronunciation
ack-ih-LEE-uh

Other Name
Sneezewort

Bloom Period and Seasonal Color
Summer; white, pink, lilac, yellow, orange, and red flowers

Mature Height × Spread
1 to 3 feet × 1 to 3 feet

Yarrow is an outstanding drought-tolerant, rhizomatous, spreading perennial with a passionate love of the hot and humid summer. It is adored by butterflies and other pollinators. Common, or native, yarrow is quite floppy and does not hold its shape well; however, many of the newer cultivars found in modern garden centers are built to have solid stems that are less prone to flopping. Additionally, contemporary hybridization for the flat-topped flowers has exploded in recent years, leading to many new color developments. Yarrow works in urban locations such as street containers and city lots because it absorbs air pollution well. While beneficial insects love this plant, its one drawback is that it is quite toxic to dogs, cats, and humans if eaten.

When, Where, and How to Plant
Yarrow grows best in a full-sun site. While it will survive in part shade, the plant will be limp and less vibrant. It prefers dry, well-drained conditions. Overly fertile soils are not required and will lead to weak stems; the plant does better with infertile locations. Consider amending clay soils with compost and gravel to loosen soil and enhance drainage. Yarrow performs better if it's planted in areas that are protected from high winds. Planting from seed is possible; be sure to sow on the surface of the soil as the seeds need light to germinate.

Growing Tips
Yarrow benefits from being well mulched; however, it does not like to be overwatered. Let the soil dry out between waterings. Do not fertilize unless the plant appears to be declining.

Regional Advice and Care
Cut a plant back if it has become overgrown. Stake the plants if they require support. Wear gloves as yarrow can sometimes cause a rash due to the plant's toxicity. Prune yarrow back to its lateral flower buds or all the way down to the basal foliage following the first flowering in order to tidy the plant and encourage more blooms. Planting in wet, overly crowded, or shady conditions can sometimes cause yarrow to completely fall over or bloom erratically. Clean up beds by cutting the stems down to the ground in fall. Divide every three to four years, or spade back if the plant's rhizomatous roots spread too quickly.

Companion Planting and Design
Yarrow works very well when planted in a butterfly garden with other plants such as butterfly bush, blazing star, coreopsis, lantana, salvia, and yarrow. Additionally, yarrow can be planted in a garden with xeric plants such as prickly pear cactus and Russian sage. Collect yarrow for cut and dried flowers.

Try These
'Paprika' is a rust-red variety that is quite vigorous. 'Moonshine' is a nonspreading, yellow-flowered plant with blue-gray foliage. 'Tutti-frutti Pineapple Mango' has a changing flower combination that ranges from pink to salmon to yellow. 'Summer Wine' is a burgundy flower the shade of red wine.

ROSES
FOR INDIANA

Roses are thrilling and can be an astoundingly showy part of your landscape design. When I was a kid I became thoroughly addicted to roses; I blame my Dad. My father was what we Midwesterners called "a yard man," and he and Mom spent a considerable amount of time in the garden every Saturday morning of summer, mowing and weeding and fussing over his roses. He had a small rose garden filled with only one variety of rose, 'Mister Lincoln', a very popular hybrid tea rose with deep red petals the texture of velvet. This rose was an experience to behold and was my first clear memory of the magic of being immersed in a plant. If you passed by at 20 feet on a warm summer's day, its powerful Damask rose scent would reach out and pull you in to the plant like an errant lover. I adored Dad's roses and remember the scent being only a part of the experience; I would touch the velvety petals and sit on the steps next to them so I could linger a bit longer and "feel" the rose. As an adult, I go out of my way to gaze at, touch, and smell any rose I can find.

Soil Preparation and Planting

Roses prefer full sun or mostly sun and need good air circulation to prevent fungus problems. Typically, more shade means more fungal issues and taller canes with less flower production. Roses prefer a soil mix rich in organic matter that drains well and does not leave their feet (roots) wet. Once planted, a rose stays in the same spot for many years, so proper soil preparation is very important. Here's how: Spade a rose bed at least 12 inches deep. Mix in one part organic matter to every two parts regular soil and be sure to add any amendments your soil is lacking based on the soil testing you have done. For a raised rose bed, mix one-half organic matter with one-quarter sand and one-quarter soil to help it retain moisture but still provide good drainage.

Planting a rose is a simple process. Select your site, making sure to space groundcovers, hybrid teas, and grandiflora roses at least 2 feet apart to maintain good air circulation. Other roses such as climbers, shrubs, floribundas, and old roses need more space, so plant them approximately 5 feet apart. If the plants are bare-root, unwrap and soak the roots in water for a couple of hours. Dig a planting hole 12 inches deep and 24 inches wide. Build a small soil mound in the center of the hole to support the roots, and then set the rose on top, draping the roots over the soil mound. Make sure the point where the canes join together, called the crown or bud union, is at ground level. Cover with soil. If the plants are container roses, do everything the same, except gently pull the rootball out of the container and tease the roots loose before planting.

Climbing roses can sometimes have challenging maintenance issues; however, this large climbing rose from the Canadian Explorer Series, 'William Baffin', is virtually maintenance free and thrives very well in the drought-tolerant garden behind my fence.

Watering, Feeding, and Double Layer Mulching

Midwestern growing conditions are fairly hot and dry most summers, which are not conducive to the successful growing of many rose varieties, so it is very important to understand your rose's watering requirements when selecting a site for a rose garden. Water requirements for a rose vary based on weather and humidity conditions; however, 1 inch of water per week is a good estimate. Water roses at the base of the plant by hand, a soaker hose, or drip irrigation system; avoid wetting the leaves as a wet leaf is usually a place fungal disease can develop. Fertilize with an organic rose food once in early spring, once in early summer, and once toward the end of summer.

Mulch is critical for roses to hold moisture at the root level for longer periods of time. While mulch decomposes into the soil, it improves the microbial activity, which is good for a rose's root system. Types of recommended mulch include shredded bark, mature wood chips, pine needles, compost, or leaf mold. Green or "hot" mulch, like new wood chips, for instance, can deplete nitrogen in the soil. By practicing double layering of mulch you can prevent green mulches from breaking down the nitrogen in the soil to help build a stronger plant. Layer 2 to 3 inches of rotted compost on the bottom, then top with a layer of mulch. By the spring of the next season, the top layer of mulch will have decomposed to become the new compost layer, so you only need to add new mulch in future years once you start the double-layering technique.

Rose Diseases and Pests

Roses can have many diseases and pests. But they can be controlled organically. Many pests can be sprayed off with a strong shot of water from the garden hose. In heavier infestations, mix your own insecticidal soap for use on aphids, whiteflies, and spider mites by mixing 2 cups of water with 1 tablespoon of regular dish soap or castile soap. Spray liberally on the invaders in the morning. Handpick Japanese beetles and place them in a bucket of soapy water. Japanese beetle traps attract more of the beetles to your garden, so for small infestations, it is simply better to pick off the offending critters rather than using a trap.

Blackspot, botrytis blight, and mildew are the most common fungal diseases present on roses. Most fungi can be controlled with an organic fungicide. Treat the fungus every two weeks until it recedes, being sure to pick dead leaves off the plant and any that remain on the ground. Do not compost these leaves; throw them away instead.

This 'Knock Out' shrub rose is mixed with nepeta to form a mass of color which looks beautiful together and also works to attract pollinators such as bees and butterflies in large quantities.

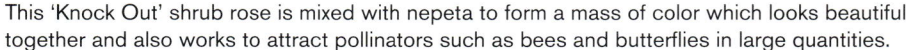

Pruning

Deadheading is the removal of spent flowers before they have time to form rose hips. As a general rule when deadheading, cut the stem just above a leaf with five leaflets. Deadhead regularly throughout the summer, and then stop deadheading in October in order to allow the plant to go into its winter sleep.

Pruning can be determined by rose type and flower blooming time. Generally speaking, spring is the best time to shape and prune roses. Once winter has passed and you see the canes begin to leaf out, trim back damaged or blackened canes, remove all weak or tiny canes, and clip off any suckers that are found at the base of the plant. If roses have been plagued by cane borers in your region, simply dab the cut with a little white glue to seal the cut end of the cane.

Winter Protection

Many hybrids and old roses are extremely hardy and do not need to be covered throughout the winter season. However, this is not true for all roses. Research each variety you plant to determine what type of winter protection is best. Depending upon the rose variety, a general practice of overwintering would include cutting the canes back to about 18 inches once roses lose their leaves in fall. Cover the bases of the plants with 12 inches of loose soil. Be sure this pile is well drained and will not soak heavily with water over the winter. Once the soil freezes hard, place as much mulch as you can over the soil, making a protective mound over the entire rose. In the spring you can spread out this organic matter as an added layer of mulch.

Many climbing roses require wrapping over winter. Remove climbers from supports, lay canes carefully down on the ground, top with 6 inches of loose soil, then another 6 to 8 inches of mulch. Alternatively, if you cannot lay the canes down, pack them with a thick layer of straw and wrap them in burlap. Unwrap in the early spring after the last of the heavy snows and below-zero temperatures.

They're Worth the Effort

Roses in the Midwest can be challenging because of our weather extremes and long winters. For most roses, the secret to success is preparing the soil well and discovering the right type of cultivar for your particular zone. Even with that, roses require considerable maintenance. If you discover the right variety for your garden, then you will have far more success. Roses are grouped into many different categories and classifications, but in this book we have listed only six: climbing, floribunda, grandiflora, groundcover, hybrid tea, and shrub—check them out to find right one for *your* garden. The rewards are great.

Climbing Rose

Rosa spp.

Botanical Pronunciation
ROZE-ah

Bloom Period and Seasonal Color
Late spring to early summer (sporadically in fall); red, white, pink, lavender, yellow, orange, and multicolor flowers

Mature Height × Spread
6 to 12 feet × 6 to 12 feet

Climbing roses have become my personal favorite rose to grow in the landscape due to their interesting architectural structure within the garden; climbing roses give the garden height, shape, and form. For years I struggled with climbing roses. They would look straggly instead of full, be smothered in blackspot and powdery mildew, and refused to be trained in the direction I wanted the plants to grow. In frustration, I dug up my climbing roses and threw them out into a native plant bed behind my fence and ignored them. We had consistent rain that season and the roses *flourished*. Within two years they became the stars of the neighborhood, growing into large rambling explosions of color every season. The secret: full sun, consistent water, and fertile, well-drained soil.

When, Where, and How to Plant

Plant the roses in rich, organic soil that is well drained in a full-sun location. Understanding the mature size and nature of a climbing rose's growth is important when planning the garden so that you give it plenty of room to grow. Plant in a rich, humusy soil with lots of natural items mixed in; rotted manure, compost, and worm castings make perfect soil amendments. Climbers produce more abundant flowers when structural rose canes grow horizontally rather than vertically. If you want to trellis the rose, be sure to select a trellis that will hold the rose's weight. Anchor the trellis on a wall, fence, or in the ground so the wind will not blow it over. Plant the rose, making sure the graft union is level with the ground. Using soft material, gently tie the canes evenly to the trellis as closely to a horizontal location as possible.

Growing Tips

Mulch the soil with a 2- to 3-inch layer of compost or organic matter. Although a climber does not like standing in water, it does like consistent medium moisture. It is better to water deeply once per week in order to build a stronger root system to help it survive the cold winter.

Regional Advice and Care

Treat powdery mildew, blackspot, and other fungal conditions with an organic fungicide. Prune out dead or diseased wood in late winter or early spring. Some climbing roses need winter protection; untie the canes, lay them on the ground, then mound soil over the canes.

Companion Planting and Design

Climbing roses look wonderful as an eye-catching vertical design solution. Place on fences, around doorways, on trellises, and at the back of a perennial bed for maximum impact.

Try These

'Fourth of July' has amazing red-and-white splotched flowers and climbs to 14 feet. Climbing roses such as 'William Baffin' and 'John Cabot', which belong to the Canadian Explorer Series, do not need winter protection and flower profusely all spring. 'Viking Queen' is a gorgeous pale pink, fragrant rose.

Floribunda Rose

Rosa spp.

Botanical Pronunciation
ROZE-ah

Bloom Period and Seasonal Color
Summer (sporadically through fall); red, white, pink, lavender, yellow, orange, and multicolor flowers

Mature Height × Spread
3 to 5 feet × 2 to 3 feet

Floribunda roses are known for their fragrant flowers that are abundantly grouped on single stems. It's a contemporary group of perennial hybridized garden roses that was created by crossing hybrid teas with polyantha roses. One branch of a floribunda has flowers that bloom smaller and in a shapelier manner than that of the hybrid tea roses, and the sprays of bloom easily resemble an extravagant bouquet of flowers. Floribunda roses are typically medium-sized bushy shrubs, which make them ideal for urban situations as they can easily be planted as low hedge bushes, flowering mass plantings, or as features in the perennial border. Many floribunda varieties flower from summer through fall, are quite tough, and come in an astounding selection of colors.

When, Where, and How to Plant

Plant these roses in fall or spring in a site that has rich, organic soil that is well drained. Amend soil with rotted manure, compost, and worm castings, or plant in raised beds if there is a lack of drainage. Floribunda roses do best in full sun. Understanding the mature size and nature of its growth is important when planning the garden so that you will not crowd the rose. Soak quite deeply after planting, watering several times a week after initial placement.

Growing Tips

Floribundas can wilt in hot or dry weather. Consistent watering at the base of the plant is very important. Keep the water off the foliage since that can encourage fungal issues. Mulch the soil with a 2- to 3-inch layer of compost or organic matter. Fertilize with organic rose fertilizer at planting time and in the spring or fall. Heavy fertilization is not necessary if the garden bed has been prepared properly and offers a nutrient-rich organic base.

Regional Advice and Care

Deadhead flowers for more consistent bloom. Treat powdery mildew, blackspot, and other fungal conditions with an organic fungicide. Prune out dead or diseased wood in late winter or early spring. Highly alkaline soils can sometimes encourage chlorosis, a condition in which the leaves yellow. This can be treated with an application of chelated iron. Test soils to determine your individual garden's needs.

Companion Planting and Design

Low-growing alyssum, lantana, nepeta and hardy geranium make attractive underplanting groundcovers for roses. Floribundas look particularly beautiful when planted *en masse*.

Try These

'Chuckles Rose' is one of the hardiest roses with pink single flowers and a white eye. 'Scentimental' is a disease-resistant, burgundy-and-white splotched rose with a spicy scent. 'Betty Boop' has interesting yellow or white blooms that are edged with a fine line of lipstick red. 'Easy Going' is a bright yellow rose with strong disease resistance. 'Sheila's Perfume' has a gorgeous pale yellow interior that fades to a burgundy red edge and has a sweet fragrance.

Grandiflora Rose

Rosa spp.

Botanical Pronunciation
ROZE-ah

Bloom Period and Seasonal Color
Summer; red, white, pink, lavender, yellow, orange, and multicolor flowers

Mature Height × Spread
3 to 6 feet × 2 to 3 feet

Grandifloras are the result of a cross between a floribunda and a hybrid tea, creating a flower that looks very much like that of a hybrid tea, yet they reside on flowering clusters. Plants tend to be rather tall and bushy, usually up to 6 feet, and therefore make extraordinary hedges exploding with flowers. Grandifloras tend to be hardier than hybrid teas and can be good tools in the landscape by hiding unsightly air conditioning equipment, cable boxes, and other utilitarian features on your property. Overall, they are not as fussy as some of the more demanding varieties of roses and bloom throughout the season. Grandifloras are highly valued for their longer stems for cut flowers, which can be rather spectacular in a vase or bouquet.

When, Where, and How to Plant

Plant these roses in fall or spring in a site that has rich, organic soil that is well drained. Grandifloras need to be planted to their appropriate depth or they will not overwinter. Amend soil with rotted manure, compost, and worm castings to improve the soil or raised beds if there is a lack of drainage. Grandifloras will tolerate some shade but much prefer full sun. Understanding the mature size and nature of its growth is important when planning the garden so that you will not crowd the rose.

Growing Tips

Soak quite deeply after planting, watering several times a week after initial placement. Mulch the soil with a 2- to 3-inch layer of compost or organic matter. Fertilize with organic rose fertilizer at planting time and in spring or fall.

Regional Advice and Care

Deadhead flowers by cutting the flower to the first five-leaflet leaf. Promote taller growth by cutting higher. For a shorter bush, cut down to the second five-leaflet leaf on a stem. It is best to wait until after the first year's growth to prune back vigorously. Keep water off the rose's foliage as wet leaves can encourage fungal issues. Treat powdery mildew, blackspot, and other fungal conditions with an organic fungicide. Prune out dead or diseased wood in late winter or early spring. Highly alkaline soils can sometimes encourage chlorosis, a condition in which the leaves yellow; treat with an application of chelated iron. Test soils to determine your individual garden's needs.

Companion Planting and Design

Grandifloras are most typically used as a large, back of the border rose hedge. They function well to hide unsightly equipment and views within the landscape; in other words, they make a good privacy screen.

Try These

'Earth Song' grows 5 feet tall and is a particularly sturdy pink variety. 'Queen Elizabeth' is an award-winning grandiflora. 'Crimson Bouquet' is a bold crimson red growing only 4 feet high. 'Radiant Perfume' is a bright yellow with a powerful citrus fragrance that grows to 5 feet.

Groundcover Rose

Rosa hybrids

Botanical Pronunciation
ROZE-ah

Bloom Period and Seasonal Color
Summer; red, white, pink, lavender, yellow, orange, and multicolor flowers

Mature Height × Spread
1½ to 3 feet × 2 to 4 feet

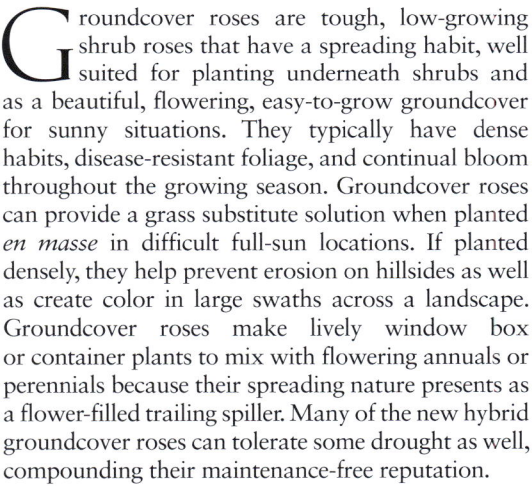

Groundcover roses are tough, low-growing shrub roses that have a spreading habit, well suited for planting underneath shrubs and as a beautiful, flowering, easy-to-grow groundcover for sunny situations. They typically have dense habits, disease-resistant foliage, and continual bloom throughout the growing season. Groundcover roses can provide a grass substitute solution when planted *en masse* in difficult full-sun locations. If planted densely, they help prevent erosion on hillsides as well as create color in large swaths across a landscape. Groundcover roses make lively window box or container plants to mix with flowering annuals or perennials because their spreading nature presents as a flower-filled trailing spiller. Many of the new hybrid groundcover roses can tolerate some drought as well, compounding their maintenance-free reputation.

When, Where, and How to Plant

Plant container or bare-root plants in fall or spring in a site that has rich, organic, well-drained soil. Amend soil with rotted manure, compost, and worm castings to improve the soil or plant in a raised bed if the soil lacks drainage. Groundcover roses will tolerate some shade but prefer six hours or more of full sun.

Growing Tips

Water a groundcover rose well upon planting and frequently throughout its first year to establish the plant. Mulch the soil with a 2- to 3-inch layer of compost or organic matter. Fertilize with organic rose fertilizer at planting time and in spring or fall.

Regional Advice and Care

While it is not necessary to deadhead most groundcover roses, it will improve the tidiness of the plant. Rake debris and old leaves out of the planting in early spring. Cut the plants back by two-thirds annually in early spring in order to refresh and invigorate the plant. Keep water off the foliage as that can encourage fungal issues. Treat powdery mildew, blackspot, and other fungal conditions with an organic fungicide. Prune out dead or diseased wood throughout the season as necessary.

Companion Planting and Design

Groundcover roses can be quite charming, but they can also be used for useful purposes such as planting in rocky areas or steep banks. They're perfect as a filler in the perennial border but also function quite nicely as an edging plants for paths and driveways. Groundcover roses look quite elegant when planted as a border around a patio.

Try These

'Popcorn Drift®' is a yellow variety that fades to white, resembling buttered popcorn with 1½-inch flowers. 'Oso Easy® Fragrant Spreader Rose' is a fragrant pink rose with a hardy nature. 'Flower Carpet® White' is a bright white variety with prolific flowers, extreme vigor, and some drought tolerancy. 'Fire Meidiland' is a red, vigorous variety growing to 24 inches tall. Oso Easy® Mango Salsa Rose requires no pruning, has attractive shades of red and mango flowers, and grows 2 to 3 feet tall.

Hybrid Tea Rose

Rosa spp.

Botanical Pronunciation
ROZE-ah

Bloom Period and Seasonal Color
Summer; red, white, pink, lavender, yellow, orange, and multicolor flowers

Mature Height × Spread
4 to 6 feet × 3 to 5 feet

Florists the world over treasure hybrid tea roses as the most popular retail gift of cut flowers. Hybrid tea roses are the classic description of what most people imagine when they think of a rose: tall, single-stemmed, fragrant, large-flowered, and colorful. Captivating attention-getters, hybrid teas flower most of the season and are totally glorious as cut flowers in vases and bouquets. While stunningly beautiful, the hybrid tea is often more challenging to maintain and can be rife with maintenance issues. The clear rewards with the hybrid tea are the gorgeous flowers, which come in a rainbow of colors and sizes. Blooms on the hybrid teas can be huge; the variety 'Parole' was once measured as having 8-inch flowers. Fragrance varies from old-world scents to lighter, more modern fragrances.

When, Where, and How to Plant
Find hybrid teas as bare-root stock or in containers at local garden centers, online, and through mail order. Plant the roses in spring in a full-sun site that has rich, organic, well-drained soil. Amend soil with rotted manure, compost, and worm castings to improve it or raise beds if there is a lack of drainage. Understanding the mature size and nature of a hybrid tea rose's growth is important when planning the garden so that you will not crowd the bush. Take note: Hybrid teas can be demanding. They need a regular regimen of fertilizing, watering, and maintenance.

Growing Tips
Soak quite deeply after planting, watering several times a week after initial placement. Fertilize organically at planting and once per month during the summer growing season. Mulch the soil with a 2- to 3-inch layer of compost or organic matter.

Regional Advice and Care
Deadhead flowers by cutting the stem back to the first five-leaflet leaf. Deadhead regularly during the growing season to encourage continued bloom. Do not prune a first-year plant except to remove dead canes. Thereafter, prune at least 70 percent of the plant back to the crown during fall, mulching heavily for winter protection or covering the rose with a cone. Keep water off the foliage. Treat powdery mildew, blackspot, and other fungal conditions with an organic fungicide. Handpick caterpillars and treat aphids using a spray of a soapy water solution.

Companion Planting and Design
Hybrid teas can be attractive in borders, cutting gardens, and perennial beds with other hybrid teas. Underplantings of low-growing nepeta and lamb's ears are appealing.

Try These
'Parole' is a cerise pink flower sometimes known as 'Buxom Beauty'. It can have 8-inch blooms and has astounding old-world rose fragrance. 'Mister Lincoln' has a powerful scent that can be smelled from 10 feet away and velvety red flowers. 'Peace', also known as 'Madame A. Meilland', is a remarkable light yellow rose that was named 'Peace' on the very day that World War II ended on April 29, 1945.

Shrub Rose

Rosa spp.

Botanical Pronunciation
ROZE-ah

Bloom Period and Seasonal Color
Summer; red, white, pink, yellow, orange,
and multicolor flowers

Mature Height × Spread
4 to 12 feet × 4 to 6 feet

Shrub roses are breathtaking rose bushes that come in all shapes and sizes. "Shrub rose" is often a description that is used to describe roses that generally do not fit into any standard rose classification. Many shrub roses are exciting because they have a natural disease resistance and capture the greatest traits of the hardiest rose varieties, and then mingle those qualities with modern, continuous blooming bushes that offer assorted fragrance, color, and flower forms. The 'Knock Out®' series, for instance, are shrub roses that have become the quintessential flowering landscape shrub because of its nonstop bloom and low maintenance needs. Like grandiflora roses, shrub roses can be good functional tools in the landscape, hiding unsightly utility issues on a property while delivering uninterrupted flowering all season.

When, Where, and How to Plant
Plant shrub roses in fall or spring on a site that has rich, organic, well-drained soil. Amend soil with rotted manure, compost, and worm castings to improve it or plant in raised beds if there is a lack of drainage. Some varieties of shrub roses will tolerate a bit of shade, but they prefer full sun. Understanding the mature size and nature of its growth is important when planning the garden so that you will not crowd this rose.

Growing Tips
Soak quite deeply after planting, watering several times a week after initial planting. Mulch the soil with a 2- to 3-inch layer of compost or organic matter. Fertilize with organic rose fertilizer at planting time and in spring or fall.

Regional Advice and Care
Maintenance issues with shrub roses are primarily related to pruning. Wait until after the first year's growth to prune back vigorously as it will take longer to recover. Cut dead canes out of the plant in spring. After the second or third year's growth, prune the plant back with hedge trimmer by one-third or as much as one-half in early spring to reinvigorate growth. Shrub roses are hybridized for disease resistance, so they have very few pest or disease problems. Handpick any Japanese beetles or caterpillars.

Companion Planting and Design
Shrub roses look magnificent planted *en masse* in large landscape designs. Mix them in with annuals, perennials, and other shrubs in garden beds and mixed borders. Create colorful hedges with them or feature one rose as a centerpiece in an island garden. Because of their nonstop color, planting shrub roses in color-themed gardens will help reinforce a specific flower color theme.

Try These
'Calypso' is an apricot pink flowering low hedge rose reaching 24 inches tall. 'Sunny Knock Out®' has dark green foliage and a cheerful yellow rose that fades to a pale cream color; it requires virtually no maintenance. 'Rainbow Knock Out®' has amazing coral blooms and grows to 4 feet tall. 'Constance Spry' is a very large, classic English rose with a tough constitution and attractive fragrance.

SHRUBS
FOR INDIANA

Strategic use of shrubs can enhance landscaping tremendously. There are many reasons to plant shrubs: they help emphasize a property boundary, hide air conditioners and garbage bins, provide a windbreak, accent homes and buildings, and can provide gorgeous flowering color and scent to highlight a landscape design. Consider planting shrubs that return something to the environment by providing food for pollinators and native wildlife.

Measuring Twice Prevents Cutting Once

One of the biggest mistakes homeowners and landscape designers make is to miscalculate a shrub's growth and climatic needs. Before purchasing a shrub, be sure to understand the shrub's long-term growth and care requirements. Measure the space where you want to plant it to understand how big the plant is *really* going to get. An easy way to do this is tape together newspaper to represent the width of a shrub. Simply move the newspaper pattern around the landscape, positioning it where you might plant the shrub for a better idea of how much space that full-grown plant is going to take up. Give it a lot of elbow room because overcrowding shrubs can lead to disease and pest problems. Measuring twice to make sure you have the right spot is important, because if you measure wrong you will be cutting the bush or shrub out in years to come if it has overgrown the spot you selected.

To get a complete idea of where a shrub can be grown, draw a plan of your garden, showing the major trees, buildings, and the entrance to your home. Mark an area in front of your home where shrubs and trees would block the entrance. Then carefully mark things you might like to hide, such as a view of trash bins, a telephone pole, a parking lot, a compost heap, or an unattractive building. Consider what bush or shrub might help you hide these particular issues. Then think about how you might plant shrubs as a windbreak or to soak up water in a boggy area. With these things in mind as a starting point, make a plan that will frame your landscapes with the proper shrubs selected for their growing needs.

Planting Shrubs

Planting shrubs where the plants will not be blocked by the eaves or utility lines is important. Double-check this by raising your shovel in a vertical fashion directly

Shrubs serve many purposes, from snow protection to feeding birds. Smoketree can be particularly gorgeous and is a wonderful large shrub feature in the front urban landscape of this Victorian home.

above the planting hole. If you see something overhead that is going to block the water, move the site to a better location. If you don't have gutters on your home, be aware that shrubs planted under the eaves of a gutterless house will get an excess amount of water during a rain storm.

Typically, prepare the soil based on your soil testing. Dig a hole that is two to three times the width of the container or rootball. Loosen roots if they're tight, and then gently place the plant in the hole and backfill. Water well and mulch immediately. Fertilize organically in the spring and fall to help keep growth strong, pruning as necessary.

Shrubs can offer waves of color and beauty throughout the entire growing season but are also useful plants that, if used properly, can offer a sustainable solution to help you use less water, encourage pollinators, and plant wisely for a better effect in the environment.

Arborvitae

Thuja occidentalis

Botanical Pronunciation
THOO-yuh ock-sih-den-TAY-liss

Other Name
Eastern white cedar

Bloom Period and Seasonal Color
Evergreen foliage

Mature Height × Spread
20 feet × 6 feet

With a tall, narrow growth habit, arborvitae is an evergreen coniferous shrub with scalelike leaves that is well loved as a hedge shrub. Because the shrub is a long-lasting plant, sometimes living decades, it is a long-term commitment to place an arborvitae in your landscape, and considerations should be made for its growth into maturity. To make a hedge seem full and more attractive during growth while giving it plenty of elbow room, consider planting a double row of shrubs with every other arborvitae being placed in an offset manner. If you prefer a perfectly straight line, try planting filler plants such as perennials or short-lived shrubs in between the arborvitae, giving plenty of space for future growth. Overcrowding an arborvitae during its growth leads to disease and dieback.

When, Where, and How to Plant

Arborvitae shrubs should be purchased from local growers and should have been planted in local soil to help guarantee growing success. Dig a hole the same depth of the rootball but at least three times as broad. Most soil needs no amending; however, if you have particularly destitute soil, consider adding a light amount of compost. Plants that are balled and burlapped should have as much of the burlap and wire basket removed as possible. Backfill around the rootball until it is about half filled. Water the rootball and backfill well. Place the rest of the soil around the rootball, forming a "well" at the base of the plant, which will help collect and hold water.

Growing Tips

Mulch the soil with a 2- to 3-inch layer of compost or organic matter, keeping it at least 2 inches from the shrub's trunk. Arborvitae like moist soils, therefore water several inches per week the first season. Let the soil dry out between waterings. Fertilize with an organic fertilizer before new growth occurs in spring.

Regional Advice and Care

Shear or prune anytime after the new growth has developed in early summer. Maintenance issues include mites, which can be treated with soapy water. Bagworms can be treated with *Bacillus thuringiensis*. Arborvitae is prone to some fungal issues, particularly when overcrowded. Although deer often browse *Thuja occidentalis*, and it is made into herbal medicinal treatments, it is considered toxic and can cause stomach upset and skin irritation.

Companion Planting and Design

Arborvitae make excellent winter windbreak shrubs. Planting the tall shrubs as a windbreak can help keep your heating bills lower, act as a fence, improve crop yields, attract birds and other native wildlife, and help control soil erosion.

Try These

'Emerald' grows 10 to 15 feet tall and is very cold hardy. 'Nigra' grows up to 30 feet tall, maintains vivid color in winter, and is very cold hardy. 'Wintergreen' grows between 20 to 30 feet tall. 'Little Gem' is a dwarf variety, only growing 3 feet tall and 6 feet wide.

Barberry

Berberis spp.

Botanical Pronunciation
BUR-bur-iss

Other Name
European barberry

Bloom Period and Seasonal Color
Fall; yellow, golden, burgundy, purple, and red foliage

Mature Height × Spread
1½ to 6 feet × 1½ to 12 feet

Barberry is a vivid, multihued shrub, found in shades that range from golden to burgundy, that keep their colorful foliage year-round. They have red berries and often have thorny barbs that act as a protection for birds that like to eat the berries and hide in safety below their prickly branches. Barberry prefers dry conditions, can tolerate part-shade, and has a superb mounding habit; this makes it an excellent solution for difficult locations. I have a little barberry that grows beneath my home's overhang, gets no direct sunshine, very little consistent water, and it has flourished for years, offering a brightly colored solution in a trouble-filled location. Certain varieties of Japanese barberry have been declared severely invasive; check local restrictions and research the appropriate cultivar before planting.

When, Where, and How to Plant
Barberry shrubs have a higher success rate if purchased from local growers that have been planted in local soil. Dig a hole in a well-drained planting area, the same depth of the rootball but 2 times as wide. Scratch the sides of the hole with a spade so the roots can break through the soil more easily. If the shrubs roots are container-bound, be sure to use a sharp knife to slice through the roots on each side of the rootball to encourage growth. Plant the top of the rootball so it is level with the ground. Backfill around the rootball until the hole is about half filled. Water the rootball and backfill well. Place the rest of the soil around the rootball, forming a "well" at the base of the plant, which will help collect and hold water.

Growing Tips
Mulch the soil with a 2- to 3-inch layer of compost or organic matter, being cautious not to smother the shrub's trunk. Barberry shrubs need about an inch of water per week upon initial planting but very little attention thereafter. Fertilize with an organic fertilizer before new growth occurs in spring only if the plant shows signs of undernourishment.

Regional Advice and Care
Shear or prune anytime after the new growth has developed in early summer. Shrubs that are over-crowded or planted in shadier, wet conditions are vulnerable to fungal problems. Keep water off the foliage and treat powdery mildew, black-spot, and other fungal conditions with an organic fungicide.

Companion Planting and Design
Colorful shrubs like barberry are an excellent choice as a feature plant, a shrubby groundcover, as well as a lovely low hedge that helps support a birding landscape.

Try These
'Sunjoy® Mini Salsa' is a tiny dwarf variety growing 18 to 24 inches that can be used in containers as well as the landscape. 'Sunjoy™ Gold Pillar' has a vertical habit, grows to 3 feet, and has golden yellow leaves that turn orange-red in fall. 'Atropurpurea Nana' is deep red throughout the season.

Black Chokeberry

Aronia melanocarpa

Botanical Pronunciation
ar-ROH-nee-uh mel-an-oh-KAR-puh

Bloom Period and Seasonal Color
Deciduous green foliage

Mature Height × Spread
3 to 6 feet × 3 to 6 feet

Grow black chokeberry for the birds; it is a native to North America and has attractive green deciduous leaves with black berries. Black chokeberry is particularly suitable for urban planting as it tolerates pollution well and can be planted with success in virtually any native soil. It is wonderful in naturalized settings and offers year-round interest for wildlife and habitat gardens. Sour, edible black berries borne in fall can be used to make jams and jellies. Black chokeberry is not to be confused with the invasive wetland shrub *Aronia arbutifolia*. While this shrub likes wet conditions and works well in low-lying areas, it will also acclimatize to drought, making black chokeberry a significantly versatile shrub that can be used to solve difficult soil conditions.

When, Where, and How to Plant

Black chokeberry is highly adaptive but prefers moist loamy or sandy soils with good drainage and full sun exposure. Plant the shrub in spring. Dig a hole in a well-drained planting area, the same depth of the rootball but twice as wide. If the shrub's roots are container-bound, be sure to use a sharp knife to slice through the roots on each size of the rootball to encourage growth. Plant so the top of the rootball is level with the ground. Backfill around the rootball until the hole is about half filled. Water, and backfill well. Place the rest of the soil around the rootball, forming a "well" at the base of the plant, which will help collect and hold water.

Growing Tips

Mulch the soil with a 2- to 3-inch layer of compost or organic matter. Keep soil moist. Only fertilize with an organic fertilizer before new growth occurs in spring if the plant shows signs of undernourishment.

Regional Advice and Care

Prune plants at any time. Maintenance includes spading any sucker roots that grow if you want to keep the bush relatively contained. If you want a more naturalized planting, let the suckers expand the shrubs into a mass. Shrubs that are overcrowded or planted in shadier, wet conditions are vulnerable to fungal problems. Keep water off the foliage and treat powdery mildew, blackspot, and other fungal conditions with an organic fungicide.

Companion Planting and Design

Black chokeberry is a great solution near rain gardens or ponds because of its love for moist soils. This shrub works well for mass plantings, but some varieties grow leggy and open, so it's not the best option for hedge rows.

Try These

'Iroquois Beauty™' has a more compact habit at 3 to 4 feet tall; it tolerates part shade; has airy, white flowers; and beautiful fall color. 'Elata' is taller at 4 to 6 feet and wide and large fruit. 'Autumn Magic' displays bold, red glossy leaves in fall and grows 4 to 6 feet.

Boxwood

Buxus spp.

Botanical Pronunciation
BUCKS-us

Other Name
European barberry

Bloom Period and Seasonal Color
Evergreen foliage

Mature Height × Spread
2½ to 4 feet × 2½ to 4 feet

Boxwood is an evergreen shrub with leathery leaves that can be mounded or tall and is relatively slow growing. There are about seventy species of *Buxus* and most of them can be sheared and clipped into creative forms. Used for topiary, container plantings, and hedge rows, boxwood has the advantage of remaining evergreen most of the year. Part sun can be advantageous for the plant as it sometimes suffers leaf burn from direct sun and cold winds in winter. Not all boxwood varieties are hardy in the northern part of the state, but new hybridization has brought a larger and hardier selection of varieties to the regional gardener. Boxwoods can be a used in a utilitarian fashion to hide air conditioning and cable boxes in the urban landscape.

When, Where, and How to Plant
Plant this shrub in fall or spring on a sheltered site that has rich, organic soil that is well drained and is protected from severe winds. Amend soil with rotted manure, compost, and worm castings to improve soil or plant in raised beds if there is a lack of drainage. Boxwood will tolerate a bit of shade to protect it from sunburn, but it also enjoys full sun. Planning is important when growing boxwood because the shape a boxwood takes on in the garden can determine its future health. Understanding the mature size and nature of its growth is important so that you will not crowd the shrub.

Growing Tips
Mulch with a 2- to 3-inch layer of compost, leaf mulch, or organic matter, keeping it at least 2 inches from the shrub's trunk. Soak quite deeply after planting, watering several times a week after initial planting. Let the soil dry out between waterings. Fertilize with an organic fertilizer before new growth occurs in spring.

Regional Advice and Care
Using pruners or shears, shape in early spring and once again in late June. Watch for random branch growth and trim as necessary. Do not trim in fall as newly cut branches can sometimes suffer winter damage. Boxwood is likely to have a leaf-filled exterior and an interior that is more sticklike. It will look more attractive if creatively pruned to allow light to penetrate in order to grow more foliage in the interior of the shrub. Boxwood can suffer root rot in wet conditions.

Companion Planting and Design
Used in formal gardens, boxwood can be sculpted into box-edging, topiary gardens, and knot gardens. Known as a hedge plant, boxwoods can bring whimsy and interest to gardens. New variegated leaf varieties look great in containers.

Try These
'Chicagoland Green™' grows 3 to 4 feet tall and wide and has shown strong winter hardiness. 'Green Gem' is globe-shaped and small at 2 ½ feet tall. 'Wedding Ring™' has an interesting variegated leaf (see photo). 'Northern Beauty' is a hardy English boxwood that grows 5 feet tall.

Burning Bush

Euonymus alatus

Botanical Pronunciation
you-ON-ih-mus eh-LAY-tus

Other Name
Winged spindle tree

Bloom Period and Seasonal Color
Spring; deciduous green foliage; bright red fall leaves

Mature Height × Spread
6 to 20 feet × 6 to 20 feet

Bold red fall leaf color is why the burning bush is so popular in the Midwest. It can be seen dotting urban landscapes throughout our region. However, in some areas it can be quite invasive, spreading vegetatively and via seed. It is important that you research your location to see if it has been declared severely invasive; check local restrictions before planting. Many homeowners think the plant is attractive in the garden center, yet are very surprised at the large size it can achieve after planting. Even the most compact burning bush can grow to over 6 feet. Many suburban homeowners try to make the plant conform to their small gardens by shearing it into unattractive shapes, but it is preferable in its natural form.

When, Where, and How to Plant

Burning bush prefers full sun in order for its fall color to develop the brightest red, but it will grow in shade with some color fade. It is tolerant of almost any soil with good drainage, and they do very well in hot and dry locations. Fertile soil makes the plant grow quite large; several varieties of burning bush shrubs grow up to 20 feet tall. When planting, dig a hole that is equal to the height of the rootball and twice as wide.

Growing Tips

Mulch the soil with a 2- to 3-inch layer of compost or organic matter. Only fertilize with an organic fertilizer before new growth occurs in the spring if the plant shows signs of undernourishment.

Regional Advice and Care

Prune plants anytime to control shape and size. Shrubs that are overcrowded or planted in shadier wet areas are vulnerable to fungal problems such as powdery mildew, fungal leaf spot, and other conditions. Plants spread by seed; birds eat the plant's berries and then excrete the seeds, causing shrubs to grow in woodlands, fields, ditches, and other unwanted locations. Seed can also drop directly below the plant and cause "seed shadows" or large patches of infant seeds that will need to be dug out. Shearing the plant before seeds develop in spring might delay or prevent seed production for that season, thereby slowing its spread.

Companion Planting and Design

This shrub looks good along foundations, fence lines, and as a fall hedge. Shorter varieties are attractive at the back of a perennial border with other shrubs as a balance. Do not plant near woodlands as the bush forms colonies that are difficult to remove. If you live in a region where burning bush is a problem, consider substituting burning bush with a different shrub that is less invasive. Consider the American cranberrybush viburnum, black chokeberry, fothergilla, or ninebark.

Try These

'Compactus' is a dwarf burning bush variety growing 6 to 8 feet high with corky wings that hold winter snow. 'Rudy Haag' grows 3 to 5 feet high.

Butterfly Bush

Buddleia davidii

Botanical Pronunciation
BUD-lee-uh duh-VID-ee-eye

Bloom Period and Seasonal Color
Summer; purple, white, pink, and red blooms;
deciduous gray-green foliage

Mature Height × Spread
30 inches to 12 feet × 2 to 12 feet

Visitors to your garden will be astounded when they come upon a butterfly bush in full bloom; it is a sight to behold, with butterflies dancing around its long arching branches and flowering panicles. An absolute essential in a butterfly or pollinator garden, this deciduous, multibranching shrub can be a long-lived plant with a life of fifteen to twenty years. Most typically, in Midwestern gardens, it only lives to be five to seven years old because of its environmental sensitivity. A butterfly bush needs direct, full sun and can suffer in shady locations or when exposed to extreme weather conditions such as drought and winter cold. Even so, the shrub's flowers can be a stunning part of the landscape if it has the consistent care it needs.

When, Where, and How to Plant
Butterfly bush needs a fertile, well-drained soil with full sun exposure. Amend soil with organic matter to improve it or employ raised beds if soil lacks drainage. Plant butterfly bush in spring by digging a hole in a well-drained planting area that is the same depth of the rootball and twice as wide. Plant at a depth so the top of the rootball is level with the ground.

Growing Tips
Water the shrub heavily upon initial planting and when it is in active growth, but water sparingly at other times of the season. Mulch the soil with a 3-inch layer of organic matter to help it hold water and protect it from winter cold. Only fertilize with an organic fertilizer before new growth occurs in spring if the plant shows signs of undernourishment. Overfertilization causes an increased growth in foliage with decreased flower development.

Regional Advice and Care
Deadhead flowers regularly to keep the plant attractive and neat. Flowers only bloom on new wood, therefore, prune back old growth and die-back to 12 inches above the ground in early spring before the new growth begins to emerge. Shrubs that are overcrowded or planted in shadier, wet conditions are vulnerable to fungal problems. Keep water off the foliage and treat fungal conditions with an organic fungicide. Mulch in winter to prevent total dieback.

Companion Planting and Design
Tall butterfly bush offers an interesting architectural feature for the back of landscapes. Low-growing varieties are wonderful near the front of a perennial border or garden walkways and encourage butterflies to dance around visitors' heads as they walk through the garden.

Try These
'Royal Red' grows to 12 feet tall and features bright red flowers. 'Summer Beauty' is a hardy pink variety that reaches 5 feet. 'Black Knight' has a deep purple flower and grows between 6 to 8 feet tall. 'Lo & Behold® Blue Chip' is a newer *Buddleia* hybrid that only grows to 30 inches high. 'Peacock™' is 4 to 5 feet tall and bushy, with bold pink flowers that also attract hummingbirds.

Cotoneaster

Cotoneaster spp.

Botanical Pronunciation
kuh-toe-nee-ASS-tur

Other Name
Chinese bearberry

Bloom Period and Seasonal Color
Spring; white and pink flowers

Mature Height × Spread
3 to 12 feet × 5 to 15 feet

Wonderful as a bird-garden shrub, cotoneaster has glossy, attractive foliage and bright red berries in autumn that persist through winter. Birds love both the berries and the foliage, which can often be dense and allows the birds a hiding place from predators. There are tall hedge shrubs or short spreading varieties, most of which flower in spring. Many of my favorite cotoneasters are the low to the ground type. For example, cranberry cotoneaster, *Cotoneaster apiculatus*, is a wide, mounding deciduous shrub with branches that are stiffly arching. It is most effectively used on hillsides or draping luxuriantly over low barriers and patio edges. From a design perspective, this unique shrub can be a tool that offers a softer transitional footstep from a hardscape to the landscape.

When, Where, and How to Plant

Cotoneaster shrubs prefer a moist, well-drained soil but are known to tolerate adverse conditions. Once planted, the shrubs do not like to be moved; therefore, make sure you have the permanent site in mind when you place the shrub. Some cotoneasters do not tolerate northern winters; research your purchase so that it will do well in your garden zone. This shrub prefers sun to part sun and a well-drained soil. Dig a hole the same depth of the rootball but twice as wide. If the shrub's roots are container-bound, use a sharp knife to slice through the roots on each side of the rootball to stimulate growth. Plant the top of the rootball so that is level with the ground. Backfill until the planting hole is about half filled. Water the rootball and backfill again.

Growing Tips

Mulch the soil with a 2- to 3-inch layer of compost or organic matter, being cautious not to smother the shrub's trunk. Fertilize with an organic fertilizer before new growth occurs in the spring only if the plant shows signs of undernourishment.

Regional Advice and Care

Prune to remove dieback. Control insects and mites with insecticidal soap. Fireblight is a bacterium that attacks cotoneaster and can kill the shrub rather quickly. Symptoms include flower blackening and wilt as well as branch browning and dieback. Treatment includes spraying with an EPA-recommended antibiotic treatment and pruning affected branches in dormancy. Be sure to sterilize pruning equipment with bleach as the bacteria are very contagious.

Companion Planting and Design

With berries that attract birds, attractive fall color, and the ability to absorb air pollution and handle environmental salt without being damaged, cotoneaster a great option for groundcovers and hedges in urban areas as well as country gardens.

Try These

Cranberry cotoneaster, *Cotoneaster apiculatus*, is a spreading groundcover that grows to 3 feet high. *C. lucidus* gets to be 6 to 10 feet high. *C. multiflorus* grows 12 to 15 feet high with more abundant blooms in spring.

Dappled Willow

Salix integra

Botanical Pronunciation
SAY-licks en-TAG-gruh

Bloom Period and Seasonal Color
Evergreen foliage

Mature Height × Spread
20 feet × 6 feet

Dappled willow is classified among the deciduous "basket willows" and can be grown in a small standard tree form but is most popular as a large shrub with arching branches that easily reach 20 feet high and wide. While most of the tree willows have extensive root systems, the dappled willow's roots can be large, but they do not compare to that of the willow tree. This shrub makes a splendid choice for suburban and urban communities because it is an easy answer for a wet area; dappled willows love damp soils and grow effusively when placed in full sun with moist conditions. When I first saw the dappled willow I was captivated by its beautiful foliage, which has an eye-catching mix of green, white, and pink on every leaf.

When, Where, and How to Plant

Partial to rich, loamy, wet soil that rarely dries out, dappled willow does best in sun to part-sun conditions. Plant the shrub either in spring or fall when conditions are wetter. Loosen the soil by digging a hole two times wider than the diameter of the planting container and mixing in organic soil amendments such as rotted manure, compost, or worm castings to enhance the soil's water retention where needed. Dappled willows need a lot of water and are well placed beneath water downspouts or near ponds and streams where they can tap into a consistent supply of water. They do not like to be swimming in pond water; simply keep the soil moist but not soggy.

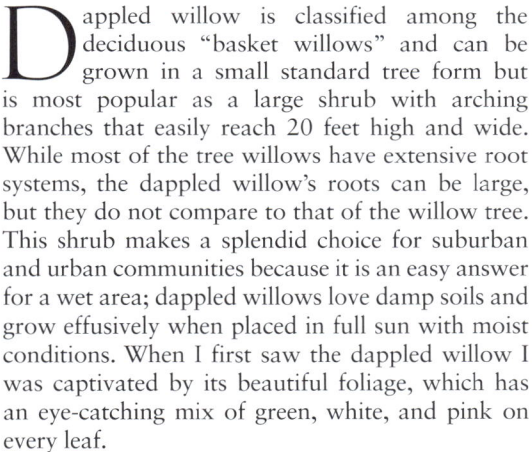

Growing Tips

Mulch the soil with a 3-inch layer of compost or organic leaf matter, keeping it at least 2 inches from the shrub's trunk. Because dappled willow likes moist soils, it needs consistent water to get established in its first year. Water the shrub several inches per week. Fertilize with an organic fertilizer before new growth occurs in spring.

Regional Advice and Care

Dappled willow looks beautiful in its natural arching form and does not need to be pruned beyond extracting any dead wood in late winter. However, if the plant grows out of bounds, prune to shape the shrub and stimulate new growth. Foliage colors are brighter on new wood, so some gardeners choose to shear the plant several times per season. If foliage browns and becomes crisp, it is most likely that the plant is not receiving enough water.

Companion Planting and Design

Dappled willow has four-season interest with yellowish catkins in the spring and red stems in the winter. Because of its size and four-season interest, this shrub makes a dazzling specimen plant and will be the center of attention in any landscape.

Try These

'Hakuro-nishiki' is the most common variety found, with variegated white, pink, and green leaves. It grows over 15 feet high. 'Flamingo' is a significantly improved mutation of 'Hakuro-nishiki' with no leaf scorch, stronger branches, and leaf colors that are considerably pinker.

Forsythia

Forsythia spp.

Botanical Pronunciation
for-SITH-ee-uh

Other Name
Golden bells

Bloom Period and Seasonal Color
Spring; yellow flowers

Mature Height × Spread
1 to 9 feet × 4 to 6 feet

A spring bloomer, forsythia is the bright beacon of yellow that shouts to the world that winter has ended and spring has arrived. Named in celebration of the Scottish botanist who was one of the founding fathers of the Royal Horticultural Society, William Forsyth, forsythia has become a popular shrub throughout the Midwest. Forsythia is a vase-shaped shrub. It has arching limbs with deciduous leaves that turn a slight purple shade late in fall. Before the leaves form in early spring, bold yellow flowers develop along the stems, smothering the shrubs in an explosion of yellow. After blooming, the stems grow light green leaves, and the shrub transforms into a rather unassuming bush that often melts into the background of landscapes.

When, Where, and How to Plant

Before selecting a planting site, understand the specific growth parameters of the variety of forsythia being planted. This will enable you to space it adequately. Forsythias prefer a well-drained site in average soil. Plant the shrub in full sun for optimum flower production. Dig a hole twice as wide as the forsythia's rootball. Place plant in the hole with the top of the rootball level with the top of the soil.

Growing Tips

Mulch the soil with a 2- to 3-inch layer of compost or organic matter. Only fertilize with an organic fertilizer before new growth occurs in spring if the plant shows signs of lacking nourishment.

Regional Advice and Care

Forsythia flower on one-year-old wood or older, so pruning or shaping the forsythia shrub in the fall or early spring before it has flowered will curtail the flowering ability of the shrub. The best time to prune forsythia is immediately after it has bloomed, this will give the shrub an entire season of growth, enabling it to bloom again the following spring. Prune one-third to one-half of the shrub's limbs back to ground level just at the finish of the spring bloom. It will be easy to discern which branches need to be cut depending upon which branches are older, with drying flowers on them. To encourage continued flowering, do not shape the shrubs into balls or squares; let the plant stay in its natural form. Plants are easy to propagate because tips that touch the soil will often develop roots. Simply dig up the rooted tips and replant.

Companion Planting and Design

Gorgeous along woodland borders, this shrub also looks good along foundations, fence lines, and as a loose hedge. Forsythia handles urban pollution and tolerates heavily alkaline soils.

Try These

'Gold Tide' is a shorter variety, only growing 1 to 2 feet high and up to 4 feet wide. 'Fiesta' has bicolor foliage and grows 3 feet tall. 'Lynnwood Gold' is 10 feet tall and wide. 'Northern Gold' grows 6 to 8 feet tall and is very cold hardy.

Fragrant Sumac

Rhus aromatica

Botanical Pronunciation
RUSS ar-oh-MAT-ih-kuh

Bloom Period and Seasonal Color
Spring; yellow flowers; intense red fall foliage

Mature Height × Spread
1 to 6 feet × 6 to 10 feet

Native to North America, fragrant sumac is an early spring bloomer with delicate yellow flowers borne on the tips of the twigs before the leaves emerge on the shrub. Foliage of the shrub is glossy, attractive, and green, and the plant holds up to air pollution and urban environments well. Fragrant sumac has an unappealing and sometimes skunkish odor when its leaves are crushed. As a relative of poison ivy, its leaves grow in groups of three, which can be confusing to Midwesterners who have learned the "leaves of three, let them be" rule. Fragrant sumac has a beautiful form, its leaves ripening to intense red tones that contribute to the fall landscape. It is fantastic for naturalizing along woodland paths or when utilized as a low border.

When, Where, and How to Plant
Plant fragrant sumac in spring or fall in a medium, well-drained soil. It will tolerate most types of soils, but do not plant in soggy or wet soil as the roots need good drainage. If soil is too heavy or wet, mix in organic ingredients such as worm castings, rotted manure, compost, or a bit of gravel. Plant the shrub in full sun for best flowering, although fragrant sumac will grow in shady woodland conditions as well. When planting, dig a hole that is equal to the height of the rootball and twice as wide.

Growing Tips
Mulch the soil with a 2- to 3-inch layer of compost or organic matter. Fragrant sumac needs consistent water throughout the first season until it gets established. Only fertilize with an organic fertilizer before new growth occurs in spring if the plant looks like it needs fertilizer.

Regional Advice and Care
Suckers can be produced freely once the plant is established and need to be spaded back annually. Shrubs that are overcrowded or planted in shadier, wet areas are vulnerable to fungal problems such as powdery mildew, rust, and other conditions. Treat with an organic fungicide. Wear gloves when pruning or handling this plant. While it is not poison ivy, some people have red and itchy skin after exposure. While the berries of the fragrant sumac are edible, they have an exceptionally tart flavor and need to be sweetened for most people to enjoy them. If you are allergic to cashews, do not consume any part of the fragrant sumac.

Companion Planting and Design
Fragrant sumac is outstanding as a hillside soil stabilizer or erosion control bush because of its tolerance for a variety of soils. It is attractive in woodlands and in urban areas, particularly for birding gardens. Birds *love* the berries and hide beneath the foliage for protection.

Try These
'Gro-Low' grows 2 feet wide and sprawls across the ground with waves of red fall color. 'Konza' is short at 2 feet tall and has reddish purple leaves in fall with berries persisting into winter.

Goji Berry

Lycium barbarum

Botanical Pronunciation
Lye-KEE-yoom bar-BAHR-oom

Other Names
Duke of Argyll's tea tree, Chinese wolfberry, matrimony vine

Bloom Period and Seasonal Color
Spring; white and purple flowers

Mature Height × Spread
8 to 12 feet × 8 to 12 feet

Native to the Himalayas, goji berries are often called "super fruit" because they possess high levels of antioxidants and are considered nutritionally superior. Berries have a sweet, yet slightly tart flavor, and can be used fresh or dried. They have been utilized for thousands of years in traditional Chinese medicine and for food. Each berry has high levels of vitamin C and nearly 13 percent protein. But it's quite ornamental too. Shrubs are deciduous and grow to 10 feet high, with glossy green leaves, quaint star-shaped blooms in spring, and fruit that ripens by midsummer. Bright orange-red and sometimes close to 1 inch around, flavorful goji berries are produced from July until frost. Once established, a goji berry shrub will tolerate drought and is easy to grow. Its interesting common names include Chinese wolfberry and matrimony vine.

When, Where, and How to Plant
Goji berry grows in nearly any type of soil but prefers medium, well-drained soil. Soggy or wet areas will drown the roots. Some goji berry roots are sensitive to fertilizers; do not mix in overly rich organic ingredients such as peat moss, rotted manure, or compost. It is better to loosen soil with a bit of gravel. Plant in any full-sun spot for best fruiting, either in the ground or in a 5-gallon container. Goji shrub has a deep taproot, so it's important to plant it where it can reach down deep to grow.

Growing Tips
It takes a while to acclimatize, so add a 3-inch layer of mulch around the base of the plant for winter protection. It is not necessary to fertilize as goji berry roots can sometimes be sensitive to fertilizers, and it can kill new plants.

Regional Advice and Care
Once established, it can grow quickly, often jumping 4 to 5 feet in one season. Heavier yields can be expected after the third year. To keep growth in check, reduce the number of branches and maintain its shape in a more shrublike form; simply prune it back annually in late spring before new growth begins. Goji berries do not like to be handled and will blacken if touched too frequently. As they ripen, pick leaves to dry for tea and berries to press for juice. Cover the plant with horticultural netting to protect berries from hungry birds. Suckers can be produced freely and need to be spaded back annually.

Companion Planting and Design
Goji shrubs are vining and generally take at least one season to establish. It's good as a background plant or up against a wall or fence. It is excellent contribution to an ornamental edible perennial garden or a birding garden. Birds and other wildlife enjoy the shrub's ripe fruit.

Try These
'Big Lifeberry®' is a 12-foot-tall sprawling shrub. 'Sweet Lifeberry™' has the same growth habit of 'Big Lifeberry®' with extra-sweet berries.

Hydrangea

Hydrangea spp.

Botanical Pronunciation
hye-DRAIN-juh

Other Name
Snowball bush

Bloom Period and Seasonal Color
Summer; white, green, pink, and blue flowers

Mature Height × Spread
2 to 15 feet × 2 to 16 feet

As a small child, I remember my grandmother picking the bright white heads of the hydrangea and placing them in my arms. She called them "snowballs," and I reveled at their gorgeous clusters and soft petals against my face. There has been a tremendous resurgence of interest in the hydrangea in recent years as hybridizers have expanded the variety of flower colors and shrub forms seen in the marketplace. Hydrangeas have large attractive leaves with beautiful bunches of long-lasting flowers in white, green, pink, or blue. Most varieties prefer full sun or part shade and can go dormant in winter, often dying back to the ground, but are reborn with vigor in spring. Hydrangeas make memorable cut flowers and can be used in fresh or dried arrangements.

When, Where, and How to Plant

Hydrangea appreciates a well-drained soil with full sun to part shade exposure. Amend soil with organic matter such as rotted manure or compost to enrich soil and improve drainage. While most hydrangeas like consistently moist conditions, *Hydrangea quercifolia*, or oakleaf hydrangea, is an exception and prefers drier feet (roots). Plant a hydrangea in spring by digging a hole that is the same depth of the rootball and twice as wide. Plant the top of the rootball so that is level with the ground.

Growing Tips

Water the shrub heavily upon initial planting and when it is in active growth in the first season. Mulch the soil each year with a 3-inch layer of organic matter to help it hold water and protect it over winter. Only fertilize with an organic fertilizer before new growth occurs in spring if the plant shows signs of needing fertilizer. Overfertilization causes an increase in foliage with a decrease in flower development.

Regional Advice and Care

Prune out dead or diseased wood in late winter, but keep in mind that certain hydrangeas produce blooms on old wood; be sure to research which type of hydrangea you have so you can prune without harming the next season's bloom. White blooms will keep their white color, while pink and blue hydrangeas can change the flower color based on the amount of acid in the soil; higher acid content means bluer flowers.

Companion Planting and Design

Tremendous as specimen plants, hydrangeas have great visual impact during their bloom time. Leave flowers on the shrub after their peak and enjoy the dried clusters of airy flowers for winter interest. Hydrangeas are wonderful planted in groups. Taller hydrangeas look good at the back of perennial borders.

Try These

'Gatsby Gal™' an oakleaf hydrangea, is 6 feet tall with long white panicles. 'Limelight' has chartreuse-green blooms that change color to a deep pink in fall. 'Tiny Tuff Stuff™' mountain hydrangea can be used as a groundcover and grows 18 to 24 inches high. 'Little Quick Fire™' is a dwarf hydrangea that blooms early with bold pinkish red blooms.

Juniper

Juniperus spp.

Botanical Pronunciation
joo-NIP-ur-us

Bloom Period and Seasonal Color
Evergreen; variety of foliage colors

Mature Height × Spread
1 to 50 feet × 5 to 50 feet

From small to very large, there is a size of coniferous juniper shrub for your landscape. Junipers also come in an amazing selection of evergreen foliage colors ranging from an intense blue, slate gray, and traditional green, all the way to bright chartreuse-green. Research the best choice of juniper because success with a juniper shrub is most dependent on selecting the appropriate-sized shrub for the correct location within your landscape. They are very drought tolerant as a species and are used in rock gardens and bonsai, although most varieties require very little pruning. The greens of these shrubs are often cut and utilized for holiday arrangements. Juniper berries are edible, and they are used for making gin.

When, Where, and How to Plant

Juniper shrubs prefer a location that has full sun and moist, well-drained soil, but they are known to tolerate adverse conditions. Amend the soil with organic matter and a couple buckets of gravel if the planting location needs increased drainage. Plants that are balled and burlapped should have as much of the burlap and wire basket removed as possible. Backfill around the rootball until the planting hole is about half filled. Water the rootball and backfill well. Place the rest of the soil around the rootball, forming a "well" at the base of the plant. Be sure to place in a location where the plant will not be overcrowded.

Growing Tips

Mulch the soil with a 2- to 3-inch layer of compost or organic matter, being cautious not to smother the shrub's trunk. Water regularly the first season to help establish junipers. Fertilize with an organic fertilizer before new growth occurs in spring.

Regional Advice and Care

Prune to remove dieback but leave the plant in its natural state. Overpruned juniper often show browning and die-off. Shrubs that are overcrowded or planted in shadier, wet conditions are vulnerable to blight and other fungal issues. Hot conditions will encourage spider mites.

Companion Planting and Design

Highly tolerant of pollution and urban environments, juniper can be a wonderful solution for the city. Its drought tolerance makes it an agreeable selection for xeriscape gardening. Dependent upon the variety, juniper can be used at all levels within the landscape. Junipers make a good low-growing transition between the front of the border and sidewalks or pathways.

Try These

'Broadmoor' is a low-growing variety at 24 inches tall, but with an 8-foot spread. 'Blue Chip' is only 12 inches tall and grows 5 feet wide; it's an excellent groundcover. 'Skyrocket' is 15 feet high and 2 feet wide with blue-green branches. 'Grey Owl' is very gray and gets 4 feet high and 8 feet wide. 'Good Vibrations®' has gold branching and grows 12 to 18 inches high and up to 9 feet wide. 'St. Mary's Broom' is a reliable and compact shrub with intense blue colors that grows 24 inches high.

Lilac

Syringa spp.

Botanical Pronunciation
si-RING-ga

Bloom Period and Seasonal Color
Late spring; white, pink, lilac, purple, sky blue, and yellow flowers

Mature Height × Spread
4 to 15 feet × 6 to 12 feet

Revered for their intense fragrance and lovely panicles of flowers, lilacs are celebrated in late spring when they bloom. Their gorgeous perfume more than makes up for their very short bloom period in May, which usually lasts about two weeks. Lilac shrubs are often challenging to incorporate into a landscape design because their woody stems are untidy and can sometimes flop; proper pruning is key to a beautiful lilac. Research the variety size and placement within your landscape as most lilacs need consistent water and can grow out of bounds in small spaces. Lilacs often suffer from mildew and fungal issues; give the plant plenty of room to enable better air circulation, and be sure to water at the base of the shrub.

When, Where, and How to Plant
Grow lilac shrubs in a fertile, well-drained soil with full sun exposure. Plant the shrub in spring by digging a hole in the planting area that is the same depth of the rootball and twice as wide.

Growing Tips
Mulch the soil with a 3-inch layer of organic matter to help it hold water and protect it from winter cold. Heavy fertilizer is not required; lilacs will not bloom if overfertilized. However, each spring consider applying a thick layer of compost, then another layer of mulch to aid in its growth.

Regional Advice and Care
Flowers only bloom on old wood, so pruning or shaping a lilac in fall or early spring before it has flowered will curtail its flowering ability. The best time to prune is immediately after it has bloomed; this will give the shrub an entire season of growth before it has to bloom again the following spring. Prune one-third of the shrub's oldest limbs back to ground level just at the finish of the spring bloom. To encourage continued flower, do not shape the shrubs into balls or squares; let the plant stay in its natural form. Lilacs sucker, some so much so that they grow into a large mass of shrubs. Spade up suckers to prevent their spread. You can easily propagate lilacs by digging up suckers and replanting them in a preferred location.

Companion Planting and Design
Plant the lilac bushes at the back of borders or as a centerpiece in a late spring perennial garden. Dwarf lilacs make great features next to walkways.

Try These
'Primrose' is a pale yellow lilac shrub that grows to 12 feet. 'Bloomerang® Dark Purple' is a mounded lilac that reaches 6 feet tall and wide. 'Sensation' has purple picotee (meaning they are edged in white) flowers and grows to 15 feet tall. 'Palibin' is a dwarf lilac with pale purple coloring and a spreading habit that grows 4 feet tall and up to 7 feet wide. 'President Lincoln' has sky blue flowers and is mildew resistant.

Mock Orange

Philadelphus spp.

Botanical Pronunciation
fill-uh-DEL-fus

Other Name
English dogwood

Bloom Period and Seasonal Color
Early summer; white flowers

Mature Height × Spread
3 to 12 feet × 3 to 12 feet

White, fragrant flowers explode on the mock orange in June. Each white bloom is bowl shaped and has prominent stamens that are quite appealing and add to the shrub's charm. Pest-free, disease-free, and hardy, mock orange is an easy-to-grow shrub with consistent early summer flowers. While it is stunning when in bloom, it often fades into the background when not blooming because its leaves are rather unremarkable; the exception to this are the varieties 'Aureus' and 'Variegatus', which have attractive foliage. Mock orange thrives well in clay or dry soils, so it can be a solution for hot dry locations in both urban and country locations. Bees and butterflies love the sweet nectar the mock orange provides; it is well placed in a pollinator garden.

When, Where, and How to Plant

Mock orange prefers fertile, well-drained, moist soil with full sun exposure; however, it can handle drought well. Improve soil with organic matter or plant in raised beds if there is a lack of drainage. This shrub handles pollution and being planted in urban environments well. Plant in spring by digging a hole in a well-drained planting area the same depth of the rootball and twice as wide. Place the top of the rootball so that is level with the ground.

Growing Tips

Water the shrub heavily upon initial planting. Mulch the soil with a 3-inch layer of organic matter to help it hold water and protect it from winter cold. Only fertilize with an organic fertilizer before new growth occurs in spring if the plant shows signs of needing nourishment.

Regional Advice and Care

Young mock oranges have a rounded shape but start to get gangly with age. Rejuvenation pruning is important to maintain the shrub's life. Prune one-third of the shrub's limbs back to ground level just at the finish of the spring bloom. There are no serious disease or pest issues, but overcrowded shrubs or those planted in wet conditions are vulnerable to fungal problems such as rust or powdery mildew.

Companion Planting and Design

Plant near walkways and public areas so that the citrusy scent of the early summer flowers can be enjoyed. The plant works well as an urban planting solution. Plant mock orange as a shrub hedge or in rows in the landscape. It's wonderful when planted at the edge of a woodland path, although be careful of deer; they are known to browse on mock orange.

Try These

'Aureus' has gorgeous yellow foliage which can extend the shrub's attractiveness in the shrub border; it grows to 7 feet. 'Variegatus' has leaves with white edges and can grow 4 feet high. 'Minnesota Snowflake' is 8 feet high and produces double white flowers. 'Miniature Snowflake' only grows to a height of 3 feet. 'Belle Etoile' grows 6 feet high and has a white flower with a maroon blotch.

Mugo Pine

Pinus mugo Subsp. *Mugo*

Botanical Pronunciation
PYE-nus MYOO-go

Other Name
Swiss mountain pine

Bloom Period and Seasonal Color
Evergreen foliage

Mature Height × Spread
1 to 10 feet × 1 to 20 feet

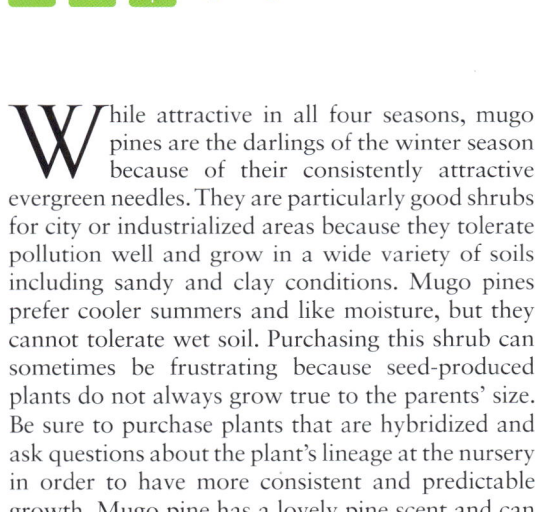

While attractive in all four seasons, mugo pines are the darlings of the winter season because of their consistently attractive evergreen needles. They are particularly good shrubs for city or industrialized areas because they tolerate pollution well and grow in a wide variety of soils including sandy and clay conditions. Mugo pines prefer cooler summers and like moisture, but they cannot tolerate wet soil. Purchasing this shrub can sometimes be frustrating because seed-produced plants do not always grow true to the parents' size. Be sure to purchase plants that are hybridized and ask questions about the plant's lineage at the nursery in order to have more consistent and predictable growth. Mugo pine has a lovely pine scent and can be used as a bonsai plant.

When, Where, and How to Plant
Plant mugo pine in spring or fall in a location that has full sun and moist, well-drained soil. Amend the soil with organic matter and a couple buckets of gravel if it needs increased drainage. Plants that are balled and burlapped should have as much of the burlap and wire basket removed as possible. Water the rootball and backfill well. Place the rest of the soil around the rootball, forming a "well" at the base of the plant to help hold moisture.

Growing Tips
Mulch the soil with a 2- to 3-inch layer of compost or organic matter, being cautious not to smother the shrub's trunk. Water regularly the first season to help establish the shrub; once it is established, it will handle drought well. Cautiously apply fertilizer because mugo pine can suffer fertilizer burn.

Regional Advice and Care
Prune mugo pine to remove dieback or to shape the plant and keep it within bounds. Shrubs that are overcrowded or planted in shadier, wet conditions are vulnerable to blight and other fungal issues. Treat with an organic fungicide. Pine sawflies and other insect pests can attack the mugo pine. Treat with an insecticidal soap and water spray.

Companion Planting and Design
Mugo pine can be used as a wonderful low-maintenance design solution in city settings, xeric landscapes, and Japanese gardens. Plant as a feature plant or *en masse*, and be sure to consider the winter snow when planting; mugo pines look *beautiful* in a winter garden. Mugos are often used as bonsai plants and are relatively easy to train into shapes.

Try These
'Teeny' is a small dwarf mugo pine growing only 18 inches tall and round. 'Carsten's Wintergold' has a small stature, only 12 inches high, and turns a gold tone when colder weather arrives. 'Mops' has a rounded form and grows to 5 feet tall. 'Jakobsen' is only 2 feet tall, has interesting branching, and resembles a bonsai-trained plant in its natural state. 'Big Tuna' grows to 8 feet tall.

Ninebark

Physocarpus opulifolius

Botanical Pronunciation
fizz-oh-KAR-pus op-you-lih-FOE-lee-us

Other Names
Common ninebark, Atlantic ninebark

Bloom Period and Seasonal Color
Early summer; white or pink flowers; fall foliage varies from chartreuse to bronze and deep burgundy

Mature Height × Spread
3 to 10 feet × 4 to 6 feet

Ninebark (sometimes called Atlantic ninebark) is a vigorous deciduous shrub native to North America with spectacular four-season interest. In spring, the shrubs bloom abundantly, with sweet-smelling, nectar-filled flowers that attract copious numbers of pollinators. During summer, ninebark has attractive foliage that comes in a wide range of colors depending upon the shrub's cultivar. They range from chartreuse, green, and copper, to red, burgundy, and deep purple. Fall brings red fruit, which mammals and birds enjoy, and even brighter leaf displays. Ninebark is named for its showy bark on young stems; it peels away in layers, revealing multiple color levels below the surface. Known for its tolerance of urban pollution, as well as wet, dry, and poor soils, ninebark makes a colorful and interesting shrub choice for demanding landscape locations.

When, Where, and How to Plant

Best grown in fertile, well-drained but moist soil, ninebark also tolerates a very wide range of soils—sandy, rocky, clay-filled, wet, or dry. Amend soil with organic matter to improve it or plant in raised beds if there is a lack of drainage. Ninebark puts up with harsh conditions such as pollution and areas that have urban environmental concerns. Plant the shrub in spring by digging a hole in a well-drained planting area that is the same depth of the rootball and twice as wide. Place the top of the rootball so that is level with the ground.

Growing Tips

Mulch the soil with a 3-inch layer of organic matter to help it hold water and protect it from winter cold.

Only fertilize with an organic fertilizer before new growth occurs in spring if the plant shows signs of undernourishment. Water regularly, especially upon initial planting.

Regional Advice and Care

Suckers can be produced freely once the plant is established and need to be spaded back annually. Some ninebark shrubs need to be cut back close to the ground for rejuvenation pruning. If you do not want to prune that harshly, cut one-third of the shrub's oldest limbs back to ground level just at the finish of their spring bloom. There are no serious disease or pest issues; however, overcrowded shrubs or those planted in wet conditions are vulnerable to fungal problems such as rust, blight, or powdery mildew.

Companion Planting and Design

With many of ninebark cultivars possessing unique foliage, it makes a delightful center feature in the shrub bed or border. When planted *en masse*, ninebark is a lovely hedge and can assist with erosion control on banks and hillsides.

Try These

'Seward', also known as 'Summerwine', has wine red foliage and pinkish white flowers. 'Diabolo®' has deep purple leaves, white flowers, and less suckering. It prefers a wetter location. 'Dart's Gold' has yellow foliage that turns a brilliant bronze in fall. 'Coppertina™' has rich copper foliage all summer. 'Tiny Wine™' is a dwarf variety that only grows 3 feet tall and wide.

Potentilla

Potentilla fruticosa

Botanical Pronunciation
po-ten-TILL-a froo-tih-KOE-sah

Other Names
Shrubby cinquefoil, bush cinquefoil

Bloom Period and Seasonal Color
Summer; yellow, pink, white, and blended colors

Mature Height × Spread
2 to 4 feet × 2 to 4 feet

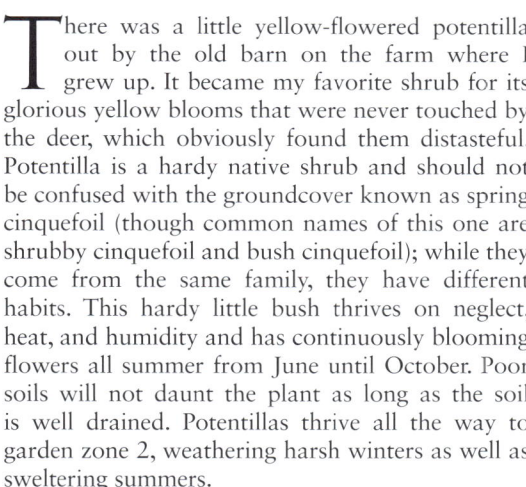

There was a little yellow-flowered potentilla out by the old barn on the farm where I grew up. It became my favorite shrub for its glorious yellow blooms that were never touched by the deer, which obviously found them distasteful. Potentilla is a hardy native shrub and should not be confused with the groundcover known as spring cinquefoil (though common names of this one are shrubby cinquefoil and bush cinquefoil); while they come from the same family, they have different habits. This hardy little bush thrives on neglect, heat, and humidity and has continuously blooming flowers all summer from June until October. Poor soils will not daunt the plant as long as the soil is well drained. Potentillas thrive all the way to garden zone 2, weathering harsh winters as well as sweltering summers.

When, Where, and How to Plant
Plant potentilla in spring in full sun to part shade. This shrub will tolerate nearly any well-draining soil; however, it does best with moderate moisture and fertility. Heavy or wet soils should be improved with rotted manure, compost, or gravel to enhance drainage. If planted in the right conditions, potentilla has been known to live for 30 years.

Growing Tips
Water consistently the first season in order to encourage a stronger root system; thereafter, only water in extreme drought. Overwatering can cause plant leaves to brown and flowers to drop; once established there is no need to water heavily. Do not fertilize; it is not needed.

Regional Advice and Care
Potentilla is a durable shrub that rarely needs pruning, although it can sometimes suffer a leggy branch or stiff old stem. Prune older branches if the bush looks a bit scraggly to encourage new growth. If an elderly potentilla still looks out-of-sorts, simply cut down the shrub a couple inches from the ground in late winter or early spring and it will grow fresh limbs. Do not round these shrubs or shear them into unnatural shapes; it's healthier to leave them in their natural form. There are no serious diseases or insect problems that attack potentilla, although excess water can cause root rot issues.

Companion Planting and Design
While the common shrub has yellow blossoms in flower during summer, new cultivars have flowers that include bright white, pink, and yellow fading to orange. This makes them quite versatile in the perennial bed or shrub border. Place them in urban landscapes or xeric gardens, which require little water. Potentilla is particularly attractive as a low hedge and functions as a bright feature in compact gardens.

Try These
'Abbotswood' has a bright white flower and grows 2 feet tall and 3 feet wide. 'Goldfinger' is a spreading shrub that grows 3 feet tall and 4 feet wide with yellow flowers. 'Sunset' has unique dark orange flowers that lighten to yellow shades. 'Pink Beauty' has delicate pink flowers that fade to a whiter shade in hot summers.

Rose of Sharon

Hibiscus syriacus

Botanical Pronunciation
hye-BISS-kiss seer-ee-AY-kus

Other Names
Shrub althea, Chinese hibiscus

Bloom Period and Seasonal Color
Late summer through late fall; white, pink
lavender, purple, red, and light blue flowers

Mature Height × Spread
5 to 12 feet × 6 to 10 feet

Hummingbirds adore rose of Sharon's beautiful flowers, which typically bloom for one day. Flowers can be as big as dinner plates and invite hummingbirds with their large red eyes in the center, much like a bull's-eye on a target. Pollinators are visually attracted to these deciduous shrubs as there is very little fragrance with this genus. Rose of Sharon had the reputation of being an old-fashioned plant until recently when hybridizers came up with new and interesting cultivars to add color to the landscape. While this shrub is quite eye-catching and long-lived, it can be a plant that demands maintenance as it is a notorious self-seeder, which can easily get out of hand. Search for newer, less-invasive hybrids. Interesting alternate common names include shrub althea and Chinese hibiscus.

When, Where, and How to Plant

Grow rose of Sharon in fertile, well-drained, moist soil in full sun. Amend soil with organic matter to improve it or plant in raised beds if drainage is a problem. Plant the shrub in spring by digging a hole that is the same depth of the rootball and twice as wide in a well-drained planting area.

Growing Tips

Rose of Sharon can be remarkably drought tolerant but appreciates consistent moisture. Add a 3-inch layer of organic mulch to help it hold water during hot summers. Yellowing leaves can be a sign of overwatering or overfertilization. Fertilize cautiously with organic low-nitrogen fertilizer in early spring.

Regional Advice and Care

Rose of Sharon can sucker and drop seed unendingly, which can develop into large masses of overgrown shrubs. Purchase cultivars that do not produce seed or spade up fast-growing suckers annually to prevent their spread. Early spring is the best time to prune, before the leaf buds open. Although pruning is not particularly required, you can cut the plant by up to half, leaving three buds on each branch, to encourage side shoot development and larger flowers. Cut out dead limbs to tidy the plant anytime.

Companion Planting and Design

Rose of Sharon is very often the last shrub to leaf out in spring. Design gardens accordingly if this bothers you; have other plants in leaf to distract from the rose of Sharon's naked arms. As a nonstop summer bloomer, it is a lovely feature planted at the back of borders. Do not plant seed-producing varieties along woodlands as their invasiveness can be damaging environmentally.

Try These

'Minerva' has beautiful bright pink flowers and a more compact growth with limited seed production due to hybridization. 'Azurri Blue Satin®' is a blue-lavender flowered seedless shrub growing to 12 feet. 'Sugar Tip®' has a dramatic variegated green-and-white leaf with pale pink double flowers that do not produce seed. 'Lil' Kim™' is a dwarf, only reaching 3 to 4 feet high with white flowers that bloom for three days instead of the standard one-day bloom.

Smoketree

Cotinus coggygria

Botanical Pronunciation
koe-TYE-nus koe-GUY-gree-uh

Other Names
Jupiter's beard, cloud tree

Bloom Period and Seasonal Color
Early summer; colorful foliage with insignificant yellow flowers

Mature Height × Spread
15 feet × 15 feet

Smoketree is a striking ornamental grown as a shrub or a small tree for its fluffy, cloudlike, hairy stalks of sterile flowers. Each panicle can be up to 10 inches long with reddish petioles that, when packed tightly together, look like smoke floating above the shrub (leading to another common name, cloud tree). Inedible berries sometimes occur on pink-tinged stems. It is often used as a specimen plant due to its four-season interest. Early spring leaves are pale, sometimes pink in tone, and very attractive. Fall leaves are explosions of bright colors. Its twisted and gnarly limbs and flaky barks make it an interesting structural addition to the winter garden. Smoketree's leaves have 30 percent tannin content and are regularly used worldwide for tannin production.

When, Where, and How to Plant
Plant smoketree in spring or fall in a medium, well-drained soil. If soil is too heavy or wet, mix in organic ingredients such as worm castings, rotted manure, compost, or a bit of gravel. Plant the shrub in full sun for best smoke flower production; also, plants in shade can be susceptible to fungal problems. When planting, dig a hole that is equal to the height of the rootball and twice as wide. Smoketree can tolerate most types of soil and does particularly well in urban situations.

Growing Tips
Although smoketree will tolerate drought, it prefers consistent moisture. Mulch the soil with a 2- to 3-inch layer of compost or organic matter.

Only fertilize with an organic fertilizer before new growth occurs in spring if the plant shows signs of undernourishment.

Regional Advice and Care
The bark of the smoketree is rather thin and should be protected from lawn mowers and weed cutting tools. Smoketree can be pruned to the ground in early spring before it leafs out to keep the plant shorter and shrublike, but it won't flower the year it is pruned. If you want the shrub to resemble a tree, simply remove key stems at the base of the plant, carefully reshaping its growth. Wear gloves when pruning or handling this plant; while it is not poison ivy, some people suffer red and itchy skin after exposure to its sap because this shrub is a member of the poison ivy family.

Companion Planting and Design
With a reputation as a survivor of tough growing conditions, this shrub makes a fantastic urban feature specimen. It is also outstanding planted as a privacy hedge row—a smoke screen, if you will.

Try These
'Ancot' or 'Golden Spirit' has unusual yellow-green leaves with coral and red leaves in the fall; its flowers are white to pinkish. 'Royal Purple' has dramatic purple foliage with pinkish purple "smoke." 'Nordine' is a very hardy purple form with yellowish copper leaves in fall. 'Daydream' is slightly more compact with green leaves and pink-tinted "smoke."

Spirea

Spirea spp.

Botanical Pronunciation
spy-REE-ah

Other Name
Chinese bearberry

Bloom Period and Seasonal Color
Spring and summer; white, red, yellow, and pink flowers

Mature Height × Spread
2 to 10 feet × 2 to 10 feet

*S*pirea is a genus of small- to medium-sized flowering shrubs with more than 80 different species and long lists of varieties within those classifications. Known as a tremendously easy shrub to grow, spireas can be very diverse and useful within the garden. There are two different types of spireas: spring blooming and summer blooming. 'Bridal Wreath' spirea is spring blooming and is often considered the quintessential plant when we refer to the shrub as a species. It has cascading white flowers that seem to bloom in explosions of pollinator-attracting flowers on arching branches. Summer-blooming varieties can produce more than one flush of flowers per season, particularly if they're deadheaded, and sometimes grow lower to the ground. Many varieties have brilliant leaves in fall.

When, Where, and How to Plant
Most spireas prefer a fertile, well-drained, moist soil with full sun exposure for best flower production. Improve soil with organic matter or plant in raised beds if there is a lack of drainage. This shrub handles pollution and being planted near urban environments well. Plant spirea in spring by digging a hole that is the same depth of the rootball and up to twice as wide in a well-drained planting area. The top of the rootball should be level with the ground.

Growing Tips
Water this shrub heavily upon initial planting. Apply several inches of organic matter, such as compost, each spring. Mulch over that layer of compost to help it hold water and protect the plant from winter cold. Only fertilize with an organic fertilizer before new growth occurs in spring if the plant shows signs of undernourishment.

Regional Advice and Care
Deadheading flowers will sometimes encourage a second round of flowering later in the season. Cut or shape most spireas after flowering at any time. Prune bumald and Japanese spireas in early spring. If the plant begins to look scraggly, prune the plant to the ground after flowering, or in the early spring. There are no serious disease or pest issues, but overcrowded shrubs or those planted in wet conditions are vulnerable to fungal problems. Treat powdery mildew, leafspot, and other fungal conditions with an organic fungicide.

Companion Planting and Design
Spirea looks quite handsome when mixed with a spring-blooming cottage garden. White-blooming shrubs are excellent in all-white-themed flower gardens. Low growers with intense fall colors can be made into low-care hedges in urban environments.

Try These
'Limemound' is grown for its leaves, which are bright chartreuse all season long. It grows to 3 feet high. 'Neon Flash' has hot pink flowers on bold green leaves on a 3-foot × 4-foot shrub. 'Goldflame' has intense gold to red leaves with red tips that fade all season. 'Renaissance' is an updated form of 'Bridal Wreath' with white flowers, improved disease resistance, and a more compact form.

Summersweet

Clethra alnifolia

Botanical Pronunciation
KLETH-ruh al-nih-FOE-lee-uh

Other Name
Sweet pepper bush

Bloom Period and Seasonal Color
Early summer; white and pink flowers

Mature Height × Spread
4 to 8 feet × 4 to 6 feet

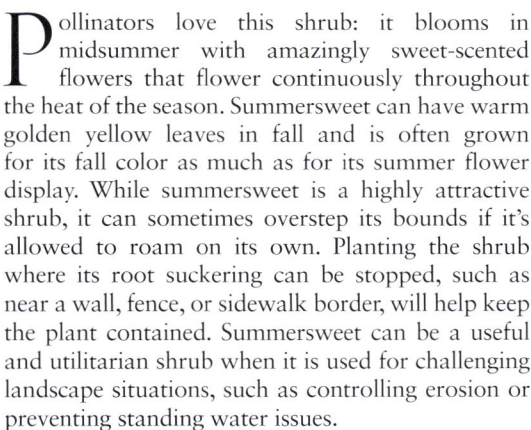

Pollinators love this shrub: it blooms in midsummer with amazingly sweet-scented flowers that flower continuously throughout the heat of the season. Summersweet can have warm golden yellow leaves in fall and is often grown for its fall color as much as for its summer flower display. While summersweet is a highly attractive shrub, it can sometimes overstep its bounds if it's allowed to roam on its own. Planting the shrub where its root suckering can be stopped, such as near a wall, fence, or sidewalk border, will help keep the plant contained. Summersweet can be a useful and utilitarian shrub when it is used for challenging landscape situations, such as controlling erosion or preventing standing water issues.

When, Where, and How to Plant
Summersweet prefers a fertile, well-drained, moist soil with full sun exposure. Amend soil with organic matter to improve it or consider raised beds if your site lacks drainage. Plant it in the spring by digging a hole in a well-drained planting area that is the same depth of the rootball and twice as wide. Place the top of the rootball so that is level with the ground.

Growing Tips
Water the root system in well upon initial planting. This shrub *loves* moist soils and should never be left to dry out. Mulch the soil with a 3-inch layer of organic matter to help it hold water and protect it from winter cold. Only fertilize with an organic fertilizer before new growth occurs in the spring if the plant shows signs of undernourishment. Heavy fertilization can increase suckering and reduce flower production.

Regional Advice and Care
Suckers can be produced freely once the plant is established and form into large colonies, so these need to be spaded back annually. Summersweet blooms on the current year's growth, so the best time to prune the bush is in late winter before the new buds have set on the limbs. Cut out dead or broken branches anytime. There are no serious disease or pest issues with summersweet.

Companion Planting and Design
Plant this shrub as a glorious blooming solution for rain gardens or to prevent erosion on hillsides. It's appealing as a naturalized plant, but be careful when naturalizing in woodlands as the suckering plant can take over large areas of the forested landscape. Summersweet is surprisingly tolerant of salt spray and makes a good choice to line walkways that will be salted.

Try These
'Ruby Spice' is a deep reddish pink-flowering shrub that grows to 6 feet tall and 4 feet wide. 'Hummingbird' attracts hummingbirds and butterflies with its white spiky flowers. This shrub requires constantly wet soils. 'Sixteen Candles' grows 3 feet tall with large, upright white flower spikes.

Sweetspire

Itea virginica

Botanical Pronunciation
eye-TEE-uh vur-JIN-ih-kuh

Other Name
Virginia sweetspire

Bloom Period and Seasonal Color
Late spring; white flowers; brilliant red fall foliage

Mature Height × Spread
4 to 8 feet × 4 to 6 feet

Sweetspire is very similar to summersweet in its growing nature, and they combine brilliantly in gardens although they are two completely different shrubs. They both have astoundingly sweet-scented blooms that flower for a large part of the summer. Pollinators adore both the shrubs; both of them spread by suckering but can be kept contained. Where they differ is that sweetspire blooms earlier in spring, has a more arching/droopy branch habit, and has intensely red leaves in fall. Planting the shrub where its root suckering can be stopped, such as near a wall, fence, or sidewalk border, will help keep the plant contained. Sweetspire, like summersweet, can be a useful and utilitarian shrub when it is used for challenging landscape situations such as to control erosion or prevent standing water issues.

When, Where, and How to Plant
Sweetspire prefers a fertile, well-drained, moist soil with full sun exposure. Amend soil with organic matter to improve it or use raised beds if your soil lacks drainage. Plant it in spring by digging a hole that is the same depth of the rootball and twice as wide in a well-drained planting site. Place the rootball so the top of it is level with the ground.

Growing Tips
Water the root system in well upon initial planting. This shrub *loves* moist soils and should never be left to dry out. Mulch the soil with a 3-inch layer of organic matter to help it hold water and protect it from winter cold. Only fertilize with an organic fertilizer

before new growth occurs in spring if the plant shows signs of undernourishment as heavy fertilization can increase suckering and reduce flower production.

Regional Advice and Care
Suckers can be produced freely once established and form into large colonies, so need to be spaded back annually. Sweetspire blooms on the current year's growth, so the best time to prune the bush is in late winter before the new buds have set on the limbs. Cut out dead or broken branches any time of the year. There are no serious disease or pest issues with sweetspire.

Companion Planting and Design
Bold red fall colors truly dominate the leaves on sweetspire from late September through early October; design the shrub plantings to take advantage of this showy demonstration. Sweetspire works wonderfully to prevent erosion and absorb water in rain gardens. While it is lovely as a naturalized plant, be careful when naturalizing in woodlands as the suckering plant can take over large areas of the landscape.

Try These
'Little Henry®' dwarf Virginia sweetspire reaches 2 to 3 feet tall and wide with bright white flowers and bright red fall foliage. 'Henry's Garnet' is 5 to 6 feet tall, has creamy off-white flowers, and intense reddish purple fall foliage. 'Merlot' has a compact 3-foot height with leaves that are red with hints of burgundy in fall.

Tree Peony

Paeonia suffruticosa

Botanical Pronunciation
pee-OH-nee-uh suh-froo-tih-KOE-zuh

Other Name
Chinese peony

Bloom Period and Seasonal Color
Late spring and early summer; white, pink,
coral, red, maroon, purple, and yellow flowers

Mature Height × Spread
4 feet × 4 feet

Tree peonies are not the herbaceous perennial peonies you remember your sweet grandmother growing. Tree peonies are woody shrubs that grow to be approximately 4 feet tall and wide that have been grown and hybridized for their fragrant flowers. They have long fibrous roots and the flowers can be 10 inches wide; plants require no staking. Some tree peonies can live exceptionally long lives, up to 100 years. So when you plant a tree peony shrub, you are really planting an investment in your landscape. Many common Chinese tree peonies go by the Latin designation, *Paeonia suffruticosa*. However, there are other species of tree peony. *P. rockii*, for instance, is a species commonly used as an herbal remedy in traditional Chinese medicine.

When, Where, and How to Plant
Tree peonies prefer rich, loamy, soil that has excellent drainage, and they perform better in part shade to full sun, requiring at least five hours of sun per day. Amend soil with rotted manure, compost, and worm castings to enrich and enhance drainage. Plant a tree peony in fall or spring, making sure the site is not located near large trees, which can pull nutrients and water away from the shrub. A tree peony typically blooms in the fifth year of its life. When purchasing the plant, be sure to discuss its age with the nursery team.

Growing Tips
Mulch the ground well around a tree peony to ensure moisture retention and provide winter protection; prolonged drought and heat stress can cause the plant to go into early dormancy. Tree peonies are heavy feeders but do not care for "hot" (fast) fertilizers, they prefer slow-release organic fertilizers applied regularly and enjoy spring treatments of fresh compost topdressings.

Regional Advice and Care
To overwinter a tree peony, mulch well. Some experts suggest wrapping the plant with burlap; however, if the soil is mulched and protected well, that should be sufficient. Do not prune except to remove dead branches because the buds will return on the stems in spring. Tree peonies can be plagued with fungal issues such as blight and powdery mildew. Be sure to water at the base of the plant to help prevent disease. Fungal issues can be controlled with an organic fungicide.

Companion Planting and Design
Tree peonies are delightful in perennial beds as specimens. They're interesting planted in groupings with other spring-flowering perennials. Because of their flowering nature, tree peonies make a wonderful contribution to a pollinator garden. Their sweet-smelling blooms make good cut flowers; one peony blossom can perfume an entire room.

Try These
'Shimanishiki' has unusual red-and-white striped flowers with yellow stamens. 'Zhao Fen' grows to 6 feet tall and has double pale pink flowers with a strong fragrance. 'Age of Gold' has pale yellow flowers with eye-catching red center flares.

Viburnum

Viburnum spp.

Botanical Pronunciation
vye-BUR-num

Other Name Arrowwood

Bloom Period and Seasonal Color
Spring and early summer; white and pink flowers

Mature Height × Spread
3 to 12 feet × 3 to 12 feet

Viburnums are a large and wide-ranging family of deciduous, semi-evergreen, and evergreen shrubs treasured for flowers that are brilliantly scented and quite prolific. They are an absolute must in bird gardens as many of the viburnum family produce berries that will entice birds to stay in the garden throughout winter. American cranberrybush (*Viburnum trilobum*) is among the favorites that are planted by bird lovers for its rich red berries and incredibly colorful crimson fall leaves. With a large range in size, sun requirements and a high tolerance for soil variance, viburnums are versatile shrubs that can fit into nearly any garden plan.

When, Where, and How to Plant

Most viburnums prefer a moist, well-drained soil; select a site in full sun to have more prolific blooms. Dig a hole the same depth of the rootball, but twice as wide. Plant deep enough so the top of the rootball is level with the ground. Be sure to give the shrub a lot of air circulation to help prevent fungal issues.

Growing Tips

Mulch the soil with a 2- to 3-inch layer of compost or organic matter. Fertilize with an organic fertilizer before new growth occurs in spring only if the plant shows signs of undernourishment. Too much fertilizer can encourage less bloom and legginess.

Regional Advice and Care

If the shrub shows signs of overgrowth, it can be given a rejuvenation prune; cut one-fourth to one-half of the older stems down to the ground in early spring. Most viburnums are not self-fertile. This means that if you want to cross-pollinate the plant to produce fruiting and even more flowers for the wildlife in the garden, you will have to install two plants within the same shrub species. Planting two of the same shrubs such as *Viburnum dentatum* 'Chicago Lustre™' together will not enable pollination. However, if you plant one 'Chicago Lustre®' with another completely different *V. dentatum* cultivar, and both plants are blooming at the same time for pollination, then the chance for successful pollination increases.

Companion Planting and Design

With berries that attract birds, attractive fall color, and a wide range of shapes and form, viburnums are a great option for landscapes. Plant these shrubs as a hedge or in a container near walkways and gate entrances where its fragrance can be absorbed by passersby.

Try These

'Korean Spice' has a gorgeous spicy scent and grows to 6 feet tall. The following are all *Viburnum dentatum* cultivars: 'Blue Muffin®' has mounds of blue fruit at the end of summer and reaches 4 to 6 feet; 'Autumn Jazz®' is a native shrub that is great for hedges, growing to 12 feet; 'Chicago Lustre™' has amazing glossy dark green foliage and a mounded habit, growing to 12 feet high.

Weigela

Weigela spp.

Botanical Pronunciation
wye-JEE-luh

Bloom Period and Seasonal Color
Spring and summer; white, pink, red, salmon, lavender, and other flower colors

Mature Height × Spread
18 inches to 10 feet × 24 inches to 12 feet

Butterflies and hummingbirds love the weigela's trumpet-shaped flowers, which makes it a fantastic shrub for pollinator or birding gardens. Weigela is dense, with coarse branching limbs that are very showy when in bloom. Modern-day hybridizations have changed the common weigela from twenty years ago, adding extensive flower color selection, interesting foliage variegation, and a broad range in sizes from the very small groundcover to the large bush. This has led to weigela being an extremely high impact shrub as well as a versatile summer bloomer that is an admirable addition to shrub borders and hedges as a foliage feature. Weigela is remarkably disease resistant when planted in full sun; crowding the shrub or planting it in shade can sometimes lead to fungal issues.

When, Where, and How to Plant
Most weigelas prefer a well-drained soil in full sun. Although it does not like standing in water, weigela does like a consistent medium moisture and a rich, humusy soil with lots of natural items mixed in: rotted manure, compost, and worm castings make perfect soil amendments. Dig a hole the same depth of the rootball but twice as wide. Plant so the top of the rootball is level with the ground. Be sure to give the shrub a lot of air circulation to help prevent fungal issues.

Growing Tips
Mulch the soil with a 2- to 3-inch layer of compost or organic matter. Supplemental water is recommended during heat and drought. Fertilize with an organic fertilizer before new growth occurs in spring only if the plant shows signs of needing fertilizer. Too much fertilizer can discourage bloom.

Regional Advice and Care
Dead branches can be cut out anytime. Pruning the entire bush too soon in the season can limit flowers and its show. Trim weigela bushes just as the flowers are fading, typically in midsummer.

Companion Planting and Design
Branches are stiff and leafy, so they can be cut as rather attractive additions to flower arrangements. As true butterfly and hummingbird shrubs, weigela make tremendous centerpieces in a summer perennial garden built to attract pollinators. Weigelas can be planted as a hedge or summer screen, but will lose its leaves in winter. Barberry and hydrangea make good companion shrubs.

Try These
'Minuet' is a diminutive variety with pink flowers that have a long bloom time through the end of August, and red-tinted foliage that only grows 18 inches high. 'Sonic Bloom™' has hot pink flowers that attract hummingbirds (see photo). 'Ghost™' has unusual foliage that changes from green to cream with bold red flowers (prune for rebloom). 'My Monet®' is a dwarf variety that tolerates part shade; it has white and pink margins on green foliage, with pink flowers. 'Wine & Roses®' has hot pink flowers that hummingbirds love and dark wine-colored foliage. 'Variegata' has outstanding bicolor foliage and pale pink flowers.

Witchhazel

Hamamelis spp.

Botanical Pronunciation
ham-uh-MEE-liss

Bloom Period and Seasonal Color
Spring; yellow or orange-red blooms

Mature Height × Spread
15 feet × 15 feet

As one of the earliest blooming native shrubs in the Midwest, witchhazel explodes in spidery yellow blossoms just as winter is ebbing. It's almost as if nature is throwing a party just when you need it the most. Witchhazel is a large shrub that tolerates many conditions including soil compaction, alkaline sites, and wet feet. In fall, most witchhazel turns yellow; exceptions include 'Autumn Embers', which has a red-purple leaf, and 'Sandra', which has orange autumnal leaves. Native Americans used witchhazel bark to make a medicinal treatment. It is still used today to produce a medicinal astringent used in over-the-counter treatments.

When, Where, and How to Plant
Grow witchhazel shrubs in a fertile, well-drained soil with full sun exposure; they can become leggy and unattractive in shadier conditions. Standing water can cause root rot, so be sure to amend soil if it is heavy or lacks drainage. Rotted manure or compost is a good amendment. Plant the shrub in spring by digging a hole that is the same depth of the rootball and twice as wide in a well-drained planting location.

Growing Tips
Mulch the soil with a 3-inch layer of organic matter to help it hold moisture and protect it from winter cold. Witchhazel does not like drought conditions and will abort flower buds if it does not regularly receive water. Consistent watering up to 1 inch per week is recommended. Fertilizer is not required; however, each spring consider applying a thick layer of compost around the root systems to encourage healthy soil conditions.

Regional Advice and Care
Prune out deadwood or weak shoots after bloom. Witchhazel can sucker, so spade out the suckers in fall or late winter to prevent its encroachment upon other parts of the garden. Do not shape witchhazel into unusual shapes; it grows best in its natural form. Fungal issues can be a problem when planted in shadier conditions.

Companion Planting and Design
Witchhazel works well when planted in a spot that will show its early flowers in shrub borders but will then fade into the background of the landscape during the main part of the season. Its rounded shape works well to soften fences and structures. Use it as a centerpiece to an early spring bulb garden; plant the witchhazel in center and surround it by yellow, white, and orange flowering bulbs.

Try These
'Arnold's Promise' reaches 12 feet high and has attractive golden fall foliage. 'Diane' grows to 15 feet and has orange-red flowers with copper leaves in fall. 'Jelena' has golden copper flowers with strong orange leaves in fall. 'Pallida' Chinese witchhazel blooms very early, has yellow flowers with plum-colored cups, and prefers a wetter location than most witchhazels.

Yew

Taxus spp.

Botanical Pronunciation
TACKS-us

Other Name
Japanese yew

Bloom Period and Seasonal Color
Evergreen foliage

Mature Height × Spread
2 to 40 feet × 5 to 40 feet

Yews have been overused as the classic Midwestern foundation planting. When I was a teenager, every home in most neighborhoods I knew had dozens of yews parked around their foundations, shaved within an inch of their life and shaped into torturous rounded balls. While they are an easy solution for hiding a home's foundation line, yew balls represent an unattractive landscaping concept. It's easy to understand how yew balls took shape; yews are surprisingly versatile and fit well into part-shade, locations, which are often found along a buildings perimeter. Yews come in a wide range of sizes and planting the wrong size means the plant will have to be pruned heavily as it grows. To prevent yew ball pruning, understand a yew's mature size and natural shape.

When, Where, and How to Plant
Plant yews in spring or fall in a location that has full sun and moist, well-drained soil. While amending the soil with organic matter and a couple buckets of gravel might help increase drainage, it might not be enough for the yew. Yews are most likely to fail because of poor drainage, so if soil is heavy clay and you cannot improve a large area significantly, consider planting the shrub's crown 2 inches above the surrounding soil. Plants that are balled and burlapped should have as much of the burlap and wire basket removed as possible. Backfill around the rootball until it is about half filled, then water. Then place the rest of the soil around the rootball.

Growing Tips
Water regularly the first season to help establish the shrub; once it is established it will handle drought well. Mulch the soil with a 2- to 3-inch layer of compost or organic matter to help prevent cold damage. No fertilizer is required.

Regional Advice and Care
Yews are often subject to winter burning. Do not plant yews where they will get harsh winter sun and wind; it can cause tip burnout. Prune yews in early spring before budding, cutting any burnt tips off. Hedges that require shearing should be pruned in early spring and again mid-year. Yews can suffer girdling and branch damage from holiday decorations; be careful about holiday light placement to prevent damage.

Companion Planting and Design
Yews can be used as a low-maintenance design answer in city settings and Japanese gardens. Plant as a hedge, feature plant, or *en masse* and be sure to consider winter snow when planting; yews look striking in a winter garden. Groundcover yews are a great transitional edging for pathways.

Try These
'Capitata' is an upright yew with a pyramidal habit that is 30 feet tall. 'Tauntonii' resists winter burn and grows 3 to 4 feet high and wide. 'Emerald Spreader' is 3 feet tall and 8 feet wide. 'Viridis' can grow to 10 feet tall and 2 feet wide, offering a solution for narrow locations.

TREES
FOR INDIANA

A s a little girl growing up in Midwestern farm country, I used to love to climb in places I was not supposed to climb. I enjoyed climbing to the big barn roof or all the way up to the top of the corncrib so I could see the flat country for miles around. And of course, I loved climbing trees. When seen from a couple stories up, trees become the backbone for all the land as far as the eye can see. From a bird's-eye view, trees are the queens of the community, and all the other shrubs and plants seem to bow down in celebration of the trees' special place.

Without a doubt, trees are the most solid structures within a garden landscape. Although no tree is permanent, many trees can live multiple generations if well taken care of and become revered by the humans who love their shade, fruit, and wildlife. There is also a more important reason to celebrate trees: oxygen. Although estimates range, trees annually produce oxygen in the hundreds of pounds. Trees are also a vital natural resource as a central control to hold pollutants, stabilize the world's climate, offset carbon dioxide buildup, cool our homes and offices, and shelter and feed a huge percentage of the world's wildlife. Trees absorb water and prevent run-off as well as make an invaluable contribution to your neighborhood landscape.

Planning Is Everything

Once planted, trees cannot easily be moved. Therefore, planning is absolutely imperative in considering the selection and planting of a tree. Additionally, by selecting new species to increase diversity, it is possible to eliminate huge and simultaneous losses of large plantings of just one species by issues such as Dutch elm disease or emerald ash borer. Diversity of tree plantings increases the chances that more trees will survive to a mature age.

Another aspect of planning is size; trees vary hugely in size, from the very small to the ginormous. Therefore, it is critical to understand a tree's mature height before selecting a sapling.

There are many varieties of trees, each with a different height and placement possibility. This small Japanese maple looks delightful mixed as an understory woodland feature next to a winding path with a stone seating area.

Trees can function as a very formal landscaping feature. Such is the case with this very formal allée of lindens, which is carefully shaped and clipped to form a unique pathway feature.

Trees can be a nuisance to a neighbor, if you plant a tree that overhangs onto their property, or to you, if you plant a tree too close to your home so the roots tap into your plumbing. They can also be the central visual appeal to your landscape design. A deciduous tree can block hot southeastern sun in summer, but once its leaves are gone, can let the sun shine on a building in winter and heat it up, thereby reducing your heating and cooling bills. If you have a busy road nearby, trees function as sound and fume filters. But avoid planting trees too close together or they can become stunted and fungus filled. Trees need to stretch.

Planting

Plant a tree in fall, when a sapling will have the least chance of heat stress. Dig a hole that is four times the width of the container or rootball, but that allows a tree's rootball to sit even with or 1 inch above the surrounding grade. Success will be more likely if you cut and remove the wire baskets, strings, burlap, or plastic covering the rootball. Do not remove soil; handle the tree by the rootball—*not* the trunk—to prevent breakage. Loosen soil that will be used as backfill, but do not add additional compost or organic matter so that the tree's roots will have to stretch out into the surrounding soil for nutrients. Water well and mulch with 2 to 3 inches of mulch immediately, keeping mulch well away from the bark at the base of the trunk. Do not fertilize the first year. Fertilize annually with an organic fertilizer thereafter.

Whether used to feed and house wildlife, build a sustainable cooling solution for your home, beautify your neighborhood, or to help with water absorption for your yard, planting a tree can absolutely make a difference for you, your landscape, and even your community.

Beech

Fagus spp.

Botanical Pronunciation
FAY-gus

Bloom Period and Seasonal Color
Fall; yellow and brown foliage; green and multicolor leaves in spring and summer

Mature Mature Height × Spread
40 to 90 feet × 40 to 90 feet

Beech trees have smooth silver trunks that stand quite straight, with glossy green leaves that turn yellow, then brown in fall. There are many varieties of beech. European beeches are typically taller than the American species, at up to 90 feet, with an affinity for full sun and browner autumnal leaves. The tree is more tolerant of pollution than other species of beech. American beeches grow to a height of 70 feet, and while they prefer full sun, they will also tolerate part shade. As a native tree, American beeches serve many positive purposes for the environment. Hollow trees house birds and small mammals. Interesting-shaped triangular beechnuts provide food for wildlife. Beech trees are also grown and harvested for flooring and furniture.

When, Where, and How to Plant
When purchasing a beech, make sure you understand if the variety prefers part shade or sun conditions before choosing your site. Beeches appreciate a rich soil that is well drained, with very consistent moisture. Water the rootball well before planting. Dig a hole at the same depth of the rootball but at least twice as broad. Plants that are balled and burlapped should have as much of the burlap and wire basket removed as possible. Do not plant beneath power lines as the tree grows too large.

Growing Tips
Mulch after planting with 3 inches of compost to help the tree get established. Beeches are susceptible to root area disturbances. Continue mulching annually to assist the beeches' shallow roots stay protected and hold more moisture. Compost or mulching material should be kept at least 3 inches away from the tree trunk to prevent rot. Do not add any amendments to the planting hole as fertilizers and some manures can burn the roots. Consistent moisture is key.

Regional Advice and Care
Aphids are easily dislodged with a spray of water from a hose. Beech bark disease happens when a tree is attacked by scale and fungus; there is no cure. It can sometimes be challenging to grow turfgrass beneath a beech due to its shallow root system and dense foliage growth.

Companion Planting and Design
Beeches do not do well in parking lots or along streets where their root structure cannot expand significantly. They are sensitive to salt so should not be planted near sidewalks that are salted. They are great in an area where the roots will have plenty of space to expand, such as large lawns, estate parkways, or as a specimen in a parklike setting.

Try These
'Roseo-Marginata' is a tricolor European beech that has green, white, and pink leaves with copper fall colors. It is best suited to part-shade. 'Asplenifolia' has an interesting fine-cut leaf with golden fall color. 'Pendula' is a weeping European beech with astounding arching branches. 'Riversii' has deep purple foliage all season that fades to coppery orange in fall.

Birch

Betula spp.

Botanical Pronunciation
BET-you-luh

Bloom Period and Seasonal Color
Fall; yellow and brown foliage

Mature Height × Spread
40 to 80 feet × 20 to 40 feet

When I moved into my first house with my husband, there was a paper birch tree outside our bedroom window. We would lie in bed on lazy Saturday mornings in our pajamas with the newspaper spread across our laps watching little yellow goldfinches eat the seeds off the tree for hours. Birch trees are typically small- to medium-sized deciduous trees with seeds that birds love. Most birches have colorful bark that peels off in thin plates; this is seen most distinctively in the "paperbark" birch, which peels abundantly. Most birches prefer moist soils, and birch trees such as the "river birch" are an effective choice for a rain garden planting due to their ability to absorb large quantities of water through the roots.

When, Where, and How to Plant

When purchasing a birch tree, make sure you understand whether the variety grows best in part shade or sun conditions before choosing a site. Birches, as a species, do not grow well in compacted soil and will not grow well planted in tight root zone locations; their roots need room to stretch out. Birches appreciate a rich soil that is well drained, with very consistent moisture. Water the rootball well before planting. Dig a hole the same depth of the rootball but at least twice as broad. Plants that are balled and burlapped should have as much of the burlap and wire basket removed as possible.

Growing Tips

Mulching the birch tree after planting with 3 to 4 inches of compost will help it get established. Birches need cool, consistently moist feet (roots); mulch them annually to help their shallow roots hold moisture. Compost or mulch should be kept at least 3 inches away from the tree trunk to prevent rot. Do not fertilize a birch tree unless there is proven soil malnutrition.

Regional Advice and Care

Birch trees can sometimes suffer drought-induced yellow leaves. All birch trees require consistent water and prefer to be planted in moist soil. River birch is particularly demanding of water and will yellow and eventually die without the proper moisture. Birch can sucker and naturalize, forming a colony; spade suckers back annually.

Companion Planting and Design

Birch trees are great trees to place in birding gardens and landscape designs. Plant birches on the north and east sides of a building or home instead of the south or west as this provides a location where they might have part-shade without the harsher afternoon sun, which can dry the soil.

Try These

Betula utilis var. *jacquemontii* is the Himalayan birch. It grows to 35 to 40 feet tall and 20 feet wide and has attractive golden leaves in fall. *B. lenta*, or black birch, has beautiful black bark; its twigs smell of wintergreen when they are broken. It prefers moist, acidic soils.

Catalpa

Catalpa speciosa

Botanical Pronunciation
kuh-TAL-puh spee-see-OH-suh

Other Names
Cigar tree, fishbait tree

Bloom Period and Seasonal Color
Early summer; white flowers with purple fringes

Mature Height × Spread
50 to 60 feet × 30 feet

On the farm I lived on as a child, there were hundreds of acres of property where trees could be planted, yet my grandparents chose to plant a giant catalpa tree immediately adjacent to the front sidewalk and driveway. After the sweet-smelling spring bloom of gorgeous orchidlike flowers erupted, catalpa worms, which are the caterpillar of the sphinx moth, would voraciously attack the tree and drop into my mother's bouffant hairstyle as she ran screaming from the car to the front door. Sphinx moths and catalpa trees have had a symbiotic relationship for centuries and, remarkably, most trees can be extremely defoliated by them yet still survive. The inedible fruit of the catalpa is a seedpod resembling a long cigar leading to its name of cigar tree. An alternate common name is fishbait tree.

When, Where, and How to Plant
Catalpas are full sun lovers that need plenty of room to stretch their legs; do not site close to a building. Plant the tree in a fertile, moist, well-drained soil. The tree is tolerant of clay soils and adapts to a variety of conditions. Water the rootball well before planting. Dig a hole the same depth of the rootball but at least twice as broad. Plants that are balled and burlapped should have as much of the burlap and wire basket removed as possible.

Growing Tips
While catalpa trees will tolerate drought and adverse conditions once established, it appreciates regular watering in its first year to help it adapt. Mulch the tree after planting with 3 inches of compost, keeping compost or mulching material at least 3 inches away from the tree trunk to prevent rot. Do not fertilize a catalpa tree unless it shows malnutrition.

Regional Advice and Care
Most catalpa trees are easy to care for and have very few disease or pest issues, beyond the ever-present summer caterpillars. Catalpa trees can be affected by fungal issues such as powdery mildew, blight, and wilt, particularly when overcrowded or planted near shade.

Companion Planting and Design
Planting the catalpa tree at the back of a landscape or property ensures beautiful flowers and a consistent supply of caterpillars for fish bait, without worries of them dropping into your bouffant hairstyle. Catalpas do very well planted along sidewalks, parking lots, and city streets, living approximately 60 years. They are rather coarse trees that do not consistently exhibit a symmetrical tree form. When designing a landscape incorporating a catalpa, keep in mind it is a heavy litter-producing plant that will require maintenance; flowers drop, caterpillars drop, giant seedpods drop, and leaves drop.

Try These
Catalpa ovata, Chinese catalpa, can grow well in colder zones and has pale yellow flowers. *C. bignonioides*, southern catalpa, is native to the southeastern United States and has slightly smaller flowers and seedpods than the northern catalpa. Southern catalpa leaves have an unpleasant aroma when they're crushed.

Crabapple

Malus spp.

Botanical Pronunciation
MAY-lus

Bloom Period and Seasonal Color
Spring; white, pink, and red blossoms

Mature Height × Spread
6 to 40 feet × 15 to 25 feet

For two weeks each spring, my front lawn vegetable garden is an explosion of white flowers thanks to a 35-year-old crabapple tree that has become the neighborhood spring queen. We love her, and she seems to flourish with the extra compost I have added to the ornamental edible garden planted amongst her roots. Most flowering crabapples begin declining between 35 to 40 years old, yet some have been known to grow to a ripe old age of 70 years. Crabapples are edible and can be made into jellies and jams. The fruit can be incredibly tart and wildlife sometimes ignore it until late winter when hungry little cedar waxwings and robins spend hours eating the remaining fruits.

When, Where, and How to Plant

Crabapple trees prefer 12 hours of sunshine per day. They like to be planted in a rich, loamy soil that is well drained. Crabapples will die if their roots are in boggy soil with poor drainage. Shady conditions encourage fungal disease, blight, and apple scab. Bare-root trees should only be planted in spring and should not be forced into curled positions. This causes girdling of the tree and can kill it. Trees that are balled and burlapped can be planted nearly anytime. Remove all burlap, rope, and wire, and then water the rootball well before planting. Dig a hole the same depth of the rootball but at least twice as broad.

Growing Tips

Mulch annually with 2 inches of compost to help the crabapple preserve moisture. Water yearling trees with 1 inch of water per week until established. Crabapples sucker directly from roots as well as around the root base; cut suckers out at any time.

Regional Advice and Care

A common disease for crabapples is apple scab. Leaves have yellowing with brown edges and black spots, and the diseased leaves drop in late summer. Many crabapple trees will continue to live with the disease but look less attractive, and some will lose all their foliage. Treating with fungicides in the spring can help prevent the appearance of the disease but cannot totally eradicate it. To prevent the disease, purchase scab-resistant crabapple cultivers.

Companion Planting and Design

Crabapples look best as the centerpiece to a garden and offer four-season interest. They cast shade in the landscape, so planting shade-loving perennials below its bounteous arms makes sense. Try heuchera, hosta, brunnera, native wild geranium, and Japanese painted fern.

Try These

'Firebird®' has a rounded form, resistance to disease, red fruit, and white flowers. It grows to 10 feet high. 'Pink Princess™' grows to 8 feet high and has red fruit, strong disease resistance, and abundant pale pink flowers. 'Golden Raindrops®' is 20 feet high and has deeply cut green leaves, yellow crabapples, and disease resistance.

Douglasfir

Pseudotsuga menziesii

Botanical Pronunciation
soo-doe-TSOO-guh MEN-zeez-ee-eye

Other Names Oregon pine, Douglas spruce

Bloom Period and Seasonal Color
Evergreen foliage; yellow catkins in spring

Mature Height × Spread 50 feet × 20 to 40 feet (much taller in more natural settings)

Douglasfir is an important tree for the environment. Typically, Douglasfir grows to 50 feet in urban settings; it can grow up to 300 feet in native settings in the United States, and its seeds feed chipmunks, voles, moles, shrews, sparrows, finches, and many others. Douglasfir is often used in the timber industry for the manufacture of plywood. Young trees smell deliciously piney and are used as Christmas trees. Within the floral industry, douglasfir is used for greenery. Deer dislike the prickly needles of the Douglasfir, so it is an excellent tree to use where deer are a nuisance. Planting a Douglasfir is a long-term investment for a landscape because the trees can easily live to be 120 years old or more. You might see it listed as Douglas spruce.

When, Where, and How to Plant

Partial to a location that has full sun and moist, well-drained soil with a higher fertility, Douglasfir can also adapt to more adverse conditions such as drought. Planting the tree in an area that has medium wet soil can reduce long-term water maintenance. Plants that are balled and burlapped should have as much of the burlap and wire basket removed as possible. Backfill around the rootball until it is about half filled. Water the rootball and backfill well. Place the rest of the soil around the rootball, forming a "well" at the base of the plant. Place in a location where the plant will not be overcrowded as air circulation decreases disease risk.

Growing Tips

Water Douglasfir consistently until well established. Fertilizer is not necessary unless tree is showing signs of disease.

Regional Advice and Care

High winds can injure the trees, so don't use the Douglasfir as a windbreak. Planting in a sheltered area will be more successful for the plant. Shape or prune out dead branches in late winter. Overcrowded trees or ones planted in shadier conditions are vulnerable to many diseases including blight and other fungal issues.

Companion Planting and Design

Young Douglasfirs make perfect Christmas trees as they are very fragrant and hold their blue-green needles for a long while. In landscapes, douglasfirs act as centerpieces as well as functional evergreen hedges. Their great girth makes them challenging to manage in a small garden once they have grown to full size, so they are better in larger landscape plantings. Douglasfir can be used for erosion control as long as the soil is not excessively rocky.

Try These

'Glauca' is a blue-needled form with more compact, upright branches. 'Graceful Grace' is a weeping form with longer needles and lovely drooping branches. 'Fastigiata' is upright with a spire form and gray-green needles. 'Fletcheri' is a common form that is also considered a shrub, growing to 6 feet tall and 3 feet wide. 'Loggerhead' has the same conifer needle foliage as the other plants, but its habit is mounded and rather dense and spreading.

Flowering Dogwood

Cornus spp.

Botanical Pronunciation
CORN-us

Bloom Period and Seasonal Color
Spring; white, pink, and red blossoms

Mature Height × Spread
12 to 30 feet × 12 to 30 feet

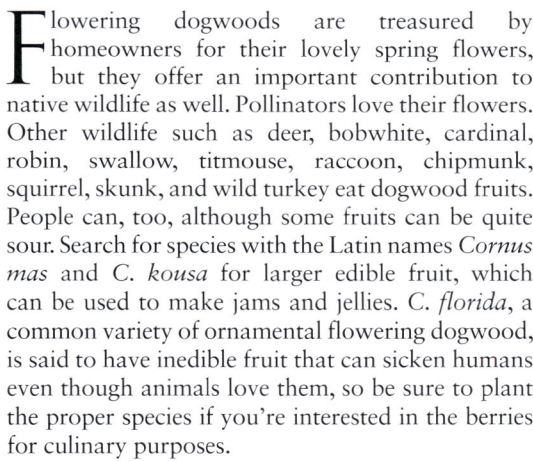

Flowering dogwoods are treasured by homeowners for their lovely spring flowers, but they offer an important contribution to native wildlife as well. Pollinators love their flowers. Other wildlife such as deer, bobwhite, cardinal, robin, swallow, titmouse, raccoon, chipmunk, squirrel, skunk, and wild turkey eat dogwood fruits. People can, too, although some fruits can be quite sour. Search for species with the Latin names *Cornus mas* and *C. kousa* for larger edible fruit, which can be used to make jams and jellies. *C. florida*, a common variety of ornamental flowering dogwood, is said to have inedible fruit that can sicken humans even though animals love them, so be sure to plant the proper species if you're interested in the berries for culinary purposes.

When, Where, and How to Plant
Dogwoods are understory trees in native woodlands around the world and can easily grow beneath maples, poplar, hickory, oak, and American beech in the Midwest. Plant dogwoods in a sunnier location; morning sun in particular will help prevent fungal problems, although it can survive shady situations well. They like to be planted in a rich, fertile soil that is high in organic matter and well drained. Remove all burlap, rope, and wire from the rootball, and then water the rootball well before planting. Dig a hole the same depth of the rootball but at least twice as broad when planting.

Growing Tips
Water consistently until the tree is established. Water the trees in droughts because dogwoods in distress are more likely to contract diseases. Mulching the tree with several inches of compost annually will help a dogwood hold moisture, but it also allow nutrients to trickle down through the soil. Do not fertilize otherwise unless the tree is showing signs of malnutrition. Be cautious when mowing because the bark of the tree is susceptible to lawn equipment damage.

Regional Advice and Care
Prune trees in spring immediately after flowering. Rainy spring weather can bring on dogwood anthracnose, caused by *Discula destructiva*, which is a fungus that kills the cambium tissue beneath the inner bark. This fungus does less damage in hot or dry weather. Good air circulation can help with prevention.

Companion Planting and Design
Because dogwoods have shallow roots, it's best to plant shallow-rooted perennials as companions such as Japanese painted fern, wild geranium, astilbe, sweet woodruff, heuchera, and ajuga. Dogwoods have brilliant red foliage in fall and look lovely when planted as a specimen in a woodland or bird garden.

Try These
'Golden Shadows' pagoda dogwood is 12 feet high and offers attractive bicolor foliage that is green and yellow. Stellar Pink® has pink flowers and reddish purple leaves in fall. It grows to 20 feet. 'Cloud 9' has showy flowers that are white with white bracts and bright red berries. 'China Girl' kousa dogwood has creamy white flowers, bumpy fruit, and grows to 20 feet.

Ginkgo

Ginkgo biloba

Botanical Pronunciation
GINK-oh by-LOE-buh

Other Name
Maidenhair tree

Bloom Period and Seasonal Color
Fall; yellow foliage

Mature Height × Spread
40 to 80 feet × 40 feet

Leaves of the ginkgo tree are captivating; bluish green in the summer, they are shaped like fans. In the fall, the leaves turn golden yellow. Fossils of the ginkgo have been found that date back to the dinosaur era. Ginkgo tolerates pollution, salt, and heat, as well as both alkaline and acid soils. With its exotic-looking leaves and remarkably tolerant nature, ginkgo is a fantastic tree both for urban and rural display. Ginkgo trees are a deciduous conifer. The female trees produce and drop noxious-smelling, messy golden fruit. Male trees will not produce the messy fruit. Its fruit is toxic to humans if eaten in large quantities. Be cautious when eating the seeds; while the seed, or "ginkgo nut," is considered edible, it must be boiled or roasted first to remove its toxicity.

When, Where, and How to Plant

While ginkgoes prefer moist, sandy, well-drained soil, it is easily grown in average soil. It is particularly suitable for urban planting as it tolerates pollution well and can be planted in virtually any native soil with success. Plant the tree in full sun. Water the rootball well before planting. Dig a hole the same depth of the rootball but at least twice as broad. Plants that are balled and burlapped should have as much of the burlap and wire basket removed as possible.

Growing Tips

Mulch after planting with 3 to 4 inches of compost all the way to the drip line to help a ginkgo get established. Compost or mulching material should be kept at least 3 inches away from the tree trunk to prevent rot. Watering consistently during the first year of growth will ensure the plant's ongoing success; only water in drought thereafter. Ginkgoes do not like boggy or constantly wet feet. Do not fertilize a ginkgo unless there is proven soil malnutrition.

Regional Advice and Care

No particular pests or diseases affect the ginkgo. Pruning is not typically needed, although cutting crossed branches can assist in developing the tree's form. Snow and ice storms can cause cracked branches; remove those limbs in spring.

Companion Planting and Design

Ginkgo trees are conversation pieces in the landscape and make stupendous specimen features. They are often referred to as "living fossils" because of their ancient heritage. Since they tolerate some winter road salt, they work well planted along sidewalks, driveways, and streets.

Try These

'Autumn Gold' is a fruitless all-male cultivar that grows to 50 feet with yellow fall color. 'Princeton Sentry®' is wider at the base than the top and is a fruitless cultivar growing to 70 feet with golden leaves in fall. 'Fairmount' is a fruitless male with a narrow, more pyramidal habit, and yellow fall color. 'Jade Butterflies' is a dwarf tree, however it can get up to 12 feet high over the course of its lifetime.

Hawthorn

Crataegus spp.

Botanical Pronunciation
kruh-TEE-gus

Bloom Period and Seasonal Color
Spring; white flowers

Mature Height × Spread
20 to 30 feet × 30 feet

Birds find refuge in the hawthorn as a nesting tree because of its vicious thorns; they form a defensive, protective perimeter for nests. The tree's crowning glory are the stunning, fragrant white blossoms that flower in spring. Hawthorn berries, which develop in fall and are commonly called "haws," are often transformed into jellies and jams. The one-seed hawthorn, *Crataegus monogyna*, has such a high pectin value that it can be made into a no-cook jelly. While hawthorn berries are edible for humans, birds, and certain wildlife, the seeds can be deadly to pets and humans alike. Strain the seeds out and do not eat them as they can be highly toxic. Flowers can be eaten raw in salads or desserts or made into a tea.

When, Where, and How to Plant

Certain varieties of hawthorns can live up to 400 years if they're planted in the appropriate location. Most urban trees live 50 years or more. Plant a hawthorn in a sunnier location; morning sun is best as it will help prevent fungal problems, although hawthorns can survive shady situations well. They will tolerate nearly any soil as long as it is well drained. Remove all burlap, rope, and wire from the rootball, and then water the rootball well before planting. Dig a hole the same depth of the rootball but at least twice as wide when planting.

Growing Tips

Water consistently until the tree is established. Also water in drought conditions because trees in distress are more likely to contract diseases. Mulching the tree with several inches of compost annually will help the hawthorn hold moisture but also allow nutrients to trickle down through the soil. Do not fertilize otherwise unless the tree shows signs of malnutrition.

Regional Advice and Care

Prune trees in spring immediately after flowering. Cut back dead wood anytime. It can be attacked by leaf spot, leaf rust, and fireblight. Fungus is the enemy of the hawthorn. Some of these fungal conditions can be controlled by planting the hawthorn in sunlight with good air circulation. Leaf conditions can be controlled with an organic fungicide.

Companion Planting and Design

Most hawthorns handle pollution well so the plant is well-used in the urban landscape as a small, flowering tree feature. It has year-round interest and functions fabulously in a birding or pollinator garden.

Try These

'Winter King' is disease resistant, grows to 25 feet, has peeling silver bark, and bright red-orange berries and burgundy leaves in fall. 'Inermis' is a thornless hawthorn growing to 25 feet. *Crataegus phaenopyrum*, or Washington hawthorn, has good form, bold red berries, lots of thorns, and grows to 25 feet. 'Ohio Pioneer' is a thornless variety growing to 30 feet. Crusader® is a cockspur hawthorn with horizontally tiered branches.

Hybrid Elm

Ulmus hybrids

Botanical Pronunciation
ULL-mus

Bloom Period and Seasonal Color
Spring; inconspicuous flowers

Mature Height × Spread
40 to 100 feet × 40 to 80 feet

Elm trees were used as street trees and truly represented Main Street USA in the beginning of the 20th century until Dutch elm disease, a wilt fungus, decimated the trees. It is reported that by 1970 over 77 million trees were dead, and a new understanding of the importance of planting diverse tree varieties within our communities became mainstream. Hybridized varieties of the elm tree have made a strong comeback because of their resistance to Dutch elm disease. Native varieties have been known to grow over 100 feet tall, but most hybrids get about 60 feet tall. Elms have winged seeds called samaras that are well loved by squirrels, chipmunks, songbirds, and game birds. Baltimore orioles love to weave their pendulous nests in elms.

When, Where, and How to Plant

Plant an elm in a sunnier location; morning sun is best as it will help prevent fungal problems, although the tree can survive shade well. Elms will tolerate most soils as long as they are well drained. Remove all burlap, rope, and wire from the rootball, and then water the rootball well before planting. Dig a hole the same depth of the rootball but at least twice as wide before planting.

Growing Tips

Water consistently until the tree is established. Also water the trees in drought conditions because plants in distress are more likely to contract fungal disease. Annually mulching the tree with several inches of compost will help an elm hold moisture but also allow nutrients to trickle down through the soil. Do not fertilize otherwise unless the tree is showing signs of malnutrition.

Regional Advice and Care

Prune trees in early spring before foliage develops. Cut back deadwood, water sprouts, and suckers at any time. Wildlife enjoys the spring seed litter, but tidy seeds by blowing or raking them up. Fungus is the enemy of the elm. While new varieties are resistant to Dutch elm disease and other fungi, they can still be attacked by fungal problems. Some of these conditions can be controlled by planting the elm in full, direct sunlight with good air circulation. Do not plant an elm in shady or crowded conditions; it will perform poorly.

Companion Planting and Design

Elms handle pollution, winter salt, and high traffic areas well. Additionally, they are very adaptable to most soils, making them a stupendous selection for the urban landscape, particularly inner city areas. Its glossy leaves make the elm ideal as a shade tree near patios and pathways.

Try These

Commendation™ has glossy green leaves, grows rapidly, and has yellow fall leaves. It grows between 40 and 60 feet. 'Triumph™' will reach 60 feet high and 40 feet wide, has good branching, and significantly improved disease and pest resistance. 'Dynasty' is a very hardy, vase-shaped, Chinese elm with leaves that turn bright orange in fall.

Japanese Tree Lilac

Syringa reticulata

Botanical Pronunciation
sur-ING-guh ruh-tick-you-LAY-tuh

Bloom Period and Seasonal Color
Early summer; white, cream, and pale yellow blooms

Mature Height × Spread
20 feet × 20 feet

    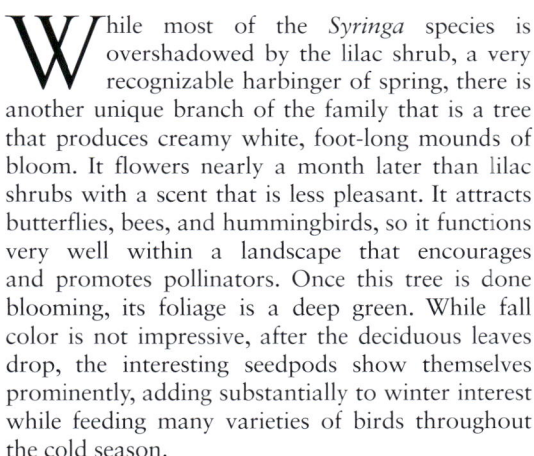

While most of the *Syringa* species is overshadowed by the lilac shrub, a very recognizable harbinger of spring, there is another unique branch of the family that is a tree that produces creamy white, foot-long mounds of bloom. It flowers nearly a month later than lilac shrubs with a scent that is less pleasant. It attracts butterflies, bees, and hummingbirds, so it functions very well within a landscape that encourages and promotes pollinators. Once this tree is done blooming, its foliage is a deep green. While fall color is not impressive, after the deciduous leaves drop, the interesting seedpods show themselves prominently, adding substantially to winter interest while feeding many varieties of birds throughout the cold season.

When, Where, and How to Plant
Grow Japanese lilac trees in a moist, fertile, well-drained soil with full sun exposure. They will survive in part shade, but flowering will be reduced considerably. Plant this tree in spring by digging a hole that is the same depth of the rootball and twice as wide in a well-drained planting area.

Growing Tips
Water consistently to encourage healthy blooming. Mulch the soil with a 3-inch layer of organic matter to help the soil hold water and protect it from winter cold. Fertilizer is not required. Japanese tree lilacs provide a heavy level of shade due to a dense growing structure, so it can be difficult to grow grass beneath the canopy. With this in mind, each spring consider applying a thick layer of compost out to the drip line, then another layer of mulch to aid in its growth.

Regional Advice and Care
Seed litter for the tree can be considerable. Trim seedpods if you would like to lessen the litter, or leave them to provide winter food for birds if you want the tree to support local wildlife. Unlike traditional shrub lilacs, Japanese tree lilacs do not sucker. Pruning is typically not necessary; however, if it needs tidying, prune the Japanese lilac tree in summer immediately following its bloom period. Overcrowding Japanese tree lilacs or planting them in shade can encourage unattractive mildew and fungal issues to develop.

Companion Planting and Design
As a relatively short tree, Japanese lilacs make a great statement as a courtyard or another small space. Most Japanese lilac trees tolerate pollution and urban environments, so it can easily work as a small tree along a building or public walkway.

Try These
'Ivory Silk' grows to 25 feet tall and has ivory-toned flowers. 'Snowdance' prefers more moisture, has an oval shape, and grows to approximately 20 feet. 'Chantilly Lace' has interesting variegated foliage that has a pale yellow perimeter. Beijing Gold™ is a Peking tree lilac that has more yellow-toned flowers and yellow leaves in fall.

Kentucky Coffeetree

Gymnocladus dioicus

Botanical Pronunciation
jim-NOCK-luh-dus dye-oh-EE-kuss

Bloom Period and Seasonal Color
Early summer; green leaves with greenish white flower panicles

Mature Height × Spread
60 to 70 feet × 90 feet

Kentucky coffeetree has astoundingly large leaves that are larger than those found on most trees in North America. Each leaf can be up to 3 feet long and is actually made of many individual leaflets. New leaf growth can be bronzy in color until it ripens to a bold green. It is one of the last trees to leaf out in spring. Although the leaves are quite large, the foliage looks airy and open because of the distinctive leaflets. Kentucky coffeetree has become a much more popular tree in the last several years because of its adaptability to various soils including heavily alkaline soils. Hummingbirds and pollinators love the fragrant, white, early-summer flower panicles. Note that the seedpods are poisonous to pets and to humans without proper culinary preparation.

When, Where, and How to Plant

While Kentucky coffeetree prefers moist, humus-rich, well-drained soil, it is easily grown in average soil and is surprisingly adaptive to environmental stresses such as compacted soils, heat, and drought. This makes it particularly suitable for urban planting as it tolerates pollution as well. Plant the tree in full sun. Water the rootball well before planting. Dig a hole the same depth of the rootball but at least twice as broad. Plants that are balled and burlapped should have as much of the burlap and wire basket removed as possible. Female Kentucky coffeetrees are attractive, but they drop the large seedpods, which are a foot long at the end of winter, and which will require tidying; consider purchasing a male tree for less litter.

Growing Tips

Watering consistently during the first year of growth will ensure the plant's ongoing success; only water in drought thereafter. Mulching the tree after planting with 4 inches of compost all the way to the drip line will help it get established. Compost or mulch should be kept at least 3 inches away from the tree trunk to prevent rot. Do not fertilize the Kentucky coffeetree unless there is proven soil malnutrition.

Regional Advice and Care

No particular pests or diseases affect the Kentucky coffeetree. Prune in winter or very early spring before buds take shape. Remove dead or broken branches anytime. Trees can sucker if their roots are disturbed and suckers should be spaded back annually.

Companion Planting and Design

Kentucky coffeetree is an attractive tree that allows grass to grow beneath its canopy. It works well in large landscapes, lawns, and parks. Since the tree tolerates some winter road salt, they work well planted along sidewalks, driveways, and streets.

Try These

'J.C McDaniel' is an upright, spreading male selection with interesting textured bark and blue-green foliage. 'Espresso' grows to 50 feet tall and has a vaselike shape. 'Stately Manor' has dark green foliage that turns gold in the fall.

Linden

Tilia spp.

Botanical Pronunciation
TILL-ee-uh

Bloom Period and Seasonal Color
Early summer; pale yellow flowers

Mature Height × Spread
30 to 80 feet × 30 to 50 feet

Lindens are known as lovely shade trees. Though a linden's flowers might not be as attractive as some, their powerful honey-lemon scent enlivens a neighborhood with fragrance when the tree is blooming. Bees and butterflies adore the sweet nectar that the tree provides, making it an excellent contributor to a pollinator garden. Nearly every part of the linden is edible, except the wood. Flowers, fruits, and even the leaves can be used raw in salads or cooked in dishes; its sap is sweet and can be utilized as a sweetener. Dropped seeds are eaten by birds and small mammals. Because of its acceptance of diverse soil types, it is well adapted in most locations beyond exceptionally wet soils.

When, Where, and How to Plant
While lindens prefer a sunny location, they can tolerate shady situations. They like most soil types as long as they are well drained; boggy soil will kill a linden tree. Remove all burlap, rope, and wire from the rootball, then water the it well before planting. Dig a hole the same depth of the rootball but at least twice as broad when planting.

Growing Tips
Water consistently until the tree is established. Also water the trees in drought conditions because plants in distress are more likely to contract disease problems. Mulch with 4 inches of compost annually to help the tree hold moisture. Do not fertilize unless the tree is showing signs of needing it.

Regional Advice and Care
Prune trees in late winter during dormancy before flowering by cutting back or shearing undesirable branches. Cut back dead wood anytime. Although lindens are relatively free of pests and disease, crowding the plants or planting in heavier shade can encourage both insect and fungal problems. Wood rot, where the center of the tree hollows out, is a fairly common problem and can weaken the tree over time.

Companion Planting and Design
Birds love the seeds of lindens, so placing the tree among a birding landscape would be most considerate. Most lindens handle pollution well, so the plant is well used in the urban landscape or inner city. A few lindens, including littleleaf linden, will not tolerate salt, so plant lindens cautiously near streets and driveways.

Try These
Tilia cordata, littleleaf linden, grows to 50 feet, has a very attractive shape, and is considered the best landscaping linden. 'Greenspire' grows to 40 feet and can be expected to live 70 years. *T. americana*, basswood, grows to 80 feet and is known as an edible tree; it prefers rich soil. *T. platyphyllos* 'Rubra' is more easily made into a hedge; its young twiggish branches are tinted red. Silver linden, *T. tomentosa*, grows 80 to 100 feet tall, has foliage with dramatic silver backsides but is only hardy to Zone 6.

London Planetree

Platanus × acerifolia

Botanical Pronunciation
PLAT-uh-nus × ass-er-ih-FOLE-ee-uh

Bloom Period and Seasonal Color
Spring; yellow and red flowers; green leaves

Mature Height × Spread
75 to 100 feet × 70 feet

Mature London planetrees are exceedingly large and can top 100 feet. The tree has grown in popularity in recent years due to its exfoliating brown-gray bark that drops off in uneven sections to reveal an off-white interior bark. While many mistake the London planetree for a sycamore tree, it is not. It is a cross between the American sycamore, *Platanus occidentalis*, and the oriental planetree, *P. orientalis*. Its name originates from the city of London, where it was planted in excess in the late 1600s because of its urban pollution tolerance and ability to tolerate root compaction. While not particularly attractive to pollinators, London planetrees do house squirrels and birds, which eat its spiky seedballs once they drop for the season.

When, Where, and How to Plant
London planetrees welcome a rich soil that is well drained but has very consistent moisture. Trees prefer full sun but will tolerate shadier conditions. Consideration should be made for its extensive size when searching for an appropriate planting site. Water the rootball well before planting. Then dig a hole the same depth of the rootball but at least twice as wide before planting. Plants that are balled and burlapped should have as much of the burlap and wire basket removed as possible.

Growing Tips
Mulch well to encourage moisture retention and water consistently throughout the first season. There's really no need to fertilize.

Regional Advice and Care
These trees can be quite messy, due to bark shedding and flower, seed, and leaf drop. London planetree foliage has a tiny hair that grows on it that is also dropped seasonally. Some asthma and allergy sufferers are sensitive to this irritant. Pruning is best done in late winter before new growth appears. London planetrees are often grown in wet and shady situations; it is susceptible to fungal diseases, particularly when crowded. It was originally thought to resist sycamore anthracnose, but that is questionable. New cultivars have improved resistance and should be chosen over older cultivars. Lace bugs and aphids are common pests found on the trees. They will not kill a tree, so they are mostly ignored.

Companion Planting and Design
This large, stately tree works in a very open landscape space meant to encourage birds and wildlife. Once the leaves drop, the bark adds seasonal winter interest. Because of its love for moisture, it is a brilliant solution in an area where water absorption is critical, such as a large rain garden or the transitional space between a waterway and dry prairie.

Try These
'Columbia' is an upright tree with orange-gray bark and deep green lobed leaves. 'Liberty' is a pyramidal tree that is not totally immune to powdery mildew and anthracnose, but it is resistant. 'Bloodgood' was bred for anthracnose resistance. It tolerates poor soil and cultural conditions, including drought and heat.

Magnolia

Magnolia spp.

Botanical Pronunciation
mag-NOLE-yuh

Bloom Period and Seasonal Color
Spring; white, yellow, pink, and burgundy-tinged blossoms

Mature Height × Spread
10 to 30 feet × 30 feet

Flowering magnolia trees have some of the most outstanding blooms in nature. Their flowers can be huge and are often fragrant. If it's an early-blooming cultivar, the flowers will be displayed on naked stems before the tree's leaves appear. If it blooms later, the tree will show both foliage and flower together. Several species are native to the Midwest, but most cultivars found at garden centers are hybridized species. Magnolia is a deciduous tree, but can be grown as a shrub, and its flowers are pollinated by beetles. Flowers can be forced indoors in vases once buds have formed on the limbs. Not all magnolias survive in northern climates, so be sure to research those cultivars that will perform better in your community.

When, Where, and How to Plant

Plant magnolias in the early spring in a rich, fertile soil that is high in organic matter and well drained. Magnolias prefer bright sun and will flower less in shadier conditions. Remove all burlap, rope, and wire from the rootball. Next, water the rootball well before planting. Dig a hole at the same depth of the rootball but at least twice as broad when planting.

Growing Tips

Water very regularly until the tree is established. Magnolias do not handle drought well; keep consistently watered. Annually mulching the tree with several inches of compost out to the drip line will help the soil hold moisture. Do not fertilize unless a tree is showing signs of malnutrition.

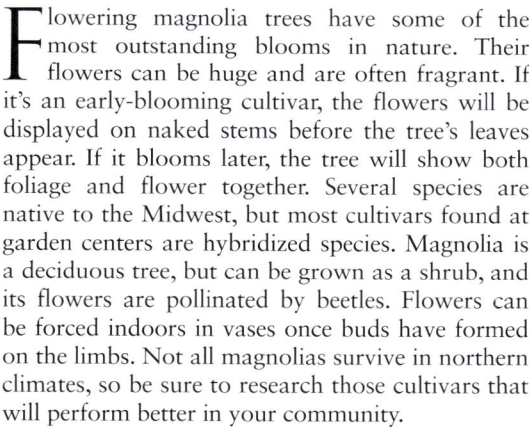

Regional Advice and Care

Pruning is not required regularly; however, if it must be done to tidy the plant, prune the trees in spring immediately after flowering. Overcrowding magnolias or planting them in heavy, damp shade can encourage unattractive mildew and fungal issues to develop such as wood rot, gray mold, and verticillium wilt. Plant the trees with plenty of room for air circulation. Magnolias can lose their flowers because of late frosts, so it may be advantageous to plant late-blooming varieties. Roots are fleshy and particularly sensitive to damage; be cautious when digging around them.

Companion Planting and Design

When magnolia trees are not blooming, their stalwart green background leaves act as a blending tool in the landscape. Magnolia seeds are enjoyed by songbirds. When trees are in bloom their color and fragrance is extraordinarily captivating. With this in mind, plan bulb gardens in partnership with the magnolia's bloom time. Yellow magnolias look fantastic with contrasting purple- and yellow-shaded bulbs below the tree.

Try These

'Yellow Lantern' has soft yellow flowers held up in a cup form, which makes them look like little lanterns on the tree. It grows to 20 feet. 'Leonard Messel' has attractive, white, star-shaped flowers that are tinged in pink, growing to 20 feet. 'Galaxy' is a late-blooming magnolia with large pinkish purple flowers and leaves that turn bronze in fall.

Maple

Acer spp.

Botanical Pronunciation
AY-sur

Bloom Period and Seasonal Color
Fall; colorful foliage

Mature Height × Spread
5 to 60 feet × 15 to 40 feet

Sap from maple trees was originally collected by the native peoples of North America, who taught the colonists how to make the delicious syrup. Sugar maple, red maple, and black maple are the primary American varieties that can be used for sugar collection. Beyond its value for sap production, though, is the spectacular fall color available with many maples. There are *dozens* of species of maples from all over the world. My favorites include the Japanese maples, many of which have interesting leaf color all spring and summer long, not just in fall. Maple trees can grow over 100 feet, but most popular varieties available at nurseries stay under 60 feet There's a wonderful maple selection for every landscape.

When, Where, and How to Plant
While maples prefer a sunny location, some varieties, such as Japanese maples. are more understory plantings and can require shadier situations. Research the tree you want before planting. Most maples like fertile, moist, but well-drained soil. Remove all burlap, rope, and wire, then water the rootball well before planting. Dig a hole the same depth of the rootball but at least three times as broad when planting to prevent root girdling.

Growing Tips
Water consistently until the tree is established. Be aware of the maple tree's water requirements because many can suffer leaf browning in drought conditions. Mulching the tree with 3 inches of compost annually will help the maple hold moisture.

Do not fertilize unless the tree is showing signs of malnutrition.

Regional Advice and Care
Prune maple trees in cool weather; never remove more than one-fifth of the tree's branches. Cut back dead wood at any time. Maple trees have winged seeds called "samaras" that are eaten by squirrels, chipmunks, and songbirds. When they drop, they can be quite messy and often self-seed all over the landscape.

Companion Planting and Design
Because maple trees are so widely varied in size and form, its best to consider the tree's mature height and width before planning the landscape. Tall, stately maples are lovely as a street or lawn tree; it needs plenty of space and full sun. Japanese maples are more likely to need some shade to prevent leaf scorch and combine well with shade-loving perennials such as hakonechloa, blue fescue, hosta, ferns, perennial geranium, and a variety of bulbs.

Try These
Acer griseum, or paperbark maple, grows to 30 feet and has interesting peeling bark. They are less likely to reseed. 'Autumn Blaze' has intense red fall color and grows to 50 feet. 'Crimson Queen' is a Japanese maple that grows to 5 feet and has burgundy foliage all season. 'Golden Full Moon' grows to 10 feet with attractive chartreuse, hand-shaped foliage turning red in fall. 'Bloodgood' grows to 20 feet and has burgundy foliage throughout the season.

Oak

Quercus spp.

Botanical Pronunciation
KWURK-us

Bloom Period and Seasonal Color
Fall; colorful foliage; flowers are inconspicuous

Mature Height × Spread
30 to 100 feet × 30 to 100 feet

Some oak trees live over 1,000 years. Native oaks are essential to the environmental structure within the Midwestern states. They are large, stately, beautiful trees that symbolize strength and unity. Oak trees support over 532 different species of moths and butterflies and over 100 species of mammals. Vertebrates that consume the acorns include squirrels, mice, voles, rabbits, deer, fox, wild turkeys, mallards, bobwhite quail, crows, and jays. Before settlement, the state featured large stands of oak forests and oak savannah prairies that supported native wildlife. With farming and urbanization of large areas in the Midwest, many of these natural areas have been destroyed. Therefore, when you plant an oak tree you are doing a service to the native environment by helping support its wildlife.

When, Where, and How to Plant
Oak trees need room to spread and prefer full sun. They like most soils as long as they are well drained. Remove all burlap, rope, and wire from the rootball, and water the rootball well before planting. Dig a hole the same depth of the rootball but at least three times as broad when planting.

Growing Tips
Water consistently until the tree is established. Mulch the tree with 4 inches of compost annually to help the soil hold moisture. Many varieties need consistent moisture; water during drought. Do not fertilize unless the tree is showing signs of malnutrition.

Regional Advice and Care
Prune trees only after November and before April. Pruning during the primary growth season encourages a devastating disease, oak wilt, to attack. Oaks can suffer from many diseases, particularly when crowded or planted in heavier shade. Bacterial leaf scorch, anthracnose, oak wilt, and root rot are a few. Help chlorotic trees with applications of chelated iron mixed in the soil in spring and fall. Many of these diseases can be quite serious; consult a professional arborist to better understand treatment.

Companion Planting and Design
Oaks are large, stately trees for a very open landscape space meant to encourage birds and wildlife. Do not plant oaks close to other large trees that will compete for nutrients, or too close to buildings. Oaks have many understory plants that can be planted nearby such as dogwoods, Japanese maples, and redbuds.

Try These
Swamp white oaks grow to 60 feet and are a species that likes wet soil. It has a leaf with a white underside. Bur oak is known as the hardiest of the species and somewhat tolerates urban situations. It grows to 60 feet and has a tough constitution. 'Green Pillar' pin oak grows to 50 feet but only grows 15 feet wide; this makes it a good selection for tight spots or to make into a hedge. Red oaks grow to 45 feet and have magnificent fall foliage. Chestnut oak has a different leaf structure than most oaks and can survive in rocky or more acidic soils.

Pine

Pinus spp.

Botanical Pronunciation
PYE-nus

Bloom Period and Seasonal Color
Evergreen foliage

Mature Height × Spread
50 to 80 feet × 20 to 35 feet

Pine trees are shallow-rooted conifers that offer gorgeous evergreen color year-round and a delicious pine scent. More important, they are a food source and residence for native wildlife. Birds, squirrels, pine martens, chipmunks, and mice are just a few of the creatures known to eat the pine nuts found in the pine cone. Pine trees grown in the proper conditions can live to be hundreds of years old. Pines are known as a needled forest tree and can be planted in stands, as windbreaks and hedges, or used as erosion control when planted *en masse* on large hillsides. Pines are notorious, however, for not tolerating urban pollution and inner city situations. They prefer open air and large growing areas that will fit their expansive girth.

When, Where, and How to Plant

Most pines are easily grown in full sun with fertile, moist, well-drained soil. Some pines suffer from harsh winter sun and wind; research varieties for the specific area where you will plant. Trees can be grown from seed but will take years to develop. Nursery-grown trees are preferable. Plants that are balled and burlapped should have as much of the burlap and wire basket removed as possible. Backfill around the rootball until it is about half filled. Water the rootball and backfill well. Place the rest of the soil around the rootball, forming a "well" at the base of the plant.

Growing Tips

Young pine trees are particularly susceptible to sunburn and dehydration. Water the pine tree consistently until well established. Mulch the tree out to the drip line to help hold moisture. Consider installing a windbreak or screen to help protect the tree in its infancy. Once it is well established, the pine tree should be strong enough to tolerate sun and wind. Prune out dead branches and shape the tree in late winter.

Regional Advice and Care

Protect young trees from foraging deer. Depending upon your location within the state, pine trees can be used for erosion control. Virginia pine, jack pine, and shortleaf pine are all species of pine trees that tolerate challenging erosion areas. Trees overcrowded or planted in shadier conditions are vulnerable to many diseases including blight and other fungal issues.

Companion Planting and Design

Young white pines, Scotch pines, and Austrian pines are all used as Christmas trees because of their fragrance and strong form. In landscapes, their large size makes them challenging to manage in a small garden once they have grown to maturity, so they are better in larger landscape plantings.

Try These

White pine makes an excellent shade tree, growing to 60 feet tall. 'Glauca' or Japanese blue pine grows to 40 feet and has interesting blue-green needles. Dragon's eye Japanese red pine is a variety that has unusual emerald green needles with yellow stripes that turn chartreuse in fall; it grows to 30 feet high.

Redbud

Cercis canadensis

Botanical Pronunciation
SUR-siss kan-uh-DEN-siss

Other Name
Judas tree

Bloom Period and Seasonal Color
Spring; white and pink flowers

Mature Height × Spread
6 to 30 feet × 6 to 30 feet

We had a giant walnut tree in my front lawn when I was a teenager and nothing of significance would tolerate the soil beneath the walnut except a gorgeous row of redbuds with happy pinkish purple buds growing on their bare branches. Their bloom heralded warm days and new possibilities. Although redbud is a native tree grown in the understory of woodlands, it is not the favorite food source for all wildlife; squirrels and songbirds will sometimes eat the seed. Once the tree is done blooming, it leafs out with beautiful dark green, heart-shaped foliage, and then produces bunches of flat brown seedpods. Leaves turn a brilliant golden orange in fall and the long seedpods stay until late winter. Flowers can be forced indoors in vases in early spring.

When, Where, and How to Plant

Plant redbuds in early spring in a rich, fertile soil that is high in organic matter and well drained. They prefer bright sun, but because of their nature as understory trees, will also tolerate varying levels of shade. Buy plants that have been grown at a local nursery so that the tree is used to the winters in your part of the state. Remove all burlap, rope, and wire from the rootball, and then water the rootball well before planting. Dig a hole the same depth of the rootball but at least twice as wide at planting.

Growing Tips

Redbud is a tree that does like fertilizer; what type and how much fertilizer is needed can be determined by a soil test and a discussion with your local County Extension Office. Typically, it should be fertilized with an organic fertilizer in spring. Each year, mulch the surrounding soil with several inches of compost out to the drip line to help enrich the soil. Water consistently throughout the season. Adding an extra layer of hay mulch the first and second season will help insulate the rootball.

Regional Advice and Care

Prune in spring immediately after it flowers. If planted at the edge of a woodland or in a shady area, redbud trees are known to lean toward the light, which might affect the shape of the tree. Overcrowding redbuds or planting them in heavy, damp shade can encourage extensive fungal issues to develop such as anthracnose, wood rot, gray mold, and verticillium wilt. Plant the trees with plenty of room for air circulation and as close to a sunny location as possible.

Companion Planting and Design

Redbuds look attractive if planted in groups of three to five. White-blooming redbuds look marvelous when planted as a white centerpiece to a very colorful bulb garden.

Try These

'Lavender Twist' has weeping branches and grows to 6 feet high. 'Alba' is a white redbud that grows to 20 feet. 'Hearts of Gold' has gold fading to green leaves, growing 15 feet high.

Spruce

Picea spp.

Botanical Pronunciation
PYE-see-uh

Other Name
Blue spruce

Bloom Period and Seasonal Color
Evergreen foliage; green or blue-gray

Mature Height × Spread
12 to 50 feet × 5 to 25 feet

Spruce is a native conifer from the Colorado Rockies that has a high ornamental value in the landscape. Many in the spruce family have a highly sought-after gray-blue foliage tone, which can show quite intensely when the tree is planted in front of deeper shades of green. Spruce looks particularly stunning in winter when its blue colors stand out against bright white snow. Spruce trees are often mistaken for pine trees, but the branching on the trees is different and the spruce is more tolerant of environmental salt and adverse conditions. As with pines, wildlife such as birds, squirrels, chipmunks, and mice are known to live in the spruce boughs and eat the nuts found in the cone of the spruce.

When, Where, and How to Plant

Spruces are easily grown in full sun with fertile, moist, well-drained soil. Different types of trees prefer different type of soil conditions; for example, white spruce handles clay soils and silt well, while others do not. Plants that are balled and burlapped should have as much of the burlap and wire basket removed as possible. Dig the hole twice as big as the rootball, place tree in the center of the planting hole, and fill in the rest of the soil around the rootball, forming a "well" at the base of the plant.

Growing Tips

Water a spruce tree consistently until it's well established. Mulch the tree out to the drip line with a 3- to 4-inch layer of compost or bark mulch to help hold moisture. There's no need to fertilize.

Regional Advice and Care

Consider installing a windbreak or screen to help protect the tree if it is particularly tiny. Once it is well established, remove the windbreak and prune regularly as needed. Prune dead branches anytime, but regular shaping should happen in late winter. Spruces are typically healthy trees. However, if planted in the wrong conditions the trees can suffer stress and then be more likely to host diseases and pests. Overcrowded trees or those planted in shadier conditions are vulnerable to many diseases including blight and other fungal issues.

Companion Planting and Design

Spruces are a long-lived species, growing over 600 years in the right location. Many spruces are highly drought tolerant and can handle environmental salt, making some spruce a better choice for planting in urban landscapes. Spruces are very effective windbreaks and hedges. Dwarf blue spruce look delightful mixed in a birding garden. Birds will nest and hide in the spruce's needles for protection.

Try These

Weeping Norway spruce grows 25 feet tall, 5 feet wide, and has a weeping shape. 'Acrocona' grows in a shorter Christmas tree shape, and reaches 12 feet. 'Tompa' dwarf spruce keeps a conical shape but only grows to 5 feet high. 'Densata' or Black Hills spruce grows to 40 feet. 'Glauca' blue spruce grows to 50 feet with an intensely blue shade of foliage.

Tuliptree

Liriodendron tulipifera

Botanical Pronunciation
leer-ee-oh-DEN-drun too-lip-IFF-ur-uh

Other Names
Yellow poplar, tulip poplar

Bloom Period and Seasonal Color
Greenish yellow and orange flowers in May

Mature Height × Spread
5 to 60 feet × 15 to 40 feet

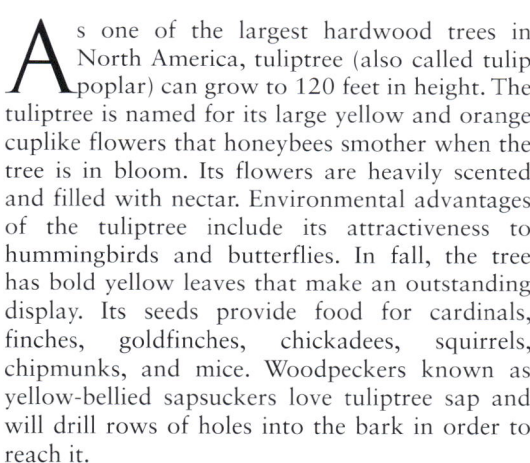

As one of the largest hardwood trees in North America, tuliptree (also called tulip poplar) can grow to 120 feet in height. The tuliptree is named for its large yellow and orange cuplike flowers that honeybees smother when the tree is in bloom. Its flowers are heavily scented and filled with nectar. Environmental advantages of the tuliptree include its attractiveness to hummingbirds and butterflies. In fall, the tree has bold yellow leaves that make an outstanding display. Its seeds provide food for cardinals, finches, goldfinches, chickadees, squirrels, chipmunks, and mice. Woodpeckers known as yellow-bellied sapsuckers love tuliptree sap and will drill rows of holes into the bark in order to reach it.

When, Where, and How to Plant

Plant tuliptrees in early spring in a rich, fertile soil that is high in organic matter and well drained. Tuliptrees prefer bright sun. They will flower less and be more susceptible to disease in shadier conditions. Tuliptrees do not do well in highly urban environments because they cannot tolerate pollution well. To plant, remove all burlap, rope, and wire from the rootball, and water the rootball well. Dig a hole the same depth of the rootball, but at least twice as wide when planting.

Growing Tips

Pruning is not regularly required; however, tuliptrees are known to have brittle branches that break in high winds. The branches, sprouts, and crossed branches can be trimmed off at any time. Annually mulching the tree with several inches of compost out to the drip line will help the soil hold moisture. No fertilizer is needed.

Regional Advice and Care

Overcrowding tuliptrees or planting them in heavy, damp shade can encourage mildew and fungal issues to develop such as wood rot, gray mold, and verticillium wilt. Plant the trees with plenty of room for air circulation. Discourage yellow-bellied sapsuckers by hanging lifelike owls or inflated snakes in the tree during early spring and late fall when the birds are migrating.

Companion Planting and Design

The tuliptree's unique leaf is somewhat tulip-shaped in profile. They are known as the "sap poplar" because its sap regularly drops off trees on windy days. This makes planting the tree near a driveway or street challenging. Design plantings in open areas, away from cars and building windows, with lots of sun exposure.

Try These

There are very few cultivars outside of the standard *Liriodendron tulipifera* species. 'Majestic Beauty®' has bright green, almost chartreuse leaves that are quite striking. It grows to 60 feet tall and 25 feet wide. 'Arnold' is a columnar tree growing 25 to 50 feet tall but only about 8 feet wide.

VINES
FOR INDIANA

Vines can be gorgeous superheroes in a well-landscaped garden, providing food for pollinators and birds, highlighting arbors, creating shade across walkways, camouflaging ugly structures, and flowering nonstop. They can also be villains that destroy buildings, fences, and trees. The secret with a vine is to understand its growing nature and place it on structures that are strong enough to support its weight. A wonderful advantage of a vine is that it takes up very little ground space, so it is particularly suited to urban gardens and landscapes where there is little ground space, so it can address utilitarian and ornamental situations.

Location, Location, Location

Perennial vines are long-term investments in your landscape design. They will thrive for years climbing up a wall or arbor and can be an excellent source of color and life. However, what if you need to paint the wood structure the vine is clinging to? Vines can make this process extremely difficult. Clematis climbs by winding petioles around

Vines such as this clematis can form a delightful stretch of color on an otherwise boring wall. Building a landscape design that incorporates structures, fences, and walls can be greatly beautified and enhanced by planting vines.

supports. Other vines latch on to things with adhesive-like suction cups, vine tendrils, and rootlets. These built-in tools of a self-supporting vine often have the strength to crack concrete, dig into brick, and pull down shutters. The suction cup-like adhesion marks are nearly impossible to get off siding. Planning ahead for the long term for your vine's location is absolutely critical.

Keep in mind that some vines are trailers, while others are powerful climbers. Vines can reach out their arms and find shrubs, perennials, and other trees to latch on to, which should be understood before you plant your vine in order to keep the vine within the landscape plan you originally envisioned.

Many vines such as wisteria and grapevine can be grown over the top of structures to form shade for walkways and patio areas. This photo shows a pink-themed garden with overhead shade created by trained vines.

Vine Care

Once you have planned the proper location for your vine, prepare the soil based on your soil testing results, adding at least 4 inches of organic matter. Be sure to place the proper support for your vine: lightweight for an annual vine or extremely sturdy for a perennial vine. Make sure the support is securely mounted. Dig an appropriate hole for your plant between 6 to 12 inches out from the support. Vines can be quite thick, and you want to be able to access the base of a plant to water and fertilize in the future. Plant the vine, water in, and mulch well. Fertilize annually with an organic fertilizer.

Once planted, training a vine up a support is quite easy to do while it's in an active growth phase. Use rubber ties, insulated wire, or loose zip ties to support and train heavier vines. For lighter-weight vines, train with loose zip ties, twine, twist-ties, or old pantyhose. Be sure to check the ties several times a year to make sure that you are not girdling the stems of the vine.

Pruning a vine is critical to its care, both to keep it from overtaking its support and also to keep it looking attractive. Vines need regular pruning to stimulate growth, and timing depends upon the individual vine. Often vines look better at the top and not as attractive at the base of the plant. This happens more often when a gardener trims the top heavily, stimulating the top growth more, and the bottom is left unattended. Pruning can help improve the overall look of the vine and balance out the top and bottom views. Most typically, vines that bloom on new growth will need cutting back in early spring before growth appears. Vines that bloom on old growth should be pruned back immediately after they flower.

Superhero or villain—it's up to you to decide.

American Bittersweet

Celastrus scandens

Botanical Pronunciation
suh-LASS-truss SKAN-dins

Bloom Period and Seasonal Color
Early summer; green-yellow flowers; bright orange or red fruits

Mature Length
20 to 50 feet, twining

Bittersweet is a vigorous native vine that grows up to 50 feet by twining. Because it is a rapidly growing vine, it is best used on sturdy supports and prevented from climbing on small trees that can be girdled or suffocated by it. Bittersweet has gorgeous red-orange seeds and fruits that represent its primary ornamental value, and which can be used in flower arrangements and crafting. In woodlands, many types of native birds enjoy the seeds including wild turkey, grouse, bobwhite, and pheasant. However, it can self-seed readily, and the vine can become thuggish and invasive. Bittersweet is also toxic to pets and humans. Therefore, be cautious when planting this groundcover near areas where small children might ingest it.

When, Where, and How to Plant

American bittersweet is easily grown in average, well-drained soil in full to part sun. To ensure pollination and strong fruit production, plant one male plant for every six female plants, all near one another. In fact, planting a male and a female plant together in the same hole ensures better pollination. Transplant from containers. Dig a hole as deep as the container the plant came in, then place plant in the hole. Although it can be planted anytime during the growing season, it does best when planted in early spring.

Growing Tips

Do not fertilize bittersweet as it is an aggressive grower. Keep the plant dry, too; regular water will encourage the plant to jump in growth.

Regional Advice and Care

While bittersweet will grow freely without any help whatsoever, it is a plant that needs consistent maintenance. The goal is to contain it and the secret is strong pruning. American bittersweet suckers at the root level; hack suckers back with a spade or small ax twice a year. Cut it back hard at the base in fall and collect the berries for flower arrangements in winter. Cut it again in spring after its first strong flush of growth. This vine becomes quite woody and difficult to compost, and the seeds will root in compost, so plant materials will have to be disposed of.

Companion Planting and Design

Do not plant oriental bittersweet, which has become incredibly invasive in some parts of the United States. American bittersweet is best used as a screen or on a fence. It can also be grown in a naturalized setting or used as a groundcover. Pollinators such as bees and butterflies seem to enjoy the plant in spring; for that reason, it would grow well as a fence screen at the back of a butterfly garden.

Try These

'Autumn Revolution' is a self-pollinating variety that prefers full sun and has very large fruit. Most nurseries simply carry the standard "American bittersweet" and do not have specific distinguishing varieties. It can sometimes be difficult to find male and females sold separately.

Boston Ivy

Parthenocissus tricuspidata

Botanical Pronunciation
par-then-oh-SISS-us try-kuss-pih-DAY-tuh

Bloom Period and Seasonal Color
Fall; red foliage

Mature Length
60 feet, twining

Boston ivy is a fast-growing, woody, deciduous vine. It should not be confused with English ivy (*Hedera helix*) and is more closely related to Virginia creeper (*Parthenocissus quinquefolia*), which are known to cover entire buildings in their aggressiveness. Because of its weight and large size, Boston ivy is best suited to masonry and brick buildings or walls. Boston ivy is well known in the Midwest as the ivy that grows on the walls at Chicago's Wrigley Field. It has lovely fall color that starts as an orange and evolves into a deep red. Boston ivy is exceptionally toxic to cats, dogs, horses, and humans. Therefore, be cautious when planting this vine where pets and small children might eat it.

When, Where, and How to Plant
Easily grown in average soil in full sun to shade, Boston ivy prefers well-drained soil. It is quite adaptable both to dry and damp circumstances, but it does not like boggy conditions. Plant Boston ivy near incredibly strong supports or permanent walls. Dig a hole as deep as the container it has come in and double its width, and then place plants in the hole, backfilling gently. Place plants at least 2 feet away from walls and other plants. Although it can be planted anytime during the growing season, it does best when planted in early spring in soil that has been amended with rotted manure or compost.

Growing Tips
Water to get established; however, once the plant is established it needs very little care. No fertilizer is needed unless the plant is suffering from an illness or problem; it can become very invasive if fertilized.

Regional Advice and Care
Boston ivy can easily climb walls by adhesive holdfasts called sucker disks. These disks are incredibly difficult to remove from walls and can damage surfaces or buildings if you try to remove them. Do not plant Boston ivy on painted walls, wood siding, or wood fences that will rot and need to be replaced. Cut or shear it back wherever it grows out of bounds. Do not fear hurting this vine; it is so abundant that it should come back with little harm done. Prevent fungal issues by watering the vine at the base of the plant and treating it with an organic fungicide

Companion Planting and Design
Use Boston ivy to help reduce energy use. During summer, a stone or brick structure can save a significant amount of energy by having the Boston ivy shade its walls. In some conditions Boston ivy can be invasive. Caution and careful consideration should be used when planting this ivy regarding its long-term maintenance.

Try These
'Green Showers' has a bright green leaf that appears yellow in early spring. Foliage turns reddish purple in fall, and the blue berries of this plant are attractive to birds.

Clematis

Clematis spp.

Botanical Pronunciation
KLEM-uh-tiss

Bloom Period and Seasonal Color
Summer; purple, white, pink, red, yellow, and bicolor flowers

Mature Length
5 to 40 feet, vining

Clematis flowers are captivating; some blooms can be 6 inches across, with bold colors and interesting structure. Once you plant clematis, you will want another and another; they become quite addicting. There is a clematis vine for nearly any planting circumstance, which makes them particularly versatile in the modern garden. 'Comtesse de Bouchard', 'Jackmanii', and 'Henryi' seemed to be the common varieties found at most nurseries up until a few years ago. But there has been an explosion of hybridization since then that has brought astounding colors, reblooming varieties, and improved selections. Vines can be very large or quite compact depending on the variety selected. All parts of the clematis are poisonous; be cautious when planting near the play areas of pets and small children.

When, Where, and How to Plant

Moist, well-drained soil in full sun is the clematis's preferred environment. Plants flower more when placed in full-sun locations. However, there is a secret to growing all clematis: While they prefer a sunny locale, their roots need to be cool and shaded. This is accomplished by planting the root base deep. In spring, dig a hole 2 to 3 inches deeper than the size of the growing container. Place the plant in the hole, then backfill loosely with soil, and water well. Cover the entire area around the base of the plant with a 3-inch layer of mulch.

Growing Tips

Clematis performs better with consistent watering and regular fertilizing. Fertilize with an organic low-nitrogen fertilizer every four to six weeks throughout its growing season.

Regional Advice and Care

Clematis grows by vining, not twining. This means the vine doesn't aggressively wrap around things and sometimes needs guidance going in the desired direction. Often trellises are large and do not have small supports for the clematis to gently grab on to. Better supports can be created by adding twine, netting, or fishing line to help this vine climb. Mid-spring bloomers grow on old wood and should be pruned at the end of flowering. Prune new wood bloomers in early spring before growth begins. Cut vines back to as much as 12 inches above the ground. Do not crowd the vines and water at the base of the plants for preventative maintenance. Vines planted in shadier conditions can suffer from fungal issues; treat with an organic fungicide.

Companion Planting and Design

Low-growing perennials planted around the base of a clematis will help keep roots cool; ornamental grasses work for this, or perennials such as perennial geranium, daylily, or nepeta. Clematis is a delightful vine that is rarely invasive although it can get large; sweet autumn clematis can grow to 20 feet.

Try These

'Praecox' has tiny flowers in shades of white edged with purple and mauve; it climbs to 20 feet. 'Duchess of Edinburgh' has double white flowers, blooming in summer. 'Niobe' has deep red flowers and climbs to 10 feet.

Honeysuckle

Lonicera spp.

Botanical Pronunciation
luh-NISS-ur-uh

Bloom Period and Seasonal Color
Summer (some varieties flower in winter);
yellow, pink, salmon, orange, and red blooms

Mature Length
20 to 40 feet, twining

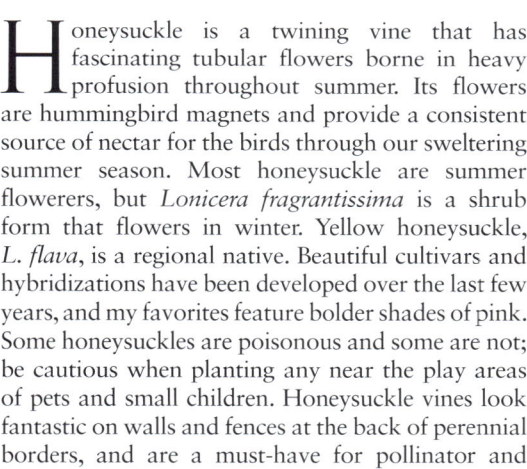

Honeysuckle is a twining vine that has fascinating tubular flowers borne in heavy profusion throughout summer. Its flowers are hummingbird magnets and provide a consistent source of nectar for the birds through our sweltering summer season. Most honeysuckle are summer flowerers, but *Lonicera fragrantissima* is a shrub form that flowers in winter. Yellow honeysuckle, *L. flava*, is a regional native. Beautiful cultivars and hybridizations have been developed over the last few years, and my favorites feature bolder shades of pink. Some honeysuckles are poisonous and some are not; be cautious when planting any near the play areas of pets and small children. Honeysuckle vines look fantastic on walls and fences at the back of perennial borders, and are a must-have for pollinator and hummingbird gardens.

When, Where, and How to Plant

Plant honeysuckle in spring in full sun. It adapts to a wide range of soils but prefers rich, fertile, well-drained soil. Consider amending heavy soil with a mixture of natural items such as rotted manure, compost, and worm castings. Dig a hole that is as deep as the container the plant came in, then place plants in the holes and gently refill.

Growing Tips

Water consistently until well-established, making sure the soil dries out between watering. Mulch to help protect its roots. Do not fertilize; the plant could take over if given too much encouragement.

Regional Advice and Care

Prune for maintenance by regularly cutting back any dead growth or occasionally shaping the plant as needed. After the first flush of bloom in summer, try lightly pruning to encourage a heavier flush later in the season. Once every three to six years, completely prune honeysuckle back to rejuvenate it; cut to within 2 to 3 feet of the ground in late winter before new growth starts. You will know when to do this because the vines will seem to be overgrown and leggy. Honeysuckle can suffer from many varieties of fungal problems such as powdery mildew and blackspot. Help prevent these by planting in full sun as shadier conditions can encourage disease. Treat fungal problems with an organic fungicide.

Companion Planting and Design

Honeysuckle often blooms for several months in summer; this makes it a long-term source of food for hummingbirds. Consider planting at the back of pollinator or hummingbird gardens. It also looks brilliant along a short fence or near a gate. Songbirds love the fruit that is produced in fall. Note: Do *not* plant Japanese honeysuckle, which has become incredibly invasive in the Midwest.

Try These

'Dropmore Scarlet' grows to 12 feet, has deep red flowers, and a slight fragrance. 'Goldflame' has reddish pink flowers with yellow tones. It grows to 12 feet and is not particularly aggressive. 'Mandarin Trumpet' has orange coloring with yellow tones with bronze fall foliage.

Morning Glory

Ipomoea purpurea

Botanical Pronunciation
ip-uh-MEE-uh pur-PUR-ee-uh

Bloom Period and Seasonal Color
Summer; purple, white, pink, red, blue, and bicolor flowers

Mature Length
5 to 40 feet, vining

Morning glories are annual flowering vines that bring back memories of my grandmother's farm. She would plant them at the base of old fence posts, and when I went out on my morning adventuring through the countryside, their heart-shaped leaves and smiling faces warmed my soul. Morning glories are known as reliable bloomers through most of the summer, thriving in heat, which is usually a time that many plants melt. Most morning glories bloom passionately in the early morning, closing their flowers by late afternoon. They come in bold colors including shades of true blue, which makes morning glory a good design solution to climb on small structures. Morning glories are quite poisonous; be cautious when planting near the play areas of pets and small children.

When, Where, and How to Plant

Sensitive to ice and cold, morning glory seeds should be planted well after the last frost. File the seeds lightly to break their seed coat, and then soak the seeds for 24 hours. Plant the seeds ¼-inch below the surface in average, loamy soil. Planting in highly fertile soil can encourage leaves and discourage blooms. They prefer consistently moist soil that drains well. It is possible to start the seeds indoors about 6 weeks before the last frost, but they need to be placed in the ground without disturbing the roots. To do this, make your own pots from newspaper, planting the newspaper pots with seedlings directly into the soil.

Growing Tips

Plants flower more when placed in full-sun locations without heavily wet soils. Let the soil dry out between watering. Do not fertilize.

Regional Advice and Care

Prune anytime to keep the plants tidy, or leave the plants to ramble if you have the space in the landscape. Morning glories will self-seed and the two-leaved babies can be seen popping up in late summer and spring. To prevent this, pop the flowers off as they wilt on the vine. Vines planted in shadier conditions can suffer from fungal issues. Do not crowd morning glory vines, and water at the base of the plants for preventative maintenance. Treat fungal problems with an organic fungicide.

Companion Planting and Design

Morning glories can be grown creatively so that they tumble out of containers. Most morning glories do not grow taller than 20 feet, so they tend to like smaller supports. Posts, low fences, and small structures all make delightful climbing locations. Consider mixing red, white, and true blue morning glories to create a Fourth of July design.

Try These

'Grandpa Ott's' is an heirloom variety of morning glory that blooms a deep purple with a pink throat. 'Scarlett O'Hara' has bold red flowers. Moonflower, *Ipomoea alba*, is a white flower that is known to open just as evening commences. *I. tricolor* 'Flying Saucer' has striped flowers.

Trumpet Vine

Campsis spp.

Botanical Pronunciation
KAMP-siss RAD-ih-kanz

Other Names
Hummingbird vine, trumpet creeper

Bloom Period and Seasonal Color
Summer; yellow, orange, and red blooms

Mature Length
30 feet, twining

Hummingbirds flock to the trumpet vine in droves in early evening. It is a thick-growing vine that is quite heavy, with bright green foliage and tubular flowers shaped like trumpet bells. Trumpet vine (also called trumpet creeper) resists deer, performs well in heavy soils like clay, and thrives in drought. While this native plant is a natural for a hummingbird garden, trumpet vine is extremely aggressive. If you plant it, be prepared to spend some time cutting it back as it easily charges through your garden by self-seeding as well as by suckers and underground runners. While climbing to 30 feet and more, it can also be used as a groundcover that can be used to disguise rocky areas or used on hillsides to prevent erosion.

When, Where, and How to Plant
Plant trumpet vine in spring in full sun. It adapts to a wide range of soils but prefers well-drained rich, fertile soil. Think about amending heavy soil with a mixture of natural materials such as rotted manure, compost, and worm castings. Dig a hole that is as deep as the container the plant came in, then place the plant in the hole and gently refill.

Growing Tips
Water consistently until well established, making sure the soil dries out between watering, and be sure to mulch to help protect its roots. Do not fertilize.

Regional Advice and Care
Prune about one-third to one-half of the plant all the way back to the first bud growth each year.

Rejuvenation pruning can happen should the entire vine begin to look ratty, suffer from disease, or become extremely invasive. Simply prune the entire vine back to the first bud growth in late winter or early spring before spring growth starts. Trumpet vine can self-seed in waves; the best way to handle this is to snip off the flowers just as they are fading, before they have had time to form seeds. Trumpet vine is slightly toxic if eaten and can cause intense skin swelling and redness when touched by mammals. It can suffer from many varieties of fungal problems such as powdery mildew and blackspot; help prevent these by planting in full sun as shadier conditions can encourage disease. Treat fungal problems with an organic fungicide.

Companion Planting and Design
Be extremely cautious when placing this plant to avoid siting near small trees or shrubs; they will quickly be smothered by a trumpet vine. Both hummingbirds and butterflies appreciate the trumpet vine's nectar, which makes the plant a good choice for a pollinator garden. Plant the vine along fence lines or on stalwart trellises.

Try These
'Balboa Sunset®' is a hearty grower with red blooms that fade to orange like a sunset. 'Flava' is a golden yellow trumpet vine. 'Indian Summer' is a less invasive variety with orange-yellow blooms.

Variegated Kiwi Vine

Actinidia kolomikta

Botanical Pronunciation
ak-tin-ID-ee-ah koe-lo-MIK-tah

Other Name Chinese gooseberry

Bloom Period and Seasonal Color
Spring; white flowers with season-long green, pink, and white foliage

Mature Length 20 feet, twining

On my very first trip to the Chicago Botanic Garden, I was flabbergasted by the variegated kiwi vine's pink, green, and white foliage. It was growing over an arbor in the ornamental edible garden and was like nothing I had ever seen before. Since then I have returned every year to see how it progresses. On years where there is more sun exposure, the leaves are filled with more variegation and color. If the season is rainy and gray, then the plant is less likely to show off its fanciness. This vine is a distant relative of the kiwi fruit we are commonly familiar with. It does produce large, yellowish, edible berries that ripen near fall, but it takes up to nine years to begin yielding.

When, Where, and How to Plant

Finding variegated kiwi vine at your local nursery might be challenging; plants can be ordered online and from mail order catalogs. Grow variegated kiwi vine in average, well-drained soil in full sun to part sun; more shade means less variegation on the leaves. Male plants have more variegation than female plants. Plant the vine in early spring in soil that has been amended with rotted manure or compost. Dig a hole the same depth as the plant's container and twice as wide, plant, and backfill the hole with soil. If you're growing for fruit production, plant one male plant for every three female plants. Variegated kiwi vines are vigorous growers and have thick, woody stems that can be immensely heavy. It will topple light supports and needs a strong structure to climb on.

Growing Tips

Placing a 3-inch layer of compost at the base of the plants will keep weeds back, protect against cold, and help hold soil moisture. These plants appreciate consistent moisture. Roots burn easily, so fertilize cautiously.

Regional Advice and Care

Vines can suffer "shoot burn" in early spring from late frosts. Simply cut the burnt shoots off; it will send new ones up. If flowers are nipped by frost, fruit will not develop although the foliage will continue to remain attractive. Pruning and training the vine is critical to its growth. Prune when dormant in late winter, then prune throughout the season as needed in order to shape the plant on its climbing structure. Should fungal diseases develop, treat with an organic fungicide.

Companion Planting and Design

Much like wisteria, this vine can be utilized as a design centerpiece for the landscape. They provide good shade and look particularly outstanding growing over pergolas, terrace walls, and large arbors. Variegated kiwi vine will grow in containers but prefers soil where its roots can take hold.

Try These

'Arctic Beauty' is a male so will not bear fruit, but it's grown for its variegated foliage. 'September Sun™' is a female that bears up to 15 pounds of fruit if fertilized by a male plant.

Wisteria

Wisteria spp.

Botanical Pronunciation
wiss-TEER-ee-uh

Bloom Period and Seasonal Color
Early spring; purple, pink, and white flowers

Mature Length
20 to 30 feet, twining

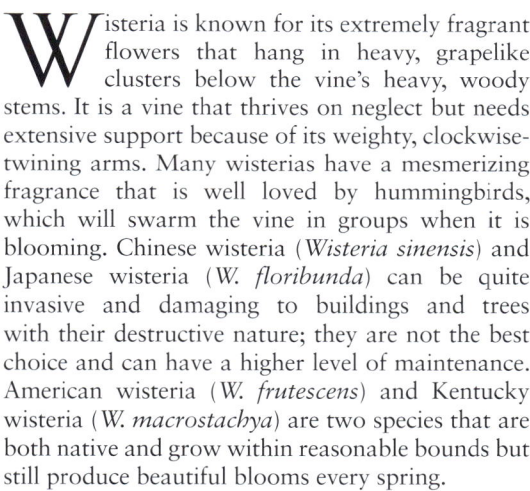

Wisteria is known for its extremely fragrant flowers that hang in heavy, grapelike clusters below the vine's heavy, woody stems. It is a vine that thrives on neglect but needs extensive support because of its weighty, clockwise-twining arms. Many wisterias have a mesmerizing fragrance that is well loved by hummingbirds, which will swarm the vine in groups when it is blooming. Chinese wisteria (*Wisteria sinensis*) and Japanese wisteria (*W. floribunda*) can be quite invasive and damaging to buildings and trees with their destructive nature; they are not the best choice and can have a higher level of maintenance. American wisteria (*W. frutescens*) and Kentucky wisteria (*W. macrostachya*) are two species that are both native and grow within reasonable bounds but still produce beautiful blooms every spring.

When, Where, and How to Plant
Plant a wisteria vine in a well thought-out site in the landscape. It needs a very strong support made of sturdy wire, metal, or stone. It is recommended that the support be able to easily hold the weight of a full-grown man; this is good advice as wisteria can be so heavy that wires drilled into walls but are not secured well can easily be ripped out. Wisteria is a poisonous plant, particularly its seedpods, so take this into consideration when planting. Keep wisteria away from play areas of pets and children. Wisteria seems to thrive on neglect and does better when planted in average soil with full sun. Dig a hole that is as deep as the container the plant came in, then place plant in hole, backfilling and mulching well.

Growing Tips
Wisterias like consistent water and can be planted in moist soil. Do not fertilize the wisteria as it will not flower if soil is overly fertile.

Regional Advice and Care
Wisterias often take a long time to flower, sometimes three to five years. Some vines in shadier conditions will never flower. Heavy pruning seems to help bring on the flowers more readily. Prune to shape after the blooms have faded. Wisteria also suckers at the root level; hack the suckers back with a spade or small ax twice a year. Prevent disease and fungal issues by watering at the base of the plant. Treat fungal problems with an organic fungicide.

Companion Planting and Design
Use as a design centerpiece for the full sun landscape. Wisteria looks particularly outstanding on pergolas, terrace walls, and large arbors. It is best grown away from homes that have loose siding; tendrils from wisteria sneak beneath siding and rip it off.

Try These
'Blue Moon' is a hardy Kentucky wisteria that grows to 30 feet and blooms with lilac-colored flowers three times per year. 'Aunt Dee' has pea-like violet flowers in large bunches with stunning yellow leaves in fall. 'Amethyst Falls' is an American wisteria that grows woodier with denser and showier foliage.

BIBLIOGRAPHY

Books

Adams, George. *Gardening for the Birds: How to Create a Bird-Friendly Backyard*
Portland, OR: Timber Press, 2013.

Ambler, Wayne. *Treasury of Gardening: Annuals, Perennials, Vegetables & Herbs, Landscape Design, Specialty Gardens*. Lincolnwood, IL: Publications International Ltd., 2000.

Beazley, Mitchell. *American Horticultural Society Encyclopedia of Gardening Techniques*. New York, NY: Octopus Publishing USA, 2013.

Brockman, C. Frank. *Trees of North America – A guide to field identification*. New York, NY: St. Martin's Press, 2002.

Dirr, Michael. *Dirr's Encyclopedia of Trees and Shrubs*. Portland, OR: Timber Press, 2011.

Dirr, Michael. *Manual of Woody Landscape Plants: Their Identification, Ornamental Characteristics, Culture, Propagation and Uses*. Champaign, IL: Stipes Publishing L.L.C., 2009.

Harrison, Lorraine. *Latin for Gardeners: Over 3,000 Plant Names Explained and Explored*. Champaign, IL: The University of Chicago Press, 2012.

Hodge, George. *Practical Botany for Gardeners: Over 3,000 Botanical Terms Explained and Explored*. Champaign, IL: The University of Chicago Press, 2013.

Kaufman, Sylvia, and Wallace Kaufman. *Invasive Plants: Guide to Identification and the Impacts and Control of Common North American Species, 2nd Edition*. Mechanicsburg, PA: Stackpole Books, 2013.

Myers, Melinda. *Midwest Gardener's Handbook: Your Complete Guide: Select - Plan – Plant – Maintain – Problem-solve*. Minneapolis, MN: Cool Springs Press, 2013.

Roth, Sally. *Attracting Butterflies & Hummingbirds to Your Backyard: Watch Your Garden Come Alive With Beauty on the Wing*. Emmaus, PA: Rodale Press, 2002.

Rothrock, Paul A. *Sedges of Indiana and the Adjacent States: The Non-Carex Species*. Indianapolis, IN: Indiana Academy of Science, 2009.

Solar, Ivette. *The Edible Front Yard: The Mow-Less, Grow-More Plan For A Beautiful Bountiful Garden*. Portland, OR: Timber Press, 2011.

Sweet, Rebecca. *Refresh Your Garden Design With Color, Texture & Form*. Cincinnati, OH: Horticulture, 2013.

Tallamy, Douglas. *Bringing Nature Home: How You Can Sustain Wildlife with Native Plants, Expanded Edition*. Portland, OR: Timber Press, 2009.

Weeks, Sally, and Harmon Weeks. *Shrubs and Woody Vines of Indiana and the Midwest. Identification, Wildlife Values, and Landscaping Use*. West Lafayette, IN: Purdue University Press, 2012.

Wilson, Andrew. *Contemporary Color In The Landscape, Top Designers, Inspiring Ideas, New Combinations*. Portland, OR: Timber Press, 2011.

Online Resources:

Chicago Botanic Garden. "Plant Profile Database," Chicago Botanic Garden's Plant Information Services, accessed September 20, 2013, www.chicagobotanic.org/plantinfo/pp/

Cornell University. "Recommended Urban Trees," Department of Horticulture College of Agriculture and Life Sciences, accessed November 1, 2013, www.hort.cornell.edu/uhi/outreach/recurbtree/index.html

Micsky, Gary. "Hardy Kiwi (Actinidia arguta, Actinidia kolomikta)," Cornell University Extension, accessed October 27, 2013, http://hwwff.cce.cornell.edu/content/crop-fact-sheets/hardy-kiwi.pdf

Missouri Botanical Garden. "Plant Finder Database," Missouri Botanical Garden Research Team, accessed November 1, 2013, www.missouribotanicalgarden.org/plantfinder/plantfindersearch.aspx

Morton Arboretum. "Quercus Plant Database," Morton Arboretum Research Team, accessed November 8, 2013, http://quercus.mortonarb.org

Purdue University Consumer Horticulture. "Prairie Wildflowers Native To Indiana," Department of Horticulture and Landscape Architecture, accessed August 28, 2013, www.hort.purdue.edu/ext/IN_prairie_wildflowers.html

USDA, NRCS. "The Plants Database," National Plant Data Team, accessed November 4, 2013, http://plants.usda.gov

University of Illinois. "Hortanswers Database," University of Illinois Extension Website and Database, accessed October 12, 2013, http://urbanext.illinois.edu/hortanswers

University of Illinois. "Horticulture," University of Illinois Extension Website and Database, accessed October 15, 2013, http://web.extension.illinois.edu/state/hort.html

University of Illinois at Urbana-Champaign. "Landscape and Human Health Laboratory," accessed October 1, 2013, http://lhhl.illinois.edu

GLOSSARY

Acidic soil: On a soil pH scale of 0 to 14, acidic soil has a pH lower than 5.5. Most garden plants prefer a soil a bit on the acidic side.

Afternoon sun: A garden receiving afternoon sun typically has full sun from 1 to 5 p.m. daily, with more shade during the morning hours.

Alkaline soil: On a soil pH scale of 0 to 14, alkaline soil has a pH higher than 7.0. Many desert plants thrive in slightly alkaline soils.

Annual: A plant that germinates (sprouts), flowers, and dies within one year or season (spring, summer, winter, or fall) is an annual.

***Bacillus thuringiensis* (B.t.):** B.t. is an organic pest control based on naturally occurring soil bacteria, often used to control harmful caterpillars such as cutworms, leaf rollers, and webworms.

Balled and burlapped (B&B): This phrase describes plants that have been grown in field nursery rows, dug up with their rootball intact, and the rootball is wrapped with burlap and tied with twine. Most of the plants sold balled-and-burlapped are large evergreen plants and deciduous trees.

Bare root: Bare-root plants are those that are shipped dormant, without being planted in soil or having soil around their roots. Roses are often shipped bare root.

Beneficial insects: These insects perform valuable services such as pollination and pest control. Ladybugs, soldier beetles, and some bees are examples.

Biennial: A plant that blooms during its second year and then dies is a biennial.

Bolting: This is a process in which a plant switches from leaf growth to producing flowers and seeds. Bolting often occurs quite suddenly and is usually undesirable, because the plant usually dies shortly after bolting.

Brown materials: A part of a well-balanced compost pile, brown materials include high-carbon materials such as brown leaves and grass, woody plant stems, dryer lint, and sawdust.

Bud: The bud is an undeveloped shoot nestled between the leaf and the stem that will eventually produce a flower or plant branch.

Bulb: A bulb is a plant with a large, rounded underground storage organ formed by the plant stem and leaves. Examples of plants that form bulbs are tulips, daffodils, and hyacinths. Bulbs that flower in spring are typically planted in fall.

Bush: *See* shrub.

Cane: A stem on a fruit shrub; usually blackberry or raspberry stems are called canes, but blueberry stems can also be referred to as canes.

Central leader: The term for the center trunk of a fruit tree.

Common name: A name that is generally used to identify a plant in a particular region, as opposed to its botanical name, which is standard throughout the world; for example, the common name for *Echinacea purpurea* is "purple coneflower."

Container: Any pot or vessel that is used for planting; containers can be ceramic, clay, steel, or plastic—or a teacup, bucket, or barrel.

Container garden: This describes a garden that is created primarily by growing plants in containers instead of in the ground.

Container grown: This describes a plant that is grown, sold, and shipped while in a pot.

Cool-season annual: This is a flowering plant, such as snapdragon or pansy that thrives during cooler months.

Cover crop: These plants are grown specifically to enrich the soil, prevent erosion, suppress weeds, and control pests and diseases.

Cross-pollinate: This describes the transfer of pollen from one plant to another plant.

Dappled shade: This is bright shade created by high tree branches or tree foliage, where patches of sunlight and shade intermingle.

Deadhead: To remove dead flowers in order to encourage further bloom and prevent the plant from going to seed.

Deciduous plant: A plant that loses its leaves seasonally, typically in fall or early winter.

Diatomaceous earth: A natural control for snails, slugs, flea beetles, and other garden pests, diatomaceous earth consists of ground-up fossilized remains of sea creatures.

Dibber: A tool consisting of a pointed wooden stick with a handle. Used for poking holes in the ground so seedlings, seeds, and small bulbs can be planted.

Divide: Technique consisting of digging up clumping perennials, separating the roots to create more plants, and replanting. Dividing plants encourages vigorous growth and is typically performed in spring or fall.

Dormancy: The period when plants stop growing in order to conserve energy; this happens naturally and seasonally, usually in winter.

Drip line: The ground area under the outer circumference of tree branches; this is where most of the tree's roots that absorb water and nutrients are found.

Dwarf: In the context of fruit gardening, a dwarf fruit tree is a tree that grows no taller than 10 feet tall and is usually a dwarf as a result of the rootstock of the tree.

Evergreen: A plant that keeps its leaves year-round, instead of dropping them seasonally.

Floating row covers: Lightweight fabric that can be used to protect plants from pests. Usually white in color.

Flower stalk: The stem that supports the flower and elevates it so that insects can reach the flower and pollinate it.

Four-inch pot: The 4-inch × 4-inch pots that many annuals and small perennials are sold in. Four-inch pots can also be sold in flats of eighteen or twenty.

Four-tine claw: Also called a cultivator, this hand tool typically has three to four curved tines and is used to break up soil clods or lumps before planting and to rake soil amendments into garden beds.

Frost: Ice crystals that form when the temperature falls below freezing (32°F).

Full sun: Areas of the garden that receive direct sunlight for six to eight hours a day or more, with no shade, are in full sun.

Fungicide: A chemical compound used to control fungal diseases. Organic fungicide is preferred for its positive environmental benefits. *See* organic fungicide.

Gallon container: A standard nursery-sized container for plants, a gallon container is roughly equivalent to a gallon container of milk.

Garden fork: A garden implement with a long handle and short tines; use a garden fork for loosening and turning soil.

Garden lime: This soil amendment lowers soil acidity and raises the pH.

Garden soil: The existing soil in a garden bed; it is generally evaluated by its nutrient content and texture. Garden soil is also sold as a bagged item at garden centers and home-improvement stores.

Germination: The process by which a plant emerges from a seed or a spore.

Grafted tree: A tree composed of two parts: the top, or scion, which bears fruit, and the bottom, or rootstock.

Graft union: The place on a fruit tree trunk where the rootstock and the scion have been joined.

Granular fertilizer: Fertilizer that comes in a dry, pellet-like form rather than a liquid or powder.

Grass clippings: The parts of grass that are removed when mowing; clippings are a valuable source of nitrogen for the lawn or the compost pile.

Green materials: An essential element in composting that includes grass clippings, kitchen scraps, and manure, and provides valuable nitrogen in the pile; green materials are high in nitrogen.

Hand pruners: An important hand tool that consists of two sharp blades that perform a scissoring motion; used for light pruning, clipping, and cutting.

Hardening off: The process of slowly acclimating seedlings and young plants grown in an indoor environment to the outdoors.

Hardiness Zone Map: This map lists average annual minimum temperature ranges of a particular area. This information is helpful in determining appropriate plants for the garden. North America is divided into 11 separate hardiness zones.

Hard rake: This tool has a long handle and rigid tines at the bottom. It is great for moving a variety of garden debris, such as soil, mulch, leaves, and pebbles.

Hedging: The practice of trimming a line of plants to create a solid mass for privacy or garden definition.

Heirloom: A plant that was more commonly grown pre-World War II.

Hoe: A long-handled garden tool with a short, narrow, flat steel blade, it is used for breaking up hard soil and removing weeds.

Hose breaker: This device screws onto the end of a garden hose to disperse the flow of water from the hose.

Host plant: A plant grown to feed caterpillars that will eventually morph into butterflies.

Hybrid: Plants produced by crossing two genetically different plants, hybrids often have desirable characteristics such as disease resistance.

Insecticide: This substance is used for destroying or controlling insects that are harmful to plants. Insecticides are available in organic and synthetic forms. Insecticides that are not organic can be harmful for the environment, therefore, organic is preferred.

Irrigation: A system of watering the landscape, irrigation can be an in-ground automatic system, soaker or drip hoses, or hand-held hoses with nozzles.

Jute twine: A natural-fiber twine, jute is used for gently staking plants or tying them to plant supports.

Larva: The immature stage of an insect that goes through complete metamorphosis; caterpillars are butterfly or moth larvae.

Larvae: Plural of larva.

Leaf rake: A long-handled rake with flexible tines on the head, a leaf rake is used for easily and efficiently raking leaves into piles.

Liquid fertilizer: Plant fertilizer in a liquid form; some types need to be mixed with water, and some types are ready to use from the bottle.

Loppers: One of the largest manual gardening tools, use the scissoring action of loppers to prune branches 1 to 3 inches in diameter.

Morning sun: Areas of the garden that have an eastern exposure and receive direct sun in the morning hours are in morning sun.

Mulch: Any type of material that is spread over the soil surface around the base of plants to suppress weeds and retain soil moisture.

Nematode: Microscopic, wormlike organisms that live in the soil, some nematodes are beneficial, while others are harmful.

Naturalized: Plants that are introduced into an area, as opposed to being native to it.

Nectar plant: Flowers that produce nectar that attracts and feed butterflies or other pollinators, encouraging a succession of blooms throughout the season.

New wood (new growth): The new growth on plants; it is characterized by a greener, more tender form than older, woodier growth.

Nozzle: A device that attaches to the end of a hose and disperses water through a number of small holes; the resulting spray covers a wider area.

Old wood: Old wood is growth that is more than one year old. Some fruit plants produce on old wood. If you prune these plants in spring before they flower and fruit, you will cut off the wood that will produce fruit.

Organic: Describes products derived from naturally occurring materials instead of materials synthesized in a lab.

Organic fungicide: Most frequently this is a fungicide control based on natural ingredients like bacteria, including streptomyces lydicus or other similar organisms.

Ornamental edible landscaping: The practical integration of plants primarily used as food within an ornamental or decorative landscape setting.

Ornamental edible plants: Typically attractive but useful herbs or vegetables that are substituted into the flower garden, container, and landscape instead of unproductive plantings.

Part shade: Areas of the garden that receive three to six hours of sun a day are in part shade. Plants requiring part shade will often require protection from the more intense afternoon sun, either from tree leaves or from a building.

Part sun: Areas of the garden that receive three to six hours of sun a day are in part sun. Although the term is often used interchangeably with "part shade," a "part sun" designation places greater emphasis on the minimal sun requirements.

Perennial: A plant that lives for more than two years. Examples include trees, shrubs, and some flowering plants.

Pesticide: A substance used for destroying or controlling insects that are harmful to plants. Pesticides are available in organic and synthetic forms. Some synthetic pesticides can be harmful for the environment, so an organic solution to pests should always be considered the first choice.

pH: A figure designating the acidity or the alkalinity of garden soil, pH is measured on a scale of 1 to 14, with 7.0 being neutral.

Pinch: A method to remove unwanted plant growth with your fingers, promoting bushier growth and increased blooming.

Pitchfork: A hand tool with a long handle and sharp metal prongs, a pitchfork is typically used for moving loose material such as mulch or hay.

Plant label: This label or sticker on a plant container provides a description of the plant and information on its care and growth habits.

Pollination: The transfer of pollen for fertilization from the male pollen-bearing structure (stamen) to the female structure (pistil), usually by wind, bees, butterflies, moths, beetles, or hummingbirds; this process is required for flower and fruit production.

Pollinator: An insect, bee, butterfly, beetle, hummingbird or any creature that carries pollen from one flower to another.

Potting soil: A mixture used to grow flowers, herbs, and vegetables in containers, potting soil provides proper drainage and extra nutrients for healthy growth.

Powdery mildew: A fungal disease characterized by white powdery spots on plant leaves and stems, this disease is worse during times of drought or when plants have poor air circulation.

Power edger: This electric or gasoline-powered edger removes grass along flower beds and walkways for a neat appearance.

Pruning: A garden task in which a variety of hand tools are used to remove dead or overgrown branches to increase plant fullness and health.

Pruning saw: This hand tool for pruning smaller branches and limbs features a long, serrated blade with an elongated handle.

Push mower: A lawn mower that is propelled by the user rather than a motor, typically having between five to eight steel blades that turn and cut as the mower is pushed.

Reel mower: A mower in which the blades spin vertically with a scissoring motion to cut grass blades.

Rhizome: An underground horizontal stem that grows side shoots, a rhizome is similar to a bulb.

Rootball: The network of roots and soil clinging to a plant when it is lifted out of the ground.

Rootstock: The bottom part of a grafted fruit tree, rootstocks are often used to create dwarf fruit trees, impart pest or disease resistance, or make a plant more cold hardy.

Rotary spreader: A garden tool that distributes seed or organic amendments in a pattern wider than the base of the spreader.

Runner: A slender creeping stem that sprouts from the center of a plant and typically puts forth roots from nodes spaced at regular intervals along its length.

Samara: Winged seeds that are released by trees in early spring and used as a nutritious food source by squirrels, chipmunks, and songbirds.

Scaffold branch: This horizontal branch emerges almost perpendicular to the trunk.

Scientific name: This two-word identification system consists of the genus and species of a plant, such as *Ilex opaca*.

Scion: The top, fruit-bearing part of a grafted fruit tree.

Scissors: A two-bladed hand tool great for cutting cloth, paper, twine, and other lightweight materials, scissors are a basic garden tool.

Seed packet: The package in which vegetable and flower seeds are sold, it typically includes growing instructions, a planting chart, and harvesting information.

Seed-starting mix: Typically a soilless blend of ingredients, seed-starting mix is specifically formulated for growing plants from seed. Organic seed-starting mix is preferred as it contains all natural ingredients.

Self-fertile: A plant that does not require cross-pollination from another plant in order to produce fruit.

Semidwarf: A fruit tree grafted onto a rootstock that restricts growth of the tree to one-half to two-thirds of its natural size.

Shade: Garden shade is the absence of any direct sunlight in a given area, usually due to tree foliage or building shadows.

Shovel: A handled tool with a broad, flat blade and slightly upturned sides, used for moving soil and other garden materials; a basic garden tool.

Shredded hardwood mulch: A mulch consisting of shredded wood that interlocks, resisting washout and suppressing weeds, hardwood mulch can change soil pH.

Shrub: This woody plant is distinguished from a tree by its multiple trunks and branches and its shorter height of less than 15 feet tall.

Shrub rake: This long-handled rake with a narrow head fits easily into tight spaces between plants.

Sidedress: To sprinkle slow-release organic fertilizer along the side of a plant row or plant stem.

Slow-release organic fertilizer: This form of fertilizer, made from natural ingredients, releases nutrients at a slower rate throughout the season, requiring less-frequent applications.

Snips: This hand tool, used for snipping small plants and flowers, is perfect for harvesting fruits, vegetables, and flowers.

Soaker hose: This is an efficient watering system in which a porous hose, usually made from recycled rubber, allows water to seep out around plant roots.

Soil knife: A garden knife with a sharp, serrated edge, used for cutting twine, plant roots, turf, and other garden materials.

Soil test: An analysis of a soil sample, this determines the level of nutrients (to identify deficiencies) and detects pH.

Spade: This short-handled tool with a sharp, rectangular metal blade is used for cutting and digging soil or turf.

Spur: A small, compressed, fruit-bearing branch on a fruit tree.

Standard: Describes a fruit tree grown on its own seedling rootstock or a nondwarfing rootstock, this is the largest of the three sizes of fruit trees.

String trimmer: A hand-held tool that uses monofilament line instead of a blade to trim grass.

Succulent: A type of plant that stores water in its leaves, stems, and roots and is acclimated for arid climates and soil conditions.

Sucker: The odd growth from the base of a tree or a woody plant, often caused by stress, this also refers to sprouts from below the graft of a rose, shrub, or tree. Suckers divert energy away from the desirable tree growth and should be removed.

Summer annual: Annuals that thrive during the warmer months of the growing season.

Taproot: This is an enlarged, tapered plant root that grows vertically downward.

Thinning: The practice of removing excess vegetables (root crops) to leave more room for the remaining vegetables to grow; also refers to the practice of removing fruits when still small from fruit trees so that the remaining fruits can grow larger.

Topdress: To spread organic fertilizer on top of the soil (usually around fruit trees or vegetables).

Transplants: Plants that are grown in one location and then moved to and replanted in another; seeds started indoors and nursery plants are two examples.

Tree: This woody perennial plant typically consists of a single trunk with multiple lateral branches.

Tree canopy: The upper layer of growth, consisting of the tree's branches and leaves.

Tropical plant: A plant that is native to a tropical region and thus acclimated to a warm, humid climate and not hardy to frost.

Trowel: A shovel-like hand tool used for digging or moving small amounts of soil.

Turf: Grass and the surface layer of soil that is held together by its roots.

Variegated: The appearance of differently colored areas on plant leaves, usually white, yellow, or a brighter green.

Vegetable: A plant or part of a plant that is used for food.

Watering wand: This hose attachment features a longer handle for watering plants beyond reach.

Water sprout: This vertical shoot emerges from a scaffold branch. It is usually nonfruiting and undesirable.

Weeping: A growth habit in plants that features drooping or downward curving branches.

Wheat straw: These dry stalks of wheat, which are used for mulch, retain soil moisture and suppress weeds.

Wood chips: Small pieces of wood made by cutting or chipping, wood chips are used as mulch in the garden.

INDEX

PHOTO CREDITS

Shawna Coronado – Cover photo and all photos within the book except those designated below.

Kylee Baumle, www.ourlittleacre.com – Crocus, pg. 65; Flowering Dogwood, pg. 199; Redbud, pg. 211; Prairie Phlox, pg. 105; Shooting Star, page 106

Karen Chapman, www.lejardinetdesigns.com – Creeping Thyme, pg. 79

Mark Fonville, www.markfonville.com – pg. 240

Jim Kleinwachter, www.theconservationfoundation.org – Wild Petunia, pg. 109

Bruce Marlin, http://commons.wikimedia.org – Bruce Marlin/cc-by-3.0 – Fragrant Sumac, pg. 173

Marcie O'Connor, www.aprairiehaven.com – American Bittersweet, pg. 216

Jimmy Randolph, http://hootowlkarma.blogspot.com – Tuliptree, pg. 213

Christina Salwitz, http://personalgardencoach.wordpress.com – Douglasfir, pg. 198

Helen Yoest, www.gardeningwithconfidence.com – Dwarf Pampas Grass, pg. 114; Mugo Pine, pg. 179; American Wisteria, pg. 223

Daderot—Public Domain, http://commons.wikimedia.org – Plume Grass, pg. 118

Courtesy of Bonnie Plants, www.bonnieplants.com – Annual Purple Basil, pg. 53

Courtesy of David Austin Roses, www.davidaustinroses.com – Floribunda Rose, pg. 157; Grandiflora Rose, pg. 158

Courtesy of Monrovia, www.monrovia.com – Tufted Hair Grass, pg. 119

Courtesy of Morton Arboretum, www.mortonarb.org – Big Bluestem, pg. 94; Black Chokeberry, pg. 166; Witchhazel, pg. 190; Hybrid Elm, pg. 202

Courtesy of Proven Winners® ColorChoice® Shrubs, www.provenwinners-shrubs.com – Wedding Ring® Boxwood, pg. 167; Sweet Lifeberry® Goji Berries, pg. 174; Spice Girl™ Viburnum, pg. 188; Sonic Bloom™ Pink Weigela, pg. 189

Courtesy of Spring Meadows Nursery, www.SpringMeadowNursery.com – Mock orange, pg. 178

MEET
SHAWNA CORONADO

Shawna Coronado began her career as a garden writer by first working as a suburban garden designer and blogger; teaching everyday homeowners creative ideas for building birding and pollinator gardens by rendering designs and telling their garden stories. A local newspaper picked Shawna up as a garden columnist and a passion for documenting nature led her on to photography as well. Since that time, her photography and organic living stories have been featured in several international home and garden magazines and multiple books. Shawna speaks internationally on building community, practical garden ideas, and green lifestyle tips for the everyday person. Shawna is an industry spokesperson and social media enthusiast with hundreds of internet-based videos and a popular blog, www.ShawnaCoronado.com.